Human Beings and their Images

Human Beings and their Images

Imagination, Mimesis, Performativity

Christoph Wulf

Translated by Elizabeth Hamilton
and Deirdre Winter

BLOOMSBURY ACADEMIC
LONDON • NEW YORK • OXFORD • NEW DELHI • SYDNEY

BLOOMSBURY ACADEMIC
Bloomsbury Publishing Plc
50 Bedford Square, London, WC1B 3DP, UK
1385 Broadway, New York, NY 10018, USA
29 Earlsfort Terrace, Dublin 2, Ireland

BLOOMSBURY, BLOOMSBURY ACADEMIC and the Diana logo are trademarks of
Bloomsbury Publishing Plc

First published in Great Britain 2022
This paperback edition published 2023

Cover image: World History Archive / Alamy Stock Photo

A catalogue record for this book is available from the British Library.

A catalog record for this book is available from the Library of Congress.

ISBN: HB: 978-1-3502-6513-4
PB: 978-1-3502-6517-2
ePDF: 978-1-3502-6514-1
eBook: 978-1-3502-6515-8

Typeset by Deanta Global Publishing Services, Chennai, India

To find out more about our authors and books visit www.bloomsbury.com and sign
up for our newsletters.

Contents

Introduction

Images, performance and human society

When we speak of 'human beings and their images', we have two meanings in mind, both of which require closer examination. The first of these is the central role that images, the imagination and the imaginary play in the constitution of the human being. The second meaning has to do with the question of the different images and conceptualizations that we have of the human being. This book illuminates the historical, cultural and philosophical aspects of the subject. Such a study is complex since these images are always changing. I will be considering images that human beings create of themselves and examining what these images mean for our perception of the world and other people, our memories and our projections of the future. Human images are generated by the social and cultural practices of everyday life and by the arts. They become part of collective and personal imaginaries and therefore play a part in shaping human actions. The capacity to produce images is common to all human beings but has emerged in very different shapes and forms over the course of history and in different cultures. Since images and the imaginary render something visible that would otherwise remain invisible, research on images is an important area of anthropology.

The word 'image' can refer to very different things; thus, the concept of the image has a very broad spectrum and needs to be more precisely defined. On the one hand, an image can be the product of visual processes of perception. Due to the influence of the neurosciences and their imaging techniques, the results of perception through other pathways are often called 'images'. We also speak of mental or 'internal' images which render something present that is actually absent. These include memory images. They differ from perceptual images in that they are less distinct. The same is true of situations we imagine happening in the future and of dreams, hallucinations and visions. Many aesthetic creations are also images. They are the products of a process that was expressly intended to create an image. Finally, as metaphors images are also a constitutive element of language. All human beings have the capacity to create images, to recognize images as images and to manipulate images in an imaginative way. However, this capacity varies depending on the culture and point of time in history, since what images we see and how we see images is determined by complex historical and cultural processes. How we perceive and handle images is also affected by the uniqueness of our personal life histories and our differing subjectivities.

Images are produced by energy processes, which transform the world of objects, actions and other people into images. These images are incorporated and become part of collective and personal imaginaries with the aid of the imagination. Many of these processes are mimetic and result in our becoming similar to other people, environments, ideas and images. In mimetic processes, the outside world becomes the inner world, which is a world of images. This world of images plays its part in shaping the outside world. Since these images are performative, they contribute to the emergence of actions and the staging and performing of our relationships with other people and the world in which we live. The imaginary is the locus of images, and it is towards this that the mimetic processes that create images are directed. And at the same time, it is where the mimetic and performative energies of the images arise.

At the present time, images, the imagination and the imaginary are more important than ever. There are several reasons for this. To begin with, the way we live in today's world is marked by the fact that we human beings have a powerful influence on the fate of the planet. This has given rise to the term 'Anthropocene' where the traditional distinction between nature and culture no longer applies. For there is hardly any nature left upon which humans have not left their mark.[1] Among the things causing this situation are the numerous destructive effects of industrialization and modernization.[2] These include global warming, destruction of biodiversity, atomic and hydrogen energy, digitalization (including the internet, robotics and AI) the cyborgization of humanity, genetics, pollution, hundreds of thousands of micro plastics, the exponential production of plastic and the eradication of non-renewable energy sources.[3] The fact that these processes take place on a global scale often prevents us from experiencing them directly. It is only by the aid of images that we find out about many of the developments that are taking place on our planet. The extremely serious effects of climate change in the Antarctic are an example of this, as without the images we would not see what is happening. In the case of such distant events, which we cannot access directly, images help us to see and experience these situations for ourselves. In view of the impact many developments in the Anthropocene have on our planet, images have come to play an increasingly important political, social and cultural role. The same is true of the digitalization of our daily lives.

When we describe our daily lives, it no longer makes sense to distinguish between online and offline activities because they are now so tightly interwoven.[4]

The presence of Covid-19 has accelerated this increase in the importance of images still further. When proximity and physical contact are not permitted because of the danger of infection, images have the important function of compensating for this. In place of physical proximity, iconic media help to create 'virtual proximity'. We see this in the situation in schools, for example, where distance learning via electronic media takes the place of classroom learning. Here images of what is being taught and of the other pupils replace their bodily presence. Media developments that have taken place in the twentieth and twenty-first centuries have resulted in images, the imagination and the imaginary becoming increasingly important in people's lives.

Image and imagination

Imagination, no less than language, is a *conditio humana*, part of our human condition, which is firmly rooted in the human body.[5] Human action is not predetermined by instinct but shaped by the imagination. With the aid of imagination, past, present and future are closely interwoven. The imagination creates the human world – social and cultural, symbolic and imaginary. It makes history and culture possible and thus also historical and cultural diversity. It creates the world of images and imaginaries, and is involved in the creation of practices of the body, such as dances, rituals and gestures. Staging and performing these practices requires more than an awareness of them – they must be incorporated and become part of a practical, body-based, implicit knowledge, the dynamic nature of which makes social and cultural changes and shaping possible. Of central importance here are mimetic processes that are rooted in the imagination. It is here that the cultural learning takes place that generates social and cultural identity, which is an essential requirement for well-being and happiness.

Imagination plays a major role in all forms of social and cultural action. It uses images, schemata and models to guide human behaviour and action. Images are determining factors of action, which become increasingly significant. This brings us to the question as to what constitutes an image and what different types of image there are. For example, a differentiation can be made between mental images and images that have been produced manually or technically, and between moving images and still images.

A glance at the traditional Chinese understanding of images helps us to realize the extent to which the Western understanding of images is historically and culturally conditioned. The half dark and the half light of the Chinese image is created by the interplay between being and non-being This to-ing and fro-ing between being and non-being can also be found in the traditional Chinese rituals in honour of the dead, in which sacrifices are made to the dead as if they were present. Chinese painting is not content with making something visible; it also wants to conceal. This movement of appearing and disappearing is typical of Chinese painting over a long period of time.

It is not only in Western and Chinese art that we see the importance of the imagination. The imagination also plays a pivotal role in the genesis of *Homo sapiens sapiens* and the associated cultures. The aesthetic shapes to be seen in bone markings, for example, go back several hundred thousand years. Human beings gain access to the world and likewise; the outside world gains access to our inner world through the medium of images, with the aid of imagination. A distinction can be made between magic, representational and simulated images. Magical images are not a reference to anything – they are what they portray. The statue of the 'golden calf' was the sacred object. In a relic it is the body part that is sacred. Representational images, which are often based on mimetic processes, are different. They refer to something that they represent without being that thing. This also includes photographs, which show situations that are in the past and not present. Simulated images are images that are created by new electronic media procedures and are playing an increasingly important role in our lives. The difference between perceptual images and mental images is important. Every mental image is indicative of the fact that an object is missing. This is obvious with remembered images and projections into the future. Both are influenced by the perceptual images that relate to objects that are actually present.

Pathological images, visions and dreams also differ from perceptual images and memory images. In all of these cases, the imagination plays its part in generating the images. Following Kant and the authors of the 'Oldest Systematic Program of German Idealism', the concept of imagination needs to be defined more precisely. It is with the aid of the imagination that mental, or 'inner' image, worlds, in which emotions are crystallized, come into being. The dynamic of the imagination connects people and creates community. Its ludic nature generates connections between images and causes new images to emerge. There is an important difference between these images, the perception of these images and the images created in the imagination.

Imagination and the imaginary

Individuals, communities and cultures all generate imaginaries with the aid of the imagination. As a concept, the imaginary can be understood as an inner world of images that includes sounds, touch sensations, smells and tastes. Human beings need the imaginary in order to be able to perceive the world in a way that is shaped by history and culture. The imagination remembers and produces, combines and projects images. It creates reality. At the same time, it uses reality to generate images. The images of the imagination have a dynamic that structures perception, memory and the future. Links are forged between the images that follow the dialectical and rhythmic movements of the imagination. Not only everyday life, but also literature, art and the performative arts have an inexhaustible reservoir of images. Some of them appear to be stable and not easily changed, while others are subject to historical and cultural changes. The imagination has a symbolizing dynamic which constantly generates new meanings, using images. People use these images that imagination has created to interpret the world.[6]

In contrast to the conventional use of the concept of the imaginary, Jacques Lacan particularly stressed the compelling quality of the imaginary. Desire, wishes and passion play a major role in our human inability to free ourselves from the imaginary. We have no direct relationship with the real. As beings endowed with language, humans can only develop a relationship with the real via the symbolic order and the imagination, a relationship which is fractured in many ways. We can use it to try to assert ourselves against the constraints of the imaginary. 'The imaginary has an effect on society and provides an "inner world-space" (*Weltinnenraum*, Rilke), that has a strong tendency to close itself off and, in a sense, to develop an infinite immanence. In contrast, human fantasy or the imagination, is the only faculty with the power to break open closed spaces and transcend them temporarily because it is identical to the discontinuous experience of time.'[7] Because we cannot resist the imaginary, it places constraints on the potentialities of human life and development. Important as it is to stress this 'coercive' quality of the imaginary, it is only one of its aspects. In the view presented in this book, the imaginary encompasses the whole spectrum of the diversity and ambivalence of cultural knowledge of the image.

The imagination has a strong performative power which stages and enacts social and cultural actions. The imagination uses this power to create the imaginary, which contains remembered images from the past, images of the present and imagined images of the future. Mimetic movements can capture the iconic character of the images. The images are absorbed into the imaginary, and we re-create this iconic character. As part of our mental worlds, they represent the outside world. Which images, structures and models become part of the imaginary is determined by many different factors. The presence and absence of the outside world are inextricably interlaced in these images. Images that emerge from the imaginary are transferred to new contexts by the imagination. Networks of images are formed with which we capture the world and which determine how we view it.

Because of the performative nature of the imagination, the greater part of the imaginary consists of images of social life. The power structures of social conditions and societal structures are represented in these images. Many of these processes begin in childhood and take place unconsciously. We already learn to perceive social constellations and arrangements at this early age. These early experiences of seeing and the images that result from them play an important and indispensable role in how we grasp the world visually. All our perceptions are influenced in some way by historical and cultural schemata and mental images that we build up over the course of our lives, enabling us to grasp what we see. We see social actions and relate to them as we perceive them. They thus take on significance for us. When other people direct their actions towards us, the impulse to establish a relationship comes from them and they expect us to respond. Whatever happens, a relationship is formed, and the images of our imaginary are an important prerequisite of this relationship. We enter into an action game and act in relation to what is expected of us in this social arrangement, be it that we respond to it, modify it or oppose it. Our actions are mimetic, less in virtue of their similarity than in virtue of the corresponding reactions that they engender. Once we have engaged in an action game, we perceive the actions of the other participants, and our own actions relate to them mimetically.

The imagination creates individual and collective images in the imaginary, images that intermingle and interconnect. An example of this is the portrayal of Covid-19 as an icon. The image takes hold of the imaginary of individuals and at the same time becomes part of a global, collective imaginary that knows no borders. At the centre is the image of the virus. Rather than being threatening, from an aesthetic point of view its portrayal is appealing and seemingly harmless. In this portrayal, some people even see an intentional playing down of the virus. This image goes round the world millions of times, continually reminding us of the pandemic. The presentation of this virus image becomes a performative gesture, relentlessly drawing our attention to the health, economic, cultural and social crisis. Everyone without exception is affected regardless of whether they are young or old, rich or poor. For some, mostly older people, the infection is fatal; for others, mostly the young, it is often hardly noticeable. Depending on the prevailing economic and social conditions, those infected have differing chances of recovering. The pandemic is global. The image of the radiant virus gives rise to many new images. In Europe, for example, there are the images of the military vehicles in Bergamo in Italy taking away the dead during the night. For many Americans, it is the photos of long queues of refrigerator trucks waiting to collect the bodies. For other people, it is the images of the town of Wuhan, hermetically sealed, that bring to our awareness the danger to democratic ways of life in pandemic situations. Later, it is more often the images of people who have had their vaccinations at last which boost our hope for an end to the pandemic. These images too take hold of the imaginary of individuals and communities and show how the imagination uses images to create an individual, regional, and global imaginary.

Imagination and practices of the body

It is from this perspective that we examine the link between the imagination and the practices of the body. Taking play and dance as examples, we investigate the importance of movement and performativity for aesthetic and social processes. In an analysis of the anthropological significance of gestures and rituals, we show how closely imagination and practices of the body are interwoven. Ludic, dance, gestural and ritual knowledge is acquired in mimetic processes, in the course of which the practices are incorporated and become firmly embedded in the imaginary. As social beings, humans have a need for cultural practices that create community. Social relations are staged in these practices, and they develop their performative nature in a dynamic way.

In games, we can distinguish between games with rules and games without rules. The imagination, with its capacity to develop images, schemata and models, plays an especially important role in games without rules, where the rules are invented by the players as they go along. Images, memories and emotions are displayed in the ludic practices of the body. They emerge in the body's enactments and the way they appear often also takes the players themselves by surprise.

In games, the players put the constraints of everyday life behind them and behave as if the actions of the game are 'serious'. This 'as if' is what makes a game a game. In order to be able to play, the players must believe in the 'fictional reality' of their game. This fiction shapes the dynamics of the game, which are essentially due to the fact that the players' bodies are duplicated. On the one hand, the players have their own personal bodies that enter into a world of play; on the other hand, there is a second body that superimposes itself on the first one, as dictated by the rules of the game. In this duplication, a play body comes into being which moves in accordance with the rules and criteria of the particular game. Each staging of a game is unique. Although it may relate to a previous staging or the same or a similar game, every staging is different because it differs in its participants and the place or the time period in which it is played. Games are staged and performed with the aid of the imagination. They are performative and therefore embodied and frequently expressive.[8]

Dance, like play, is also an important cultural practice. It is a field of action in which people portray and express themselves and discover something about themselves. The body is at the very core of dance. It is the body that stages and performs movements. The relationship between body and movement gives rise to rhythmic formations. There are very many different dances, and they cannot all be categorized under a few headings. In order to develop and construct them, it is necessary to imagine the formations and how they can be executed by the body by using our imagination of movement. Dance formations are developed in an interplay between movement, rhythm and space and give us a knowledge of human beings that we would not otherwise have. They create collective, aesthetic experiences and thus also community. In many cultures, they are associated with sacrifice, ecstasy and death. In its freedom from conventional constraints, contemporary dance draws attention to the functionalization of movement by society. In its performances, the imagination constantly draws on structures, schemata and images of the imaginary.[9]

In addition to games and dance, rituals are among those practices that are most effective in the shaping of human imaginaries. A practical, body-based knowledge, in which images, schemata, performances, body images and bodily movements play a central role, is needed to stage and perform rituals. This practical knowledge is an *implicit knowledge* that is only partially accessible to the conscious mind. Imagination is a constitutive element in the process of interpreting ritual images, movements and experiences. Its effects derive not only from images that can be remembered but also from movements and social practices that have been carried out and from the performance of rituals. Rituals condense and stage social events. They generate feelings of belonging and inscribe these in the imaginary with the aid of images. Rituals and mental images of rituals become the starting points for further rituals and social practices.[10]

Rituals render something visible that would otherwise be invisible. They generate images that find their way into the human imaginary where they develop their effects. For example, they play an important part in shaping the transition from one social role to another. They develop a magical power which comes about because all the participants of a ritual believe in the appropriateness of the ritual arrangement in which the change in status takes place. In these rituals, during the first phase the participants still identify with the initial situation. In the second, middle or liminal phase, they undergo the transition. In the third phase, they accept the adjustment of the images to the new situation. These ritual sequences of action lead to the establishment of the corresponding image sequences in the imaginaries of the participants. The example of a wedding ritual illustrates this. The ritual stages and performs the transition from being an unmarried couple to acquiring the social status of a married couple. In all the phases of the ritual arrangement, images that are produced are inscribed in the imaginaries of the participants, forging a connection between them.

Rituals are dynamic. If they were not, then they would degenerate into stereotypes and lose their social function. It is from their dynamism and performativity that their social effects arise. Rituals generate feelings. They are expressive and demonstrative and create social structures. Many of them contain implicit hierarchies and power structures together with the imaginary images associated with them.[11]

Gestures are often key components of rituals. The iconic nature of a gesture such as when Willy Brandt fell to his knees at the monument to those who died in the Warsaw Ghetto Uprising captures the essence of the meaning of a ritual. Gestures are often wordless actions in which meanings are created by the arrangement of the bodies. These actions relate back to familiar patterns, schemata and images. Some of them are incorporated and thus form part of an implicit knowledge. Others are consciously deployed in interactions between people. Gestures are linked to spoken language without being subordinate to it. They are used in various 'performance styles',[12] including: firstly, unspecific *beat gestures*, which serve to accentuate linguistic meaning; secondly, *iconic gestures*, which are of a pictorial nature; thirdly, *metaphoric gestures*, whose basic structure is also iconic. In order to understand metaphoric gestures, it is necessary to be familiar with their cultural context. The gestures in Indian dances that cannot be understood without a knowledge of their cultural meanings are an example. The role of gestures and their images in the imaginary in child-rearing, education and socialization in families, schools, peer cultures and the media has been explored in extensive ethnographic studies.[13] The social and cultural significance of gestures is based on the fact that phylogenetically they are far older than spoken language and contain elements that are distinctly iconic. Gestures convey social values in an elementary, embodied form. Because gestures are performative and iconic, it is very important to consider the context when interpreting and analysing their complexity.[14]

If we accept that the Covid-19 pandemic is also an expression of the destructive nature of the Anthropocene, then it is clear that the imagination and practices of the body have the task of designing and bringing about the changes in human attitudes and behaviour that are necessary if the situation is to improve. Changes in regard to sustainable development play an important role in this process. It is essential that we should design and create new social and cultural practices based on the goals of sustainable development. Here it is quite clear to us that it is essential for our daily rituals to change in, for example, what we consume and in travel and tourism. Rituals also enable us to develop permanent new attitudes towards the use of plastics and energy which will help to bring about large-scale changes in society. If we are to develop new practices of the body appropriate to the altered social conditions, then cultural learning processes must take place in which a mimetic approach plays an important role.[15]

Mimesis and cultural learning

Mimetic processes create images of games, dances, rituals, gestures and other social and cultural actions with the aid of the imagination and make them into part of both the collective imaginary and our personal imaginaries. Mimetic processes are forms of productive imitation in which people make themselves similar to other people. As a result of the mimetic impulse, people who are behaving mimetically take what one could call an iconic 'impression' of the person to whom they want to become similar. These processes are particularly important in childhood. Children learn to feel, express their feelings and modify them in mimetic processes. We know from reports about 'wild children' who have grown up outside human society that upright gait and the ability to speak are acquired mimetically. If the social prerequisites are lacking, these potentials remain undeveloped. However, children have mimetic relationships not only with other people, but also with their environments, to which they become more similar and which they absorb into their imaginaries in the form of mental images. Images of other people and other worlds are incorporated with the aid of imagination and movement. Mimetic processes also play an important role in the production, mediation and modification of the intangible cultural heritage that is so important for identity formation. The medium of the intangible cultural heritage is the human body with its temporality and transience. Important components of the intangible cultural heritage are play, dance, ritual, gesture and traditional modes of living and working. These are all integrated into the practical knowledge that is required for the performativity of these cultural forms. This takes place in mimetic processes by means of which this practical knowledge is passed down from one generation to the next. Performances in the arts are a good example of this. They are staged in mimetic processes with the aid of the imagination. In these processes, people learn how to act in social situations, thus acquiring practical knowledge. They need to be able to generate a new body-based knowledge and put on new performances.[16]

Family rituals are also forms of cultural knowledge which contribute to the creation of social and cultural identity. The spectrum ranges from rituals carried out at important events such as weddings, births and funerals to everyday rituals such as shared mealtimes, family outings and going shopping. In the middle range, there are the rituals that are repeated every year at family celebrations. It is not just the ritual practices, but also the associated mental images that ensure that these rituals have lasting effects. This is confirmed by ethnographic studies on what people remember particularly vividly from their childhoods. Study participants frequently mention images of ritual situations and arrangements in which they experienced strong feelings as children. Family rituals and the mental images that arise from them enact the family's collective symbolic knowledge, support the image they convey to the outside world and confirm the way they operate as a family. They are social practices which are of major importance for the development of a family style and a family identity.

Ethnographic studies carried out in a collaborative German Japanese research project investigated the role of mental images of happiness in engendering feelings of happiness in families.[17] A major goal of these studies was to establish how families create their happiness in Christmas and New Year's rituals and what role mental and 'internal' images play in this. What elements and images are used to create feelings of satisfaction, well-being, belonging and happiness at Christmas and the New Year? Despite large differences between the two cultures, it was possible to identify five transcultural complexes of behaviours and ideas that are important for creating family happiness. These include religious ideas and practices which are rooted in collective and personal imaginaries and ideas, memories and practices involved in eating and drinking together in the family. The exchange of gifts also belongs in this context. In the Christian families, there is an important analogy between the mutual exchange of gifts and God's gift of his Son to redeem humanity, which shows the transcendental dimension of present-giving. The specific narratives and mental images that each family uses to reaffirm its uniqueness and the open-ended periods of time that are not planned and within which unexpected things can happen also contribute much to a feeling of well-being and family happiness.

I

Image and imagination

The world as image

The great image without form

In our everyday consciousness, we assume that our perception of the world is 'natural' and that there is no other way to perceive it. Our way of seeing the world seems to us to be reliable and well founded. It gives us security and the capacity to act. We find it hard to grasp that our senses were not always structured in the way we experience them today, but that this structure results from historical and cultural change processes. This chapter aims to elucidate this further. As central or one-point perspective became prevalent during the Renaissance, and the controlling gaze came into being, a development was set in motion which eventually brought about a fundamental change in the human mentality: our perception of the world in the modern era is characterized by the fact that the world is there for us human beings as an object and thus becomes for us an image. Looking at other cultures helps us to see that the Western order of the senses is culturally determined. The way the Chinese perceive images demonstrates how European images and the way they are perceived are determined by historical and cultural factors.

1.1 The world as an image or picture

We still find it hard to grasp that our way of seeing the world as an image and in images is determined by our history and culture. Heidegger understood this when he emphasized that the way we perceive the world as an image is the result of the historical developments that we call the modern age. Whereas in antiquity we saw ourselves as part of the *physis*, that is, of nature, and in the Middle Ages as part of the world created by God, in the modern age we are moving away from this embeddedness. As we do so, the world presents itself to us as an object and becomes an image to us. We do not simply get an understanding of the world by picturing it; the world itself becomes an image for us. In his 1938 essay, 'The Age of the World Picture', Heidegger states:

> But a decisive condition in the essence of the picture is still missing. That we are 'in the picture' about something means not just that the being is placed before, represented by us. It means, rather, that it stands before us together with what belongs to and stands together with it as a system. To 'be in the picture' resonates with: being well informed, being equipped and prepared. Where the world becomes picture beings are set in place as that for which man is prepared, that which, therefore, he correspondingly intends to bring before him, have before him, and, thereby, in a decisive sense, place before him. Understood in an essential way, 'world picture' does not mean 'picture of the world' but rather the world grasped as picture. Beings as a whole are now taken in such a way that a being is first and only in being insofar as it is set in place by representing-producing humanity.[1]

We human beings have now adopted a completely new stance towards the world. This is connected with our attempt to picture the world to ourselves and use it to orientate ourselves and see ourselves in this new stance. With this new stance, 'that which is' (*das Seiende*) becomes a world of objects, and we human beings develop a new relationship to ourselves.

> What begins is that mode of human being which occupies the realm of human capacity as the domain of measuring and execution for the purpose of the mastery of beings as a whole. The age that is determined by this event is not only new in retrospective comparison with what had preceded it. It is new, rather, in that it explicitly sets itself up as the new. To be 'new' belongs to a world that has become picture.[2]

Our relationship to the world and our relationship to ourselves are interdependent. In the modern age, the world becomes an image and the human being a subject. The more we conquer the world the more the subject evolves, and the more the engagement with the world becomes anthropology.

> The interweaving of these two processes (that the world becomes picture and the man subject) – which is decisive for the essence of modernity, illuminates the founding process of modern history, a process, that, at first sight, seems almost nonsensical. The process, namely, whereby the more completely and comprehensively the world, as conquered, stands at man's disposal, and the more objectively the object appears, all the more subjectively (i.e. peremptorily) does the *subiectum* rise up, and all the more inexorably, too, do observations and teachings about the world transform themselves into a doctrine of man, into an anthropology.[3]

How images are seen and grasped is, therefore, of importance not only for aesthetics but also for anthropology. It is this new understanding of the relationship between subject and image that was responsible for the evolution of the modern notion of art and aesthetics. The emergence of such a cultural subsystem is closely linked to this development. In many other cultures there is no such comparably distinct field of art with such a long-lasting effect on our understanding of images.

Of course, this view of Heidegger's is more complex than this. However, for our purposes here, this particular aspect does support the argument that the way we understand the image in the modern Western world is determined by historical and cultural factors. Images are experienced differently depending on the cultural context. Thus, before the 'Age of Art' (Belting) they were perceived differently from the way they were perceived after the Renaissance and are perceived now in the modern day, where the boundaries between artistic and everyday images have dissolved and new images have arisen under the influence of the digital media.

1.2 Forms and types of image

Human beings interpret themselves and the world not only with the aid of speech but also with the aid of images. As they do this, it is not only in metaphors that we find an overlap between linguistic and iconic images. Images hold a position between the concrete and the abstract, the real and the unreal. They permit us to internalize the world and embody it; they form a yoke between the world of the senses and the imagination. They represent while at the same time being more than mere representations. They are media and as such have the quality of being 'in between'. In spite of these characteristics, not all images are the same. Depending on what criteria we are judging them by, we can distinguish between many different types and forms of image, and there are many possible perspectives from which we can categorize and understand them. As well as the distinction between linguistic and iconic images and between images that present, represent or simulate, the nature and intensity of the imagination required to generate and distinguish between different types of image is also important. Do images manifest something or do they embody the outside world in the world inside us? Do they result from an imagination that is reproducing something or one that is producing something for the first time? To what extent does their historical and cultural nature determine how they can express and portray something?

Images can be understood as being representations that are closely linked to sensory perception; they relate to all objects of contemplation and how they appear to us. As soon as we go a step further than merely perceiving what is in front of us, images arise. This is different from another view of the image, which, in the empirical tradition, suggests that there are no representations (including representations of abstract thoughts and ideas) which do not have their origin in the images of our perception. There is a middle position between these two views according to which the most important thing about the images is that they use imagination to make absent people and things 'present'. Thus, the image occupies a position between the perception of the object(s) and the idea of the object(s) that has or have been perceived. According to this view, to put it in the terms of cognitive psychology, 'What makes imagery a specific modality for the representation of information is that it can maintain perceptual information in a form having high structural similarity with perception.'[4]

In order to make the invisible visible, an image needs a medium. The human body is one of the most important vehicles for images. It uses its senses and movements to create multisensory images. By means of these, the outside world and its objects become the inner world of humans and are shaped by the images of our inner worlds. In our perception of the world, our different senses overlap and produce a multisensory complexity. 'Images', or rather the impressions of touch, smell and taste in our body, are clearly important, and these senses have gradually come to be valued more highly in the humanities,[5] but it is equally clear that hearing[6] and seeing have special importance as do also the auditory and visual images that are transmitted by these two senses and the optical and auditory bipolarity that arises from the way they overlap with each other.

There are also the sensomotor images of movement, which are closely linked to the imagination of movement and are particularly important for the imaginary of the body. For (as images of movement) stances, gestures and other forms of bodily expression not only find their way into our inner world of images but also become part of the 'memory of movement' (or muscle memory) that plays an important role in dance and sport, for example.[7] In addition, there are also the kinetic images of movement associated with bodily reflexes and muscle movements and the images of bodily expression produced by the emotions. In these images of the human body, that are perceived and processed mimetically, the body expresses its feelings and also the changes that are taking place in it. These images play a central part in the way we humans construct our identities and form images of ourselves.

The reciprocal interweaving of auditory and iconic images is of considerable importance for the development of culture. It is not only that visual and linguistic images are primarily formed in different areas of the brain,[8] but the way they relate to objects is also different. Whereas the iconic images are first and foremost representations of the objects to which they refer, before any interpretation takes place, this sensory relationship is lacking in linguistic images. They are evoked by random conventional signs and, inasmuch as they are rather more abstract in nature, are different from visual images, which have a representational relationship with the world of human beings and objects. Iconic images are directly connected to what we see; linguistic images first have to create an inner view. Whereas in iconic images relationships are portrayed simultaneously, the linguistic images arise over the period of time we are in the process of talking, reading or writing. As we speak, the linguistic signs and the images that they help to evoke inside us continually overlap. Iconic and linguistic images refer to each other, and our imagination helps to fill in the gaps. Consequently, as we contemplate the images, we interpret them linguistically, and our interpretations are reflected upon; likewise, we produce images as we speak, images that make sense of what we are saying. Historically, there have been different views of how to interpret the relationship between iconic and verbal images, and right up to the present day this relationship is still a central issue in linguistics and image science.

Depending on the criteria we apply, there are various typologies of images that can be developed. In 1986, Mitchell proposed distinguishing between categories of image as follows:

- Graphic (pictures, statues, designs)
- Optical (mirrors, projections)
- Perceptual (sense data, 'species', appearances)
- Mental images (dreams, memories, ideas, fantasmata)
- Verbal images (metaphors, descriptions).[9]

This does not yet take into consideration the moving images produced by the New Media or digital images. If we try to work these into a typology of images, then, inspired by Mitchell, we arrive at a typology which includes the characteristic features of the New Media and gives a useful overview of the variety that exists in today's world of images. Its starting point is the basic difference between the internal and the external, according to which images that come about in a non-material way inside the human body, where the human body is the medium, differ from externally produced images, which may be created either 'manually' or 'technically'. Within manually produced images we find a distinction between still and moving images. A further subdivision can be made in still manual images which may be either graphic images (panel painting, panorama, etc.) or sculptures. Moving manual images would include such things as stage sets or wheels of life.

In the case of technical images as well, we find a distinction between unmoving and moving images. Here again there are subdivisions. Unmoving technical images would be, for example, mirrors, camera obscura, still photographs, or, in a further subdivision, holographs. Moving technical images can also be divided into analogue (which include film, TV, video) or digital (e.g. computer simulations and Virtual Reality).

Mental images, such as dreams, ideas, memories and projections differ from both the manual and technical images.[10]

The mental images can also be subdivided according to their relationship to time (present, past, future), their degree of consciousness (waking or sleeping state) and also their degree of truth (true, false, an illusion).[11] In the first group, the question is how perceived images should be differentiated from remembered and imagined images. For example, what role do images arising within us, from our memories and imaginations, play in our perception? How much do they determine our perception? How important is desire or what we want to see when it comes to how we perceive the world? At the very moment of perception, the images are (mimetically) duplicated, and in this process mental images are created in which the outside world becomes our inner world. It is a matter of debate to what extent it is the 'inherent' quality of things and people that enters our inner world of images and to what extent this process is a 'construction' that is essentially determined by the prevailing collective and personal historical and cultural circumstances. There is no doubt that both elements are fundamental for perception. But how much of one and how much of the other? There is no general answer to this question. We can only determine the ratio of these two elements of perception to each other by analysing individual cases. When we try to do this, we come across situations such as those of Proust's 'madeleine', where we can no longer decide whether it is a description of a perception or a memory.

Memory images can differ greatly. In some cases, the objects to which the memory refers are remembered in their entirety; in other cases, they are only partially accessible to the memory. In yet other cases they slip out of the memory's grasp completely or are overlayered by screen-memories (Freud). In such cases, we realize the extent to which memory images are continually being reconstructed and thus also change. It is clear that mimetic processes play a central role in this. The process of memory reconstruction can therefore be described as a mimetic process in which the person remembering draws on the existing traces and uses them to create his or her memory. Since this is a reconstructive process, it is clear that the result will be different each time. Motor processes, which play a large part in the creation and shaping of memories, are important here. The social framing of the memory and the inclusion of current social factors are even more important. Memory images can only be consciously produced to a limited extent. Many of them, therefore, tend to follow the dynamic of 'mémoire involonté' (Bergson), which stresses the impulsive, spontaneous and volatile nature of imagination.

Images projected into the future bring the imagination into play in a special way. Such images are pictorial projections of situations, actions and social behaviour which have not yet become reality. These anticipatory images have an 'as if quality'. They behave as if they were real and ignore the fact that they still have to take place in reality. These projections of the future incorporate images of past experiences that mingle with collective and personal image worlds. The origins of these projected images can vary. Anticipatory images can be the result of a need to act, a wish or desire. Desire plays a particularly important role in many cases.

From the images of desire and projection, it is just a small step to the unconscious images of dreams and daydreams. Today we have moved beyond the idea that the images of dreams are merely wish fulfilment. It is true that in many cases they are a way of processing conflicts and anticipating the solutions to problems but there is far more to them than this. Dream images are forms of expression and representation in which the collective also plays an important role. Even if we do not share C. G. Jung's idea that there are archetypes that are firmly anchored in the body, anthropological research takes seriously the question of the existence of universal dream images (Jung, Bachelard, Durand). Such background images influence human emotions and the way we orientate ourselves in the world. As archetypes or schemata, they shape how we perceive things, the way we conjure up images through our imagination and also create scripts for how we plan our lives. They combine the general with the particular. In addition to the forces that produce and shape the internal images, we can also distinguish between lasting forms of images. Likewise, there are prototypes that shape the production of images. Here the spectrum ranges from the production of icons to that of advertising images. Images also serve as models which help to simplify complex webs of (inter-)relationships. The same is true of stereotypes and clichés. These too are simplifications, inadmissible oversimplifications which do not fully correspond to situations and circumstances.

In contrast to these various kinds of mental image, there are also images that use a medium in order to become visible and to materialize. Images can appear on liquids, such as water, or on stone, canvas, paper, film and so on; they can be still or in motion. Images can, however, also be produced by representational forms. These might be figures, contours or traces which relate to a point of reference or a word without copying it. These reference points can be visible or even fictitious. They can be sketches, schemata, silhouettes or geometrical simplifications such as monograms, diagrams, pictograms, plans and maps. We can also differentiate between images by referring to the different means that media use to produce them. The spectrum ranges from simple tools such as a pencil or paintbrush, to cameras and computers. Finally, images can be analysed in terms of how they are reproduced. Mirror images are among the earliest and simplest forms of pictorial reproduction. These were followed by the printing of books and pictures and then eventually by the new forms of mass media image production that exist today. Regardless of which criterion we choose to subdivide the image worlds, each one only captures a small part of the complexity of images.

1.3 The cultural nature of the order of the senses

This expansion of the spectrum of images goes hand in hand with a differentiation between the senses. It leads to the senses being independent of each other, the sense of sight and the images perceived by this sense, in particular. This has been accompanied by a *hypertrophy of the sense of sight* at the expense of the other senses. This development has led to a growing devaluation of the sense of hearing and even more so of the senses of touch, smell and taste. This development is a characteristic of the Western modern age, and the fact that it is culture-specific is often ignored. In many other cultures, the sense of sight does not have the same importance as in the Western modern age; other senses are dominant there. Despite the dominance of certain forms of seeing in Western culture, there have been repeated attempts to emphasize the 'unity of the senses' and to bring to the fore the central importance of the little regarded senses of touch and taste.

Erwin Straus saw the unity of the senses as being due to the fact that humans experience them as linked, despite all culturally conditioned differences.[12] For Straus, sensing is 'sympathetic experiencing', in which man and the world are interwoven and both the unity and the diversity of the senses have a role to play.

It is true that the individual senses convey different sensations, yet what unites them is the connection that each forges between the human being and the world. One criterion for differentiating between the senses is that each one of them has a different relationship to space and also to time.[13] Seeing occurs because there is an inner link between sensing and moving. Seeing creates sensations through movement, without which it becomes staring, when neither visual images nor sensations are evoked. Sensations arise through movement. This becomes very clear if we consider dance which comes into being through the unity of music and movement. Hearing is tied to the temporal sequence of noises and sounds. Movement helps us to be able to follow the fleetingness of the sounds and their temporality in space.

With our focus on seeing since the times of ancient Greece, which has been intensified as we have moved increasingly to a culture of literacy, and with seeing becoming more important with the invention of the New Media, it is above all touching and tasting that are losing importance. There are many more reasons for this development which we can do no more than touch on here. The links between modernization and the development of science and individualization, to which Norbert Elias and Michel Foucault have drawn attention, are also part of it, although they do not offer sufficient explanation.

The cultural dependency of the hypertrophy of seeing in Western culture becomes evident if we remember that the weighting of the senses can also be quite different. This is clear in the following example:

> Blood has a variety of sensory properties: it is warm, viscous, red, salty and odorous. Which of these gets emphasized depends on the order within which they are perceived. Thus North Americans, for instance, tend to think of blood in terms of its *visual appearance*, its redness, In South India, practitioners of Siddha medicine give priority to the *tactile* dimension of blood, the pulse it produces within the body.
>
> [. . .] This holds true in Guatemala as well, although there the pulse is said to be the 'voice' of blood, suggesting an audio-tactile perceptual framework. [. . .] Among the Ainu of Japan it is the *odor* of blood that is the most salient, as the smell of blood is thought to repel spirits. In the myth of the Wauwalak sisters as told in Northern Australia, there is reference to both the smell of blood and to 'blood containing sound' [. . .], which implies an audio-olfactory bias.[14]

This example shows how different sensory perceptions are. The order of the senses in any given culture decides how something is perceived and the role played by the individual senses. Upon closer scrutiny of these differences we see that there are also many other cultural characteristics at play in the order of the senses. There are, for example, linguistic differences in the varieties of different words connected with the senses. In the Indo-Germanic languages, there are far more words relating to sight, for example, than to smell or taste. Furthermore, the senses are involved in different ways in the shaping of the aisthetic and aesthetic norms of a society. Here again sight predominates in our culture, which makes an object of what we are looking at. It is a completely different situation with the Navajo Indians, who, unlike the American tourists who try to achieve a bird's-eye view of pictures they have made in the sand, enter into the middle of the sand pictures. In other cultures, the perception of beauty, which in Western culture occurs predominantly through seeing, also often takes place much more via the other senses such as hearing or smell. As a rule the differences between the cultural modes of using the senses correspond to the way these are used in the different social fields. The order of the senses results from the staging and performing of each of the senses.

1.4 'The great image has no form'

Research in cultural anthropology has elucidated how different the relationship of the senses to each other can be in different cultures.[15] Just as there are differences in the way we see things, there are also major differences in our understanding of images, which in turn come back to affect our seeing and the order of the senses in society. The example of the Chinese image shows how different our understanding of images can be.[16] Their alterity clarifies once more how in Europe the world becomes object and image and how this process contributes to the emergence of the European subject.

In François Jullien's interpretation, Chinese pictures of landscapes are a product of an interplay between presence and absence; they appear and disappear in a movement that is situated somewhere between being and non-being. Laotse puts it in a general way (§ 40): 'In the world all beings and things are born out of the "there is", and the "there is" is born out of the "there is not"'. This interplay between being and non-being gives rise to the half dark and the half light of the Chinese image. This interplay between being and non-being can also be found in the Chinese rituals in honour of the dead, in which sacrifices are made to the dead as if they were present. This 'as if' is an essential part of the mystery of the picture and painting. Thus, in a traditional text by Wang Wei, 'Of the pagodas whose rooftops vanish into the sky, one need not have the rooms at the base appear: it's as if there were – as if there were not; either high or low'.[17] This movement of appearing and disappearing is typical of Chinese painting, whose aim is not to depict objects but to execute movements which capture and exert an effect on the observer of the picture. Chinese painting is not content with making something visible; it also wants to veil and conceal and make the simultaneous presence of both movements experienceable.

> The *yin* and *yang* factors, which both oppose and complement each other, are at the beginning of any reality, and the 'way', or *tao*, is born from their alternation – 'one time *yin*, one time *yang*' ('now *yin* – now *yang*'), in the canonical formulation. Hence it falls to the *yang* to promote the obvious, its role being to unfold and to 'display outside', whereas the 'hidden' is the *yin*, the *yin* factor's role being to 'enclose within the figuration'.[18]

Revealing and concealing, and form and formlessness, are the elements of the Chinese picture. However, how should we understand this formlessness, on which the pictorial forms depend and which would not come into being without it? In Chinese paintings what is important is not that the painter paints what he sees but that he portrays what is given him and what he receives. The opposition between presence and absence must be dissolved. For the *tao* is the basis of the visible; it is at the boundary of the visible, as if it existed. Accordingly, painting is a happening at the boundary of not-painting, the creation of a picture an event on the boundary of the non-picture, or, in the words of Laotse (§ 41), 'The great image has no form'.

In view of the aforementioned, it is no surprise that in Chinese the word *xiang* means both picture and phenomenon, and so there is no difference between what appears and what is created as the picture. There is no representational relationship between the appearances in the world and the pictures. The view that there is, therefore, no mimetic relationship between the phenomena of the world and painting, as Jullien maintains, can be explained only by the fact that this argument is based on far too narrow a concept of mimesis which relates mimesis to the idea of *natura naturata* (i.e. nature which is static or already completed) rather than to *natura naturans* (i.e. nature as self-generating or dynamic). My own understanding of mimesis is different, and I believe that in this process of creating Chinese pictures, which is described as a to-ing and fro-ing between revealing and concealing, mimetic processes are central.[19] The idea of an object that stands facing the subject, for which the Chinese have coined the neologism *dui-xiang* (phenomenon facing us), but only under the influence of Western culture, suggests that when someone paints a picture there is a mimetic process in the search for a picture that is between appearance and non-appearance. The mimetic process does not focus on an object, but on the 'great image that has no form' and which arises in the encounter with Chinese pictures of landscapes.

Chinese pictures are neither reproductions nor representations or repetitions, but rather reflect something that is neither an image nor an object.

> The old man reminds the neophyte who believes that 'resemblance' suffices to achieve 'truth' that he must first fully consider the 'phenomena' (xiang) of beings and things to achieve both the 'flower' (of external resemblance) and the 'fruit' (constituted by breath-energy). Otherwise, resemblance, in its superficiality, lies in achieving the material form but abandoning the breath-energy that permeates it, and makes it vibrate. The term 'vibrate' is not metaphorical here, nor more or less aptly poetic, but rather expresses the vibratory phenomenon of reality.[20]

The breath-energy, which is similar to the force of *natura naturans*, produces the image; it gives life to its forms and enables it to come into being between the void and plenty. This powerful force creates the image on the boundary of the non-visible, regardless of whether it portrays clouds, wind and rain or rivers, paths and trees. Alien to this way of painting is the object that remains constant, which Alberti and the painters of the Renaissance were striving for and which persisted for a long time, with the one-point perspective and the associated idea that the gaze would always remain the same. In European painting of the Renaissance the godlike creative force of the painter is expressed in the 'disegno', which creates the artistic work out of nothing. In contrast to this, the Chinese painter does not consider that he possesses the power to create things. In his painting speaks the energy of nature; it is incumbent upon him, merely as part of this force, to keep expressing this energy in new pictures, to modify and transform it. Whereas the intensification of the difference between subject and object, image and phenomenon has had a considerable effect on the emergence of European culture in the modern age,[21] for Chinese culture it was important not to enhance these differences. In contrast to European painters, traditional Chinese painters seek harmony with nature, and their 'paintings are appreciated in direct proportion to their capacity to make *something* of life express itself between the bamboo leaves or the rock structure, distilling the moment that promotes it, and starting to become once more, through that refound fluidity, available and unspecified'.[22]

Whereas in European culture man is perceived as a creator of images, *homo pictor*, pictures in Chinese painting have been understood not so much as objects but as process. 'Being able to relate to pictures is essential if living a good life in the world is to succeed.'[23] Thus, in Chinese art we are not confronted with pictures as objects; it is far more of the question of the interplay between us and the image. We ourselves are part of the pictures, which are not simply objects but performative processes. Images are perceived not so much in terms of their appearance but rather in the way they affect us. It is by means of these ethical effects that they create 'a community between people'. The effect of the picture becomes possible through the *qi* or *chi* (Jap. *ki*), or the life force which reveals itself in different forms.[24] According to Chinese ideas, pictures are infused with a breath which also gives them expression. This expression is sensed by the person looking at the picture; it is via this expression that the pictures are able to affect and influence those who look at them.

Since Chinese pictures of landscapes are often scroll paintings, we view them in a different way from the pictures of the Renaissance that use a one-point perspective. They cannot be perceived simultaneously in one look but have to be unrolled to be 'experienced' or read. 'As we look at the picture, our relationship with the world is to be transformed in such a way as to make us enter what is really going on in the world, through our looking.'[25] What is important in these pictures is not a representation of the world as a picture but that the picture should have the effect on the observer of making him or her an integral part of the picture. Instead of a distancing relationship, in which picture and observer face each other, the result is intended to be a relationship to the world. A complex mimetic process takes place which results in the picture becoming a place of life.

2

Imagination and the development of human beings

In the Western visual culture of the modern age, images, through the mass media, have penetrated all areas of human life and exercise their influence there. With the spread of the visual culture, we can no longer deny that images play a key role in our understanding of the present day. A new interest in images has led to a 'pictorial turn' in the humanities. 'What is an image?' is the key question, followed by the equally important questions: 'How are images used?' and 'What do images do to us?' Is there even any point in talking about *the* image?[1] Do we not need to make complex differentiations between different kinds of image? The question arises, for example, whether *presence or representation* are still important in digital images. Digital, that is, mathematically produced, images are often simulations, whose representational character comes into question because of the digital IT procedures used to produce them. The situation with regard to the imaging procedures in the natural sciences is particularly complicated. Here images are the result of complex calculations, the various iconic representations of which are often not yet compatible. In all sciences, images have appeared alongside language which has made it clear that they are conveying iconic information which cannot be expressed by language alone. In other words, images have an intrinsic value which is irreplaceable. The fact that there is now a greater awareness of this by academics in the fields of culture and science is a consequence of the 'pictorial turn'. What is the anthropological significance of this capacity to produce images? How can we understand this ability to create, to remember and to restructure images? What significance does this have for our phylogenetic and ontogenetic development?

Imagination is a *conditio humana*, without which neither the phylogenetic nor the ontogenetic development of humanity is possible. We could start by saying that imagination can be described as a force which makes the world appear before human beings, in the sense of the Greek word *phainestai*.[2] Here we can differentiate between two different dimensions of meaning. One meaning of 'to make appear' is that the world appears to humans in a way that is determined by the human condition, and is perceived accordingly. Another meaning of 'to make appear' is that humans use mental images to construct the world and create it accordingly. Images are thus the medium that connect humans with the world and the world with humans. They act as a bridge between outside and inside, inside and outside; they are *chiastic*, and it is this that defines them. The Romans transformed the 'fantasy' of the Greeks into 'imagination'. Here language stresses the capacity of imagination to transform the outside world into images and convey these to the inner image world. In the German language, Paracelsus used the word '*Einbildungskraft*' for '*imagination*', seeing it, therefore, as a power or force which brings the world inside people, thus making the inner world hold the outside world within it. Without this possibility there would be no human world of culture, no imaginary and no language.[3]

2.1 Hominization and imagination

Little is known about the origins of fantasy. There are indications that it is very old. It is doubtlessly closely linked to the marked increase in the size of the human brain, which began with *Homo erectus*, 800–500,000 years ago. *Homo erectus* underwent some decisive developments – these early humans stood up and their hands were freed. The interplay between brain growth, liberation of the hands, development of the front part of the cranium and language resulted in a new evolutionary complexity characteristic of human beings in which fantasy played an important part. However, it was not just the increase in brain size (which was 3 times larger in relation to body weight in *Australopithecus*, 4.5 times larger in *Homo erectus* and 7.2 times larger in *Homo sapiens*) but in particular the quality of neuronal networking that was important for the development of fantasy. This development in the brain was embedded in a number of further changes. Most important among these were upright gait, the change in habitat with an increase in the meat content of the diet due to hunting, the cultivation of fire and the gradual development of language and culture. *Hominization can be conceived as a multifaceted morphogenesis deriving from the interaction of ecological, genetic, cerebral, social and cultural factors*, of which the evolution of the imagination, which has an important part to play in the further development of human beings, was an integral part.

We can see imagination, with its ability to construct images, at work in the process which turns a piece of nature into an aesthetically formed tool. In this process, a stone is selected according to a mental image and processed to fashion a tool which has to perform certain functions and also fulfil aesthetic demands. A further stage of aesthetic creation was reached when human beings translated their reality into drawings, as we see in the bone markings in Bilzingsleben in the Artern district in Thuringia in Germany that date to about 300,000 years ago in the Palaeolithic Age. Some interpreters have tried to see figures in these markings, while others have seen no more than markings that are hardly possible to interpret. Another new stage in the forming of images is to be found in the figurines of animals and humans that were produced roughly 35,000 years ago in the area around the Danube and the Rhine. Here *Homo pictor*, the image-creating human being, can be seen.

Complex works of the imagination are to be seen in the rock paintings of this era, most of which are to be found in Europe, the most beautiful examples existing in the Franco-Cantabrian region. If we accept André Leroi-Gourhan's interpretation, 'we see art as split away from writing, as it were, and follow a trajectory that, starting in abstraction, gradually establishes conventions of form and movement, and then, at the end of the curve, achieves realism and then eventually collapses'.[4] These rock paintings are pictures that date from before the artistic era over whose meaning there has been much speculation and which have continued to defy interpretation. What is certain, however, is that these pictures were perceived completely differently by their contemporaries from the way we see them today. Our limited capacity to grasp such rock images is an example of the basic methodological problem of how we should understand cultural phenomena of a particular period without our own cultural preconceptions getting in the way. This is one of the main challenges that historical anthropology has to deal with.[5] According to this, it is important to relate the historicity and culturality of the works to the historicity and culturality of their observers. Only if we do this can we understand these works in a way that includes our own historicity as a constitutive element.

How were these pictures perceived? Were they seen as being based on living creatures? Did the presence of the animals in the picture make it possible to conjure up the absent animals as though they were present? We don't know. As we view them today, these pictures bring something into the present; they portray absent animals and figures and intensify the portrayal through the act of showing, the deictic gesture, of which we have only a tenuous grasp. The rock pictures can be repeatedly viewed and reanimated, thus intensifying the way we perceive them. We see pictures as pictures and the things depicted in them as *pictorial objects*. At the same time, we see their reference to the world outside the picture. What we see as a picture points to something outside the picture that stands in relation to what is portrayed. This relationship is sometimes magical, sometimes characterized by similarity and sometimes there is a causal connection. This superimposing of different images in our perception results from our imagination, without which it would not be possible for us to look at the picture and for the picture to look back at us.

2.2 Images of the dead and imagination

Burial objects from Neanderthal graves provide further evidence of the development of human imagination. This includes colours, equipment and provisions which lead us to conclude that the Neanderthals believed in a life after death. Relics of a man, woman and child were found in the La Ferrassie rock cave in the department of the Dordogne in France that were strewn with ochre. In the Shanidar cave in North Iraq, rose, carnation and hyacinth pollen was found beneath and over the skeletons, which leads us to conclude that the dead lay on a bed of flowers. From these finds, it can be deduced that the living looked after the dead and saw them as still belonging to them. They knew pain and grief and had conceptions of the finiteness of human life that they hoped to offset through a belief in a life on the other side. The Neanderthals had not only clear ideas of past and future but also ideas of an imaginary and the possibility that the dead could live on in a world on the other side. Death represents a frontier presenting people with a strong challenge to produce imaginary images. This is true for this early period of human development and still holds true today. Much of the religious imaginary is a response to human transitoriness and our extinguishing by death.

There is a close link between the experience of death and the production of sculptures. We see this in the sculpture of a skull from the Melanesian island of New Ireland which, as part of a death cult, was probably placed on a carved wooden figure and was the skull of the person who was being commemorated in the death rite. It was coated with wax and chalk paste and painted with ochre. The skull was treated in such a way that it was not simply a mummy but was removed into a different imaginary sphere whereby it became the bearer of other forces, which cannot be perceived without imagination. Skulls and images of the dead only become possible when there is a collective imaginary relating to the beyond. This is evident from early works such as the Jericho skull, which is about 7,000 years old. Communities would use them to create images of the deceased, enabling the absent deceased to be present in the community again, albeit only as an image. In the image, there is an intermingling of the absence of the deceased and their presence as an image. The image is an indication that something is absent and renders it visible. The point of the image is to represent something that is absent and which can therefore only be present in the image.

> The image of a dead person is, therefore, no anomaly but rather the quintessence of what an image in fact is. The dead person is always absent, death an unbearable absence that people wanted to fill with an image to make it bearable. This is why people banished their dead, who are nowhere, to a chosen place (the grave) and gave them an *immortal body*: a *symbolic body*, with which they could be reintegrated into society while their *mortal body* dissolved into nothingness.[6]

The image makes something appear that *is* not in the image but can only *appear* in the image. This is precisely what is expressed by the Greek word *phantasia*. Fantasy makes something that does not exist appear in the image, thereby anticipating the development of the field of aesthetics. What we see in the image is not merely shapes, colours and configurations, that is, the pictorial elements of the picture; we see them *as* the image. This seeing *in* and seeing *as* only is only possible through fantasy, which makes the world appear and is constitutive of our human relationship with the world.

From this discussion of the role played by imagination in aesthetics, it is Without imagination there would be no *memories* and no *projections of what the future may hold*. According to Kant's definition in Paragraph 24 of his *Critique of Pure Reason*, 'Imagination is the faculty for representing an object even without its presence in intuition.'[7] According to Kant, the power of imagination is tied to what we have perceived with our senses. If concepts are to denote reality, they must be accompanied by 'intuition'. Whereas with empirical concepts this is no problem, concepts of understanding or reason need schemata or symbols to render them appreciable by the senses. In Kant's view, concepts such as the state, love and death are not based on intuition gained from experience. Nevertheless, imagination can clearly mediate between a concept and our perception of it by reminding us of similar objects that we have perceived.

From this discussion of the role played by imagination in aesthetics, it is evident that imagination is more than the ability to make present what is absent and to conjure up an internal image of the world. No less important is the ability of the imagination to reorganize existing structures and create something novel. Imagination permits us to *invent* things and become *creative*. What remains uncertain is the extent to which imagination, when producing its works, is bound to the prerequisites of nature or culture. Even if we assume that the artist acts as the *natura naturans*, that is, as the creative force of nature, this metaphor does not explain how originality, creativity and novelty arise. The creativity of imagination is based on the act of *inventio* in which the 'freedom of subjectivity' is expressed. Imagination is neither 'without origin nor not without origin' but is indebted to the medial paradoxes and the productivity of the paradox.

2.3 Presence – representation – simulation

As we have seen, human beings are characterized by our ability to use fantasy to create images. The images range from images with a hieratic, magical character, where the image is identical with what it depicts, to those images that no longer represent anything but simply simulate. In between these two types of image are images based on a representational relationship and whose relationship to the world and other images is mimetic. We can, therefore, differentiate between three types of image:

- The image as magical presence
- The image as mimetic representation
- The image as technical simulation

Although there are many overlaps, it is important to make this distinction. It enables us to identify different, sometimes contradictory, iconic characteristics.

The image as magical presence. Images that came about in an era when images had not yet become works of art include *figurines, masks, cult images and sacred images*. Among these, images that suggest that the gods have a magical presence, that is, images of gods or idols, are particularly important. These include early portrayals of fertility goddesses from ancient cultures in clay or stone. Many idols, figurines and masks of early times serve to ensure through their existence the presence of the divine. The Golden Calf, referred to in the Old Testament, was also a cult image in which god and image become one and the presence of a god is embodied and symbolized in the calf. While Moses was on Mount Sinai receiving God's commandments which expressly forbade the creation of any image of God and the worship of images, the people had followed their old need to worship an image under the leadership of Moses's older brother Aaron. Aaron is an example of an image-worshipping iconodule and Moses of an image-combatting iconoclast. The two of them represent fundamental ways of relating to images that are still valid today. What they have in common is that they are convinced of the power of images. This power emerges from their ability to envision an impalpable and distant being and make it so vivid that it can completely fill the space of human attention. The power of the image lies in the fact that it is a 'becoming similar', it creates something that is the same as the one portrayed. The Golden Calf *is* (from the perspective of the ritual) *the god.* The image and its content fuse together until they are indistinguishable.[8]

In the medieval cult of relics a small body part attributed to a saint sufficed to make the saint present. 'Here lie the bodies of many saints', we read in the Conques relic collection. The saints are actually present; they are not represented by their relics. They develop their healing powers for the faithful in the place where parts of their bodies are to be found. The relics consecrate the place and the participants in the ritual actions. Ritual actions are performed to produce a connection between the relic as a pictorial embodiment of the saint and the awaited salvation. The salvation is seen as being the consequence of the ritual action, which in other cultures would have been called magical.

Many modern works of art do not represent anything beyond the work itself, but rather create a presence which can be compared to early (cult) works from the age before art. Mark Rothko and Barnett Newman use images with the express intention of invoking a sense of the sacred or of inner mystery, for example in the Rothko Chapel in Houston, where the colours of the pictures leave the observer in a diffuse floating state where there is a mysterious balance between 'presence and diffusion'. Newman's pictures also test our limits and make us aware of our powerlessness. In Newman's view, this makes it possible for us to experience the sublime. This experience is characterized by the excessive demands made on our cognitive capacity by something vast. Our feeling of being overwhelmed by this vastness turns into an unexpected gain. In this respect a picture by Newman wants to *show nothing* at all (not even just areas of colour); it wants to *affect* us in pure form and to *release* something in the observer. It cancels itself out as a picture completely the moment this succeeds.[9]

The image as mimetic representation. In the works of Plato, *images become representations* of something that they themselves are not. They portray something, express something and point towards to something. According to Plato, painters and poets do not produce ideas like God, or useful objects like craftsmen. They create the *appearances* of things. Painting and poetry are not, however, restricted to portraying things artistically, but also portray how things appear. The aim is not to portray the idea or truth, but phantasms. Thus, painting and mimetic poetry can make what is visible appear. What we are concerned with here is mimesis, which creates images and illusions, and in which the difference between the model and the depiction of it is unimportant. The aim is not similarity but the *appearance of what is appearing*. In Plato, art and aesthetics are a domain of their own where the artist, or the poet, is the master. According to Plato, the artist does not have the ability to produce things that exist and is free of the truth claim to which philosophy has to do justice and which is fundamental to the 'State'. Thus, art and aesthetics gain independence from the demands of philosophy, from its search for truth and insight and its striving for goodness and beauty. The price they have to pay for that is excommunication from the 'State', which does not accept the incalculable nature of art and poetry.

The artistic creative process, therefore, is directed towards the creation of an inner image that painters or poets see before their eyes. The conception behind the creation merges more and more into the image, which is formed in a different medium from the idea imagined. In this process, changes, omissions, additions and so on are made so that there is only a limited degree of similarity. In most cases the 'proto-images' which preceded the images created by the artists are unknown to us, either because they never existed or because they have not been preserved. The focus of the artistic process is the image, which contains references to a 'proto-image' and which comes into being through a process of transformation.

The (mimetic) production of representational images is an elementary anthropological skill. The human body is a central theme. Renaissance portraits and contemporary photographs depict human bodies that represent human beings. As pictures of bodies, photographs portray human beings in important situations in their lives. Tied up with these and other forms of representational images are the issues involved in how we conceive of ourselves as human beings. Without pictures of ourselves, that is, representations of ourselves, we cannot comprehend ourselves. Insight into the pictorial nature of such representations is essential if we are to grasp the limits of the possibilities of human self-perception.

Humans have been creating images of the human body since the earliest times. These images of the body are human images, just as human portrayals are always body portrayals. The images portray the body, whose biology has not changed over time, in various ways. A history of these images is representative of a history of the human body. At the same time, it is a history of representations and images of humans. From this, we can conclude that human beings are just as they appear in their bodies. The body itself is an image even before it is replicated in images. The depiction is not what it claims to be, that is, a *reproduction* of the body. In truth it is a *production* of a body image which is already predefined in the self-portrayal of the body. The *triad human being – body – image* cannot be dissolved if we do not want to lose all three reference points.[10]

The image as technical simulation. Everything today has a tendency to become an image. Even opaque bodies are transformed; they lose their opacity and solidity and become transparent and fleeting. Processes of abstraction result in images and pictograms. We come across them everywhere; nothing is strange or overwhelming any more. Images make things, 'realities', disappear. As well as the handing down of texts, for the first time in human history a large number of images are also being saved and traded. Photos, films and videos become aide-memoires, and image memories evolve. Whereas up until now texts have required imagined images to complement them, nowadays imagination is curbed by the production and passing on of captions. Fewer and fewer people are producing images and more and more people are consuming them, images that are prefabricated and hardly challenge the imagination at all.

Images are a specific form of abstraction; their two-dimensionality transforms space. The fact that TV images are electronic means that they can be ubiquitous and speeded up. These images can be simultaneously distributed all over the world. They miniaturize the world and allow us to experience the world specifically as an image. They represent a new form of commodity and are subject to the economic principles of the marketplace. They are even produced and traded if the objects on which they are based do not become commodities. Images are exchanged with others and are related to others; they select elements and rearrange them; fractal images are produced which each time form a new whole with each iteration. They move and relate to each other. The very fact that they are accelerating means that they become more similar to each other: mimesis of speed. Because they are essentially two-dimensional, electronic and reduce the size of things, images are growing increasingly similar to each other, despite differences in content. They sweep the observer along with them. They fascinate and frighten. They dissolve the relationships that have evolved between things and humans and convert them into a world of appearance. The world, political and social relations are aestheticized. In a mimetic process, images seek models upon which to base themselves; they are transformed into new fractal images with no frame of reference. This results in a promiscuity of images. Intoxicating games with simulacra and simulations are produced: extreme differentiation between images with a simultaneous implosion of their differences. The images as images are the message.[11]

Images are spread at the speed of light. The result is a world of appearance and fascination which detaches itself from 'reality'. The world of appearance is expanding, tending to detach the reality content from the other 'worlds'. Ever more images are being produced that have only themselves as reference point and have no basis in reality. Ultimately, everything is becoming a game of images in which all is possible, so that even ethical questions are becoming unimportant. If everything becomes a game of images, arbitrariness and lack of commitment are inevitable. The worlds of images thus produced must in turn exert an influence on how we live. It is becoming increasingly difficult to differentiate between life and art, fantasy and reality. Both areas are growing alike. Life is becoming a 'proto-image' for the world of appearance and vice versa. Visual elements are multiplying exponentially. The world is becoming transparent; time is compressed as though the only thing left is the present with its accelerated images. The images attract desire, bind it, dissolve its boundaries and diminish the differences. At the same time, they elude desire and direct our attention to what is absent while at the same time remaining present. Things and people demand transcendence in images.

Images become simulacra.[12] They relate to something, make themselves similar and are the product of mimicry behaviour. Political debates are often not conducted for their own sake but staged so that they can be transformed into images to be broadcast on the television. All political debate is conducted with an eye as to how it is going to be converted into images. The television images become the medium of political argument. The viewers see the simulation of a political controversy in the course of which everything is staged to make them believe that the political argument is authentic. Everything is always designed for transformation into the world of appearance. The success of the controversy is dependent on the success of the transformation. The effects of politics arise out of the simulation of politics. The impacts that politics have result from how they have been simulated. Simulations are more effective than 'real' political debates.

Simulacra are constantly in search of 'proto-images' that need them to come into being. Simulations become pictograms that have repercussions on the nature of the political controversies. It becomes difficult to distinguish clearly between reality and simulacrum; the dissolution of boundaries has led to renewed overlapping and intermingling. Mimetic processes bring about a circular flow between 'proto-images', 'likenesses' and 'after-images' or 'post-images'. The aim of the images is no longer to be like 'proto-images', but to be like themselves. A similar thing happens with human beings. The aim is to attain an extraordinary similarity of individuals with themselves, attainable as an effect of productive mimesis, while at the same time we find extensive differentiation within the same subject.

2.4 Looking at pictures: Pictures looking

Images of presence, representation, simulation and also many of our mental images do not come into existence until they, or the figurative properties they contain, are looked at. But what does 'looked at' mean? Looks can vary greatly. They can be modest, kind, impatient, evil, angry and so on. Looks are closely connected with the history of the subject and subjectivity and also with knowledge. They express power, control and self-control. They reveal our relationship to the world, to other people and to ourselves. Our social life is constituted by other people's looks. We can differentiate between intimate looks and public looks. They are not merely individual, but also social, and linked to the collective imaginary and the human images expressed in this. Descriptions of the look or gaze as a flame, without which the world would remain invisible, or as a mirror which simply takes the world in and reflects it back, do not do it justice. The look is both active and passive; it is directed towards the world and receives the world at the same time. In the history of seeing, there have been different interpretations of the extent to which it is active and the extent to which it is passive. Since Maurice Merleau-Ponty at the latest, we have had to assume that the world, together with the images created by human beings, is also looking at us. The look is chiastic; in it world and human being meet and cross over. Human beings can express many things in a look and then instantly deny it. This is because the look is spontaneous and ephemeral. It makes things visible and at the same time is an expression of our humanness.

With regard to artistic images, we find the following thoughts about art: 'Gazes are already in the picture before they fall upon a picture. This alone permits the use of the *history of the image* in support of a *history of the gaze*'.[13] Therefore, an iconology of the look or gaze gives useful insights into the diversity of historical and cultural image praxes. The gaze moves back and forth between image, body and medium; it comes to rest neither in the body nor in the image but unfolds in the field between the two; it cannot be pinned down and can choose how it wants to behave towards the medium. Images entice the gaze and make it 'an object itself, in our desire for images'. In works of art, the primary image praxis of the body merges into a secondary image praxis. As we look at images which have no life of their own, our imagination comes into play. When we look in the mirror or through a window, we can become aware of our looking. 'The look through the window is echoed by the computer screen, the look in the mirror by the video.'[14]

The way we approach images is substantially affected by what is called the *mimetic look*. As observers we use this mode of looking to open ourselves up to the world. By making ourselves similar to it, we expand our world of experience. We absorb an impression of the world and incorporate it into our mental image world. We reconstruct shapes and colours, and material and its structures, by looking and transform them into our inner worlds where they become part of the imaginary. In this process, the uniqueness of the world is absorbed in all its different historical and cultural forms. What this does is slow down our interpretations of world and image, interpretations which transform them into language and meaning but at the same time destroy them as 'images'. The point is to endure the uncertainties, ambiguities and complexities of the world and not seek to achieve clarity. By reproducing things mimetically, we expose ourselves to the ambivalence of the world and images. In this process, it is a matter of learning 'by heart' this piece of the world, that is, the image. In the case of images, this means closing our eyes and using our imagination, creating the image we have seen in our mind's eye and focusing our attention on it. We must then protect it from other images streaming in and use our concentration and power of thought to 'hold onto' the image. The re-creation of an image in an act of contemplation is the first step; holding onto it, working on it and allowing it to unfold in our imagination are further steps in a mimetic processing of images. Reproducing an image in our mind's eye, staying a while with it attentively, is just as important as the interpretative approach.

3

Iconic forms of imagination

We can begin to understand imagination if we describe it as an energy which helps us to make absent people, objects and states of affairs present. What is absent becomes present in the medium of the image. In the image, on the one hand what is absent is present; on the other hand, viewed in concrete terms, it is absent at the same time. This paradox is responsible for the fact that many images are representational, which is essential for the development of mental images. It is the representational structure of the image that makes it possible to make the outside world the inner world and the inner world the outside world.

Mental images do, however, vary in the intensity in which the outside world appears in them. A comparison between perceptual images and the images of our imagination makes this clear. In general, imagined images do not attain the intensity of perceptual images. The objects of imagined images are unreal; they are present but unattainable at the same time. Unlike perceptual images, which show the objects upon which they are based from a single perspective, images of our imagination are seen from several sides at once. It is hardly possible to keep to a single perspective, because our imagination completes it and transmits the idea of the whole. 'The act of imagination is [. . .] a magical one. It is an incantation, destined to produce the object of one's thought, the thing one desires, in such a way that one can take possession of it.'[1]

However, this is only one aspect of how we deal with mental images. In addition, mental images resist our intent to make them appear and force us to wait for them to form. Here our attention is focused on a vacuum that has been created deliberately, which has to be endured and in which the inner images evolve. They are often hesitant; they make us wait for them to appear. Sometimes they are clear and then they lose their power again and have to be evoked once more. At other times, they arise spontaneously and with great intensity. Our wish for the desired images to appear confronts us with the limits of our capacities. Every time we imagine an image an object is missing; whatever we do, the object will never really be there, even if we are successful in imagining it. In what follows we will examine the difference between images of the imagination and perceptual images. With images of the imagination, we can distinguish between remembered images, images that project into the future, images based on perceptions, pathological images of the imaginary and dreams. We will demonstrate the importance of the imagination in the production of these different types of image by comparing them with each other and especially by differentiating them from perceptual images. It will become clear that here too we are looking at different ways in which the imagination appears and articulates itself.

3.1 Memory

Let us recall what was said by using our memory. *Yesterday* I had dinner in a pizzeria with my best friend. I try to remember what happened. To begin with, I can hardly remember a thing. Instead, images constantly come into my head reminding me of all the things I still have to do today. After a while, I manage to push aside these distracting images – I see the pizzeria and my friend sitting at a table waiting for me. I feel the atmosphere, see the restaurant, hear the sounds and relive my feeling of guilt at being late. Arbitrarily I can choose which of the images conjured up by my memory I want to get clearer – I can see my friend's pullover, his face, his slightly flushed cheeks; I can see him drinking a glass of red wine, hear him calling the waiter and relive the intimacy of our conversation. I can expand the scene as I wish; in so doing I can keep strictly to what happened last night; I can, however, also embellish the scene: I remember what I didn't tell him, although I should have done; I correct my tendency to eat too fast – nice to eat more slowly than him for once; I see myself in the room and sense the gradual passing of time over the course of the evening. By making myself into an imagined image of myself, I can now take part in what have now become the unreal events of last night. I can swap chairs and sit next to my friend. I can suppress and change my memory images almost arbitrarily by replacing them with imagined images that change the situation. Almost imperceptibly there is a shift in boundaries between what happened yesterday and what could also have happened. I enjoy this playful approach to memory and changing it. My conscious mind can differentiate between what really happened and what could have happened. I know what memory is and where the game of changing it starts. Despite the freedom I grant my memory to reshape last night's situation by embellishing what happened, the whole of last night is condensed into the few minutes in my memory. I believe in the fact that our meeting took place in the pizzeria and that everything happened exactly as I remember it. A consistency develops between me last night at the pizzeria and me as the rememberer of everything. I can distinguish between my memory images of last night and what I now perceive in my study – including the distant sounds of a young musician playing the trumpet. There is the space of my study and the time as I am experiencing it in the present and alongside that the space in the pizzeria with the events that took place last night. Last night's memory world arises in me; it is accessible to no one else and can only be entered by me if I am prepared to become an imagined image of myself. Likewise, I can also end the memories of last night. They don't force me to keep repeating the events in my imagination. Even if I enjoy intervening to change my memories, I sense how arbitrary this is. I also feel that the world of perception around me has a quality of concrete reality that resists me and that I cannot change at will.

In memory, therefore, images that have once been perceived can be reconstructed. We often judge how accurate our memories are by comparing how remembered images match up with perceptual images. Every memory is a reconstruction of the past. For various reasons, however, the memories can change, for example if there is a painful occurrence that I have 'forgotten' over the course of time or for which I have forgiven the person who caused it. In this case, the memories do not have the intensity of what happened at the time. If the context within which the event that was so painful for me occurred has changed, then the memory images will also be influenced by this change in context. As memory images are reconstructions, I can also consciously influence them. I can evaluate certain events differently, more or less deliberately. David Hume differentiated between the memory, which as a rule aims to remember what has passed as exactly as possible, and the imagination, which is given free rein to embellish memory with projections and changes. He described it as follows: 'For tho' it be a peculiar property of the memory to preserve the original order and position of its ideas, while the imagination transposes and changes them, as it pleases; yet this difference is not sufficient to distinguish them in their operation, or make us know the one from the other.'[2]

Bergson makes the distinction between a 'mémoire d'automatismes' and a 'mémoire-souvenir',[3] of which only the latter can distinguish between perception and imagination. In the 'mémoire involontaire', the relationship of memory to perception is different again. An example of this type of memory identified by Bergson is the madeleine passage in Proust's *Du côté de chez Swan*, where memory becomes, as it were, a resurrection of the past. This allows the I to step out of the sequential order of time and dip into the past, of which it is later said:

> the truth was that the being within me who was enjoying this impression was enjoying it because of something shared between a day in the past and the present moment, something extra-temporal, and this being appeared only when, through one of those moments of identity between the present and the past, it was able to find itself in the only milieu in which it could live and enjoy the essence of things, that is to say outside of time.[4]

Conflicts can arise between the images of memories and those of imagination. This occurs when the memory weighs so heavily that it can prevent the individual from freeing himself or herself from the weight of the past in order to be able to live a creative life. This weight of the past can be due, for example, to a period of guilt from which the individual can hardly free himself or herself, if at all. An example of this is the recurrent debate about our relationship with the past, or rather history.

We can draw together all these thoughts and ideas in these observations about imagination and memory images as follows:

1. Memory images can be deliberately produced with the aid of the imagination.
2. Compared with perception, memory images have an 'essential poverty' (Sartre), which makes it difficult to form them clearly and preserve them in our mental image world.
3. The process of creating memory images requires effort. Distracting images have to be pushed aside, and resistance has to be overcome for memory images to be able to inhabit a space that has been emptied of other images.
4. Memory images vary in the clarity and speed with which they occur; their appearance can only be controlled to a limited extent.
5. Memory images are not restricted to the visual; they are also bound up with atmospheres, sounds, smells, sensations of touch and taste.
6. Memory images are not unchangeable. Their structural properties can change, depending on the time and context of the memory.
7. The boundaries between memory images and imagined images which change them are fluid.
8. The game of modifying memory images can be enjoyable and even pleasurable. Transitions to a free play of fantasies are fluid.

9. Memory images are reconstructions produced by recreating past events through mimesis.
10. Memory images are interwoven with many other images of the mental image world and are constantly interacting with them, so that they are often not easily distinguishable from other images.

3.2 Projection of future events

The imagination does not produce memory images alone. We need the imagination when we are *projecting future events*. If I try to imagine a future event that has not yet happened and that bears no resemblance to anything that has happened up until now, it is generally more difficult for the imagination than if the event has already happened and simply needs to be remembered. In this case, as well, we can consciously differentiate between the future event and a past one or one that has simply been imagined without our really intending it to happen. Of course, greater effort is required for the imagination to retain a mental image of the image of the future and give it more substance. As we try to make these projected images more precise, we are more likely to be distracted by other images and resistance than is the case with memory images. Although both kinds of image are products of the imagination, the event that is the subject of the memory image is different in status from the event that has not yet happened; a far greater effort is required to develop an image of future events. Here the imagination cannot relate to a situation that has already been perceived; instead, in the case of the imagined event all further concrete details of the image are missing and have to be devised by the imagination. When we remember a past event, we know that the event took place in specific conditions and that it resulted in corresponding effects. In contrast, when we imagine a future event, our image can carry all our hopes and desires; however, these feelings are always focused on something that has not yet become concrete, unlike a past event. Therefore, the images are often still indistinct and need more clarity. At the same time, with this image of a future happening there is also the idea that everything could still turn out quite differently, since the future event is just one of many possibilities that are still awaiting realization. The memory image, on the other hand, relates to a possibility that has already been selected and realized. And yet the image of a future event also contains sensory elements and other painful or joyful feelings; often these are not as strong as is the case with memories; the extent to which these arise, are displaced, or rather replaced by completely different emotional impulses is still uncertain. The images of projected events are determined by the range of possibilities they offer, whereas those of real events are determined by the context and framing of how they actually happened.

It is only by using imagination that we can gain an idea of what could be.[5] As 'the as yet undetermined animal' (Nietzsche), we have no choice but to make images of the future for ourselves. With the help of these images, we construct ourselves in order to become the person we can be. Imagining our future is a way of gaining some control over our uncertainty. Anticipating the future is an attempt to divest ourselves of fear of uncertainty, that is, ultimately of our fear of death. Even if images of the future are not accurate and the associated disappointments are painful, for most people life is only bearable if it has a future that we can access through images. Imagination can free us from past and present and open us up to our future. In Gaston Bachelard's words:

> By the swiftness of its actions the imagination separates us from the past as well as from reality; it faces the future. To the *function of reality*, wise in experience of the past, as it is defined by traditional psychology, should be added a *function of unreality*, which is equally positive as I tried to show in certain of my earlier works. Any weakness in the function of unreality will hamper the productive psyche. If we cannot imagine we cannot foresee.[6]

Inasmuch as action is part of human nature, we have to use our imagination to plan our actions. This is true both of individuals and of communities and societies. 'Both individual and collective acts are crucial for imagining the future; here pure fiction and adequate anticipation are so closely linked that only the event, once the day comes, will allow us to judge retrospectively the level of truth or falsity in the images produced'.[7] As desiring beings, we humans are never content with the lives we lead; instead, we constantly devise alternatives and form images of what we lack. As finite beings, we are never satisfied with ourselves as we are and we experience this lack as a fact of life. In the words of Rousseau: 'It is imagination which extends for us the measure of the possible, whether for good or bad, and which consequently excites and nourishes the desires by the hope of satisfying them'; as a result, we form images of satisfaction that are sometimes more intense than the images that we perceive.[8] The images of the future anticipate a world that may or may not be fully or partially realized. In the way it anticipates the future, imagination is spontaneous, often radical and hard to control. In any event, it is geared towards constructing the future and as such also towards anticipating cultural practices.

If we now attempt to summarize the most important aspects, we can formulate the following theses:

1. Images projected onto the future are images of possibilities where all is uncertain and lacking in sharpness.
2. If and how these projections can be realized is completely open.
3. Images produced by projection are an attempt to catch up with the future and to prepare us for it.
4. They cannot be other than indistinct and await clearer definition.
5. Images produced by projection are images of yearning, desire and anticipation, and are threatened with failure.

3.3 Perceptual images

Perceptual images are processed not only by memory images but also by imagined images which are projected on to future events and actions. In the case of memory images, the relationship to perception is quite clear. First of all, we remember what happened, what we saw, heard, smelled, touched or tasted, along with the associated sensations and feelings, and what is brought into our conscious minds through imagination. In the process of reconstruction that takes place as we remember, the social environment in which the event took place and the actions associated with it are very important.[9] We use memory images to bring the past into the present of our conscious minds. In such reconstruction processes, what actually happened is often changed, particularly when our imagination is no longer powerful enough to reconstruct the event precisely. This is how mistakes, errors and illusions come about.

Perception also plays an important role when we envisage future actions and events. Although we do not in general expect the scene that we are imagining to be the same as a past one, when we envisage a future happening, we do need elements that have their origins in our perception and which are incorporated into our mental image world with the assistance of our imagination. Without imagination, we cannot process what we perceive.

As developments in perceptual psychology[10] and brain research in recent years have demonstrated,[11] we even need imagination *in order to perceive*. The two disciplines use different languages to describe this. Perceptual psychology has demonstrated that especially in situations in which the object of perception cannot be seen clearly, we complete its shape. This cannot be explained purely by the act of perception alone; rather, there is the suggestion that we use our imagination to fill in the gaps in incomplete images. Brain researchers believe that we are not born with the ability to see but that we acquire this ability in early childhood. A small child's brain generates a complex system of switches and connections that are essential for seeing and that cannot be acquired later in life. Many people who were cured of blindness in adulthood report that they were still not capable of learning to see, which shows that it is not possible to learn to see later in life. Instead, they felt overwhelmed and tortured by the visual stimuli. From these reports, we can see that there are many processes going on in the human brain, processes which must be considered to be switching and construction mechanisms, for which imagination is indispensable. It is as yet still uncertain as to exactly which neuronal activities are involved in these processes and the extent to which they overlap with what we are here calling imagination.

These approaches share the view that perception cannot be explained either by Euclid's emission theory or by Kepler's receptor theory, both of which held sway for several centuries. Gérard Simon summarizes Euclid's emission theory thus:

> The visual ray is conceived of as a kind of outgrowth of the soul which is related to light and fire, and touches things, as it were, at a distance. The theory is based on a spontaneous comparison with touch, as if it is a sensitive psycho-podium emanating from the pupil. From this it can be concluded that the visual ray is, quite literally, an unthinkable entity in our culture. It is spatial, more or less fiery, it reproduces itself in a straight line and is diverted by obstacles – all of these, for us in the modern era, are characteristics of a physical object. And yet it is intrinsically endowed with sensitivity, with a sensitivity that is active outside the body – which makes it at the same time a physical object, which, however, over and beyond that, corresponds to nothing that anatomy and physiology have taught us about our body. For a person from the ancient world visual sensation takes place where the object itself is, where the angle of view comes into contact with its surface and takes on its form.[12]

Neither this model of vision nor that of Johannes Kepler, influenced by Arabic optics, that took over from Euclid's model in the seventeenth century, took into account the fact that perception requires culturally shaped schemata which are applied in the act of perception. For Euclid, it was the touching of things by the angle of vision, whereas now it is a reception model of vision, in which 'the emanation of a ray' is replaced by 'mirroring' and which Kepler describes as follows: 'I say that vision occurs when an image of the whole hemisphere of the world that is before the eye, and a little more, is set up at the white wall, tinged with red, of the concave surface of the retina.'[13] He goes on to distinguish between an inner and an outer phase of vision. In the outer phase the objects are reproduced on the retina; in the inner phase, the images received by the 'soul' are processed. The introduction of this second phase prepares us for the insight that perception can no longer be grasped as a process in which objects are simply reproduced on the retina but that these images must also be processed by the 'soul'.

This ties in with our proposal that the outside world as we perceive it is processed with the aid of the imagination in such a way as to produce gestalts and configurations that can become a starting point for meanings and symbolizations that are cultural in origin. In this process, a merging of outside and inner worlds, of the sociocultural world and of the collective and individual imaginary occurs which makes it impossible to continue assuming that there are two separate phases that take place in sequence. Rather, as perception proceeds it includes memory and the actualization and application of schemata, experiences and habits that have been acquired in the past to the objects and situations that we actually perceive. It is imagination that causes this interweaving of the outside world, perception and consciousness. In this process, our consciousness has a clear task. We can understand it as

> a double relationship: on the one hand as an 'internal' relationship (between the memory, reflection and our relationship to ourselves), and on the other as an 'outward' relationship (to people, objects, world situations). Consciousness would be the 'interior' (as 'second order seeing') without which there can be no 'exterior' ('first order seeing'): that 'inner eye' that permits us to gaze upon an 'outer' world and to be aware of it.[14]

This view repudiates the idea that perception is neutral, something that comes 'naturally', is common to everyone and is not influenced by culture until later.[15] Instead, we assume that our perception is culturally shaped through our imagination which is itself shaped by culture. We understand perception to be a performative act in which, right from the start, our imagination interweaves the outside world and consciousness so closely that an inner image world can be produced, containing elements that can shape both memories and projections of future situations and events. Since perception is learnt in historical and cultural contexts, it can be seen as a cultural practice, like speaking and thinking. It follows from this that perception differs from one culture to another more than is generally thought. In any event, perception is learnt though social and cultural customs. It takes place in 'perception games' in which we receive mental images in which and with which we perceive the world, other people and ourselves, without our being aware of the fact that we are perceiving.

Memories, ideas of the future and perceptions differ from each other in that we are aware of their game quality, and as a rule we can distinguish relatively easily between them. Thus, memory images are generally not as clear as perceptual images and yet clearer than the images of scenes that we anticipate in the future. In the case of memory and anticipation of the future, imagination makes what is absent present; and in the case of the present, it enables us to turn the outside world into our inner world. But this is just an initial attempt to capture what imagination is.

3.4 Pathologies of the imagination

Another aspect of imagination is possible if we consider what happens when it becomes dysfunctional. Here people are not in control of their imaginary images but in their power, and they force them to behave in accordance with their mental images. One such image type is obsessive images. People feel they are at their mercy and have no power to resist them. They force people to perform and repeat certain actions. By performing such actions, they ward off fears against which they would otherwise be completely defenceless. By enacting and performing actions and scenes over and over again, they can protect themselves from the threat but at the same time, through their compulsive actions, they succumb to it.

People diagnosed with borderline personality disorder also live with similar splits in their imagination to those from which schizophrenic people suffer, as in Sartre's example:

> I recall the crisis I went through once: I said that I was the queen of Spain. At heart I knew well that this was untrue. I was like a child that plays with its doll and who is well aware that its doll is not alive but who wants to believe it. . . . Everything seemed to me to be enchanted. . . . I was like a comedian who played a role and identified himself with his character. I was conquered . . . but not entirely. I lived in an imaginary world.[16]

In this report, we are struck by the fact that the client is suffering from a delusion but that at the same time she is aware of being possessed by it. On the one hand, the patient takes the imagined idea that she is the Queen of Spain to be a perception of her situation, while on the other hand she knows that this idea is incorrect and therefore not identical with the perception. The client is held captive by her imagination and is unable to tell herself that it is a delusion. Nor can she rid herself of the awareness that accompanies her imaginings and enter completely into the world of her imagination. She lives in an imaginary world in which 'the object of the image differs from the object of perception: (a) in that it has its own space, whereas there exists an infinite space which is common to all perceived objects; (b) in that it occurs immediately as unreal, whereas the object of perception originally set up, as Husserl says, a claim to reality *(Seinsanspruch)*'.[17] It is characteristic of the client's situation that her perception and her imagining consciousness are two alternating positions which the client merges, whereas a 'normal' person can separate the two worlds. A 'normal' person can also imagine he is the king of Spain and enjoy this image so much that he devotes much time and space to it in his daydreams. Unlike Sartre's client, however, he is not the object of these imaginings and he can let go of them at any time and pursue a different activity of his daily life.

The hallucinations of a state of delirium or psychosis are different. Here there is no awareness of anything outside, not even the faintest sign of one. The patient is in the world of delirium and its hallucinations, and is completely absorbed in it and cannot escape. The space and time of the delirium become all that there is; nothing exists outside of any happening that occurs in the delirium, and there is no hope of its ending. The events take on a compulsive power, which is beyond anything we know in everyday life. This applies both to objects, persons and actions and to figurations, colours and sounds. A person in a state of delirium experiences the events so intensely that he or she cannot escape them. The event is so powerful that the patient loses all capacity to resist and all ability to speak. The result is almost unimaginable feelings of powerlessness and anxiety – which arise from the hermetic nature of this world from which there is no escape. In this state normal human capacities are lost. A perception or a thought can be observed, but the hallucinations of delirium cannot. The patient cannot distance himself, cannot change his perspective; he is incapable of using language to drive out the frightening images, resist their attack and organize them as he wishes. He cannot look at the images objectively and put himself outside of them. They have taken possession of him so that he is no longer but exists merely in the images that have mastery over him, that do with him as they will. The patient can no longer act, cannot develop any spontaneity that would help him to free himself from the hallucinations. In this world of delirium, the hallucinations appear in an absurd form. They do not follow the logic and order of everyday consciousness. They cannot be symbolized; they are 'the correlatives of an impersonal consciousness.'[18] Only in his memory, when the patient has left the state of delirium, can he attempt to express what is happening and what he experienced. Only in memory can the hallucination be categorized and become something experienced; only retrospectively can it be put into words so that it is comprehensible in its incomprehensibility and can be imparted to other people.

We can use our imaginations to recall not only real but also unreal states such as hallucinations. When we remember these, we also reconstruct and revive their images, although they do not attain their original intensity in the process. Now the hallucinatory images follow the dynamic of recollection; within this they are reconstructed on the level of everyday consciousness, captured and become available. Seeing the images that now appear, the person remembering is hardly able to recall what the hallucinations once did to him. The remembered images of past happenings are now only pale likenesses of the hallucinations, which, although their figurative details can still be remembered, have lost the power and the compulsion that they exerted as hallucinations. In the patient's memory, all that is left is mere shadows of what went on in the state of delirium, and as he looks back at them he experiences his newly won freedom as a gift of life.

3.5 Visions

Whereas there is no doubt that in episodes of psychosis and delirium hallucinations are pathological, where the imagination plays a significant role, the status of *visions* is controversial.[19] The term *vision* denotes mainly religious or quasi-religious imaginings. Visions play an important role in all religions but they also extend into the area of parapsychology and secular images of salvation or happiness. Regardless of whether these phenomena are considered to be in principle possible, likely or impossible, based on some criterion of human rationality, it is important first and foremost to regard *visions as ways in which the human imagination expresses itself.* In many cases, visions are reported in ways that remind us of the hallucinations experienced in psychosis or delirium. For example, the visionary is overcome by the visions; they force themselves upon her and leave her with no alternative but to surrender herself to them. Visions are also generally only spoken of as memories; we can only tell people about them once they are over. They differ from hallucinations inasmuch as the visionary believes them to have been given to her by a higher being that is using her as its mouthpiece. Visions are also intended to be communicated to other people.

They bear witness to the visionary's having been transported into an altered state, which is also of significance for other people. These visions are not experienced by everyone but by a select few. They cannot be deliberately invoked but are bestowed upon one. What they have in common is that they contain a message, an insight or enlightenment that is life-changing for the visionary and worthy of being conveyed to other people, so that they too can change their lives. Visions are associated with belief systems that are more or less closed, and they herald the attainment of a higher state in which both the visionary and the community must believe. Visions often happen completely unexpectedly. They burst in on our everyday life and imperiously demand that it change. Visions are not only visual but also involve the other senses. Thus, hearing, touch and also smell and taste come into play when it comes to emphasizing the special nature of the occurrence. Visions rupture the sequentiality of time; they occur at a particular moment, a *kairos*. When they appear, not only is time altered, being divided into a time before and a time after the vision, but there is also an alteration in space, together with its social structures. Visions are often heralded by a special light or a special sound or sounds. The weather changes. Nothing is the same after the vision as it was before. Visions also make use of certain rhetorical forms of topographical representations and images, without which it is not possible to portray what is special about the visionary occurrence. In the case of visions, the imagination serves a higher purpose which has no other way of communicating itself. The imaginary happening of the vision allows us to perceive something that transcends reality which would otherwise remain invisible and inaccessible, and this makes it possible for us to experience what makes us human. It remains an open question from whom these visions originate or where they might stem from and what significance they have for the community.

3.6 Dreams

Daydreams. Another place where we see how productive the imagination can be is in *dreams*, which we can divide into daydreaming and dreaming at night. It is clear how important *daydreams* are for the way we conduct our lives. In the dreams we dream during the day, our imagination conveys numerous images into our semi-consciousness. Some of these become conscious; others slip past without crossing the threshold of consciousness, so that we remain unaware of them. In daydreams, we reflect on problems in our lives and are sometimes able to find a solution. Daydreams are not goal oriented – they have no specific focus.

We are preoccupied with something and suddenly up comes the solution to a problem that we have not thought about for a long time. These dreams enter our consciousness in moments when we are not absorbed in what we are doing and when our attention is not on anything in particular. Daydreams seek unimpeded consciousness to settle in so that we can become aware of them. They articulate our desire, and images play with our longings and wishes. Sometimes there are shadows that are suppressed when our consciousness is fully focused. In daydreams the images follow their own dynamic and not the logic of our waking consciousness. Sometimes it is snippets of language, fragments of feelings, sounds and smells which we cannot decode and yet which suddenly coalesce into something that we grasp, and which takes on meaning. The daydreams fluctuate between memories and fantasies about the future. They are like guests who come to stay but want to remain strangers.[20] Sometimes fears intensify in them, urging us to come out of them so that they do not upset us too much, and sometimes they also bring us premonitions. We sense that something is threatening us without actually being able to grasp it; we suspect something, we receive a warning, sometimes in time to protect ourselves from it. These daydreams offer us alternatives to the way we are living our lives, corrections to unsuccessful or blameworthy actions. Sometimes we escape into these dreams that suppress the demands of everyday life and fill us for hours with images of a different life. Is it we who are dreaming? Or, are we being dreamt? Do we dissolve in the floods of images and longings? Usually we are able to free ourselves from these images, to hold them at arm's length and continue with our daily lives.

Dreams of the night-time. In night-time dreams, the situation is different. In his first meditation, Descartes wrote,

> I must remember that I am a man, and that consequently I am in the habit of sleeping, and in my dreams representing to myself the same things or sometimes even less probable things, than do those who are insane in their waking moments. How often has it happened to me that in the night I dreamt that I found myself in this particular place, that I was dressed and seated near the fire, whilst in reality I was lying undressed in bed! At this moment it does indeed seem to me that it is with eyes awake that I am looking at this paper; that this head which I move is not asleep, that it is deliberately and of set purpose that I extend my hand and perceive it; what happens in sleep does not appear so clear nor so distinct as does all this. But in thinking over this I remind myself that on many occasions I have in sleep been deceived by similar illusions, and in dwelling carefully on this reflection I see so manifestly that there are no certain indications by which we may clearly distinguish wakefulness from sleep that I am lost in astonishment.

And my astonishment is such that it is almost capable of persuading me that I now dream.[21]

The difficulty of distinguishing between being awake and being asleep that Descartes describes here is to be found in many testimonies about dreams in many cultures, and it would therefore seem to be a basic human experience. Nevertheless, in what follows I shall define the qualitative difference between the world of our waking consciousness and the imaginary world of the dream by looking at the different forms of imagination in the two states.

In a dream we are unable to step out of the imagined world. If we do, we wake up. As long as we are dreaming, however, we are immersed in the images of the dream, in its imaginary world. In a dream we are living in an unreal world and go along with the events of the dream. A dream is an enclosed imaginary world that we have to enter in order to participate in the events that take place in it. It is impossible to assume an external stance on these events. This would be the case if we were to have some awareness of the world. Yet as long as we are dreaming, we cannot perceive. The world of the dream is an isolated world; it has no past or future; there is nothing outside its imaginary space and the figures and events contained within it.

Because of the fact that a dream carries us suddenly into a temporal world, every dream appears to us as *a story* [. . .] Naturally the spatio-temporal world in which the story unrolls is purely imaginary, it is the object of no position of existence [. . . .] As the imaginary world it is the correlative of a *belief*, the sleeper *believes* that the scene unrolls in a world; that is that this world is the object of empty intentions which are directed upon him beginning with the central image.[22]

Every dream image surrounds itself with a 'worldly atmosphere', that is, it becomes a vehicle for all the things that preoccupy us outside the dream as well, but these things are projected into the imaginary world of our dream. As long as the dream lasts, we are unable to consciously reflect. Nor can we consciously perceive; because our consciousness has lost the function of distinguishing what is real, and it cannot make any changes to its experiences and sensations. Nor can it remember. If this were possible, our consciousness would grasp what is real – the world of the dream and its imaginary would shatter. The dream images, on the other hand, only possess the qualities that our imagination bestows on them. Because they are not real, the images of the dream are opaque and unattainable, and it is precisely this quality that fascinates the dreamer. The dreamer is unable to distance herself from her images and stories. Therefore, in the dream there are no possibilities but simply the unreality of what happens in the dream. In the dream, all the figures are unreal and imaginary, including also the imaginary I, whom the dreamer uses to be able to act and who can also have an effect on the real I of the sleeper.

> In fact what constitutes the nature of the dream is that reality altogether eludes the consciousness which desires to recapture it; all the effort of consciousness turns in spite of itself to produce the imaginary. The dream is not fiction taken for reality, it is the Odyssey of a consciousness dedicated by itself, and in spite of itself, to build only an unreal world.[23]

However, unlike the hallucinations of delirium and psychosis, in dreams there is an awakening that puts an end to nightmares and makes it possible for us to perceive, distance ourselves and reflect again.

4

Theories and concepts of imagination

4.1 The etymology of the term

In Greek, the classical expression for imagining is *plattein*. This word denotes the practice of producing and modelling things and representations and can also include simulating things. Plato refers to the corresponding mental activity as *eidôlopoiein*, the production of images. However, the activity of taking something into one's mind in order to examine it is called *ennoein*. If the purpose of the activity is to anticipate an action, it is referred to as *epinoein*. If the emphasis is on representing something as an image, then the activity is termed *eikazein*, a verb which also contains within it *eikôn*, the Greek word for image. In this context, the following Greek words are also used: *phantazein*, for making visible or making something appear; *phantasma*, for appearance; and *phantazesthai*, to 'have an appearance'. Unlike the activity that is referred to as imagination, the object of which is to internalize images or bring images into oneself, which Paracelsus then translated into German as *Einbildungskraft* (literally: the power to bring a picture inside or internalize an image), Greek words in the word family of *phainesthai* stress the appearance of things.

In Latin, to begin with the activity of imagining is denoted as *fingere*, in line with the entirely practical activity of producing and modelling images, an activity which corresponds to the Greek *plattein* and which is different from the mental activity of inventing, which is termed *invenire* or *excogitare*. Later on there is reference to a *vis imaginativa* and, from the eighteenth century onwards, a *facultas fingendi*, which describes the power to produce images, phenomena, replicas and simulacra. This term describes the creative power of imagination which has been a subject of debate in the modern world since the Renaissance. In German, this creative aspect of imagination is termed *Einbildungskraft*. From an etymological point of view, the words *Bild* (picture or image) and *bilden* (to form, shape, build and configure) and also *hineinbilden* (literally draw a form inside) are important.

In English, there are two main terms that are important for the purposes of this study: *fantasy* and *imagination*. *Fantasy* is the faculty or activity of imagining impossible or improbable things. The words *imagination* and *imagine* refer to productive processes, often where something new is created. 'Imagination' can include processes in which images that already exist are reproduced, even though they are absent, and also processes which produce images, creating them for the first time. Both words can be used to emphasize that what is experienced subjectively cannot (easily) be intersubjectively corroborated by others and is thus not objectively present in the outside world. There is no clear dividing line between the meanings of these two words. It is also not possible to draw a clear distinction between the terms *Fantasie, Imagination* and *Einbildungskraft* in German, so they are usually used as synonyms, the differences between them being defined in the contexts in which they are used.

4.2 Historical positions

As we have already seen, imagination can be understood as the ability to make absent things present. In order to do this, the imagination has to reproduce something that was once actually there but is now absent. In order to do this, it has to have a connection with the senses. The imagination cannot reproduce things unless they have at some time already been perceived and processed. Diderot sums up the imagination thus: 'I have a different idea of the imagination; it is the capacity to paint absent objects for oneself as if they were present. It is the capacity to borrow from perceived objects images which serve as a comparison. It is the capacity to link an abstraction notion to a body.'[1] Hobbes and Locke also have no doubt that imagination exists independently of sensory perception. For how could the imagination make something become present if this were not already within it? For Hobbes, imagination (or 'fancy') originates in sensory impressions. In Chapter II of Part One of *Leviathan*, he writes: 'Imagination therefore is nothing but *decaying sense*.'[2] And Malebranche clarifies this process further when he states that for the process of imagination to take place, we require certain objects and the images of these objects. He describes these as being nothing other than impressions engraved on our brains by the events that have taken place in our lives. The more deeply imprinted the images are and the stronger and more rapid the sequence of events, the more powerfully are we able to imagine something.

In order to understand completely all the changes the different conditions produce in the imagination, it is absolutely necessary to be reminded that we imagine objects only by forming images of them, and that these images are nothing other than the traces the animal spirits make in the brain; that we imagine things more strongly in proportion as these traces are deeper and better engraved, and as the animal spirits have passed through them more often and more violently.[3]

However, seeing the imagination purely as a faculty that is dependent on and subordinate to the senses cannot explain how such things as invention, inspiration, change, modification, spontaneity or innovation arise.

As early as Aristotle, we find an objection to conceiving *phantasia* purely as a movement of the soul that is engendered by a direct sensory impulse. Instead, Aristotle already understands *phantasia* as an ability to relate images to each other that do not derive directly from sensory perceptions and which are mental rather than sensory in nature. Furthermore, in *De anima* (431b 39) he states that there is no thought 'without images'. Descartes also sees the imagination as having a certain independence of the senses and spontaneity of its own:

For even when painters try to create sirens and satyrs with the most extraordinary bodies, they cannot give them natures which are new in all respects; they simply jumble up the limbs of different animals. Or if perhaps they manage to think up something so new that nothing remotely similar has ever been seen before – something which is therefore completely fictitious and unreal – at least the colours used in the composition must be real.[4]

Descartes therefore identifies two types of imagination. One type is an 'imagination involontaire' which arises 'simply from the fact that the [animal] spirits, being agitated in various different ways and coming upon the traces of various impressions which have preceded them in the brain, make their way by chance through certain pores rather than others. Such are the illusions of our dreams and also the daydreams we often have when we are awake and our mind wanders idly without applying itself to anything of its own accord'.[5] On the other hand, there is a real intentionality of the imagination which permits the soul through a particular 'effort of mind'[6] to imagine a 'palais enchanté ou une chimère', 'an enchanted palace or a chimera'.[7] These images can be evoked without the aid of external objects, without looking at the outside world and can make absent objects present. Without this it is simply a question of replicating.

Paracelsus translated both 'phantasia' and 'imaginatio' into German as 'Einbildungskraft' (see aforementioned text), which emphasizes the active role of the subject in producing images. The subject uses this power (Kraft) to bring an image into himself or herself (Ein-Bildung), so the world is taken inside the subject. In the Pre-Romantic and Romantic eras, this term was used increasingly, Christian Wolff being one of the first to use it in that period. Also, in their work on the theory of literature and art, the Zurich aestheticians Johann Jakob Bodmer and Johann Jakob Breitinger referred expressly to 'Einbildungskraft'.[8] 'Einbildungskraft' as a concept of interest to anthropology was used at this time in connection with self-empowerment and becoming a subject; this aspect of the use of the term is still valid today. Kant's reflections, to which scholars keep returning, are of particular importance here. In Paragraph 10 of his *Critique of Pure Reason*, Kant links 'Einbildungskraft' to our capacity for synthesis which precedes the coining of the term: 'Synthesis in general is, as we shall subsequently see, the mere effect of the imagination' (*Einbildungskraft*) 'of a blind though indispensable function of the soul, without which we would have no cognition at all, but of which we are seldom even conscious. Yet to bring this synthesis to concepts is a function that pertains to the understanding, and by means of which it first provides cognition in the proper sense.'[9] Here 'the imagination (reflecting the abstract characteristics of the idea of reason) must mediate between the concept and perception by remembering objects that have been perceived by the senses to which comparable rules were applied'.[10] This possibility of imagination is of great anthropological significance.

Imagination is an important element of *creativity* (*vis creativa*). Since the beginning of the modern age, we have been fascinated and inspired by the possibility it offers for us to become creators, like God. The artist of the Renaissance who, in *disegno*, designs and forms a world, came to be a model of the creative human being who realized his likeness to God through his creativity. The *disegno* is an idea that has assumed a form and is realized on paper with the aid of the imagination. It is because of their imagination that human beings were only a little later to behave like nature, not *natura naturata* (i.e. nature which is static or already completed) but *natura naturans* (i.e. nature as self-generating or dynamic). It was not a question of copying the products, shapes and expressions of nature but rather of being creative like nature. Three centuries later, it was genius that helped human beings to realize their divinity, and which became the ideal for human creativity. Goethe masterfully described this feeling for life and idea of creativity in his poem 'Prometheus': 'Cover your heaven, Zeus, with cloudy vapours, and test your strength, like the boy chopping the heads off thistles, on oak trees and mountain tops! But my earth you must leave to me.'[11] We human beings challenge the old gods; we want to outdo them and design and shape our own stories. A few years later, Novalis referred directly to imagination in his studies in Freiberg: 'The imagination is the marvelous sense that can *replace* all senses for us – and which already is so much directed by our will. If the external senses seem to be entirely governed by mechanical laws – then the imagination is obviously not bound to the present and to contact with external stimuli.'[12]

It was during this period (probably in 1797) that the 'Oldest Systematic Program of German Idealism' appeared, the authorship of which is uncertain but is thought to have been Hegel, probably influenced by Schelling and Hölderlin. This work demands a 'poeticization' of the world – how else than with the aid of the imagination. There is a call for a new mythology. The object of this study was to make the poetic aspect of imagination the defining aspect of human life. This idea of the creative power of the imagination is still alive today in twenty-first century avant-garde art. It is this that brings novelty into the world and enables human beings to fulfil their potential. In this view, imagination is the force that makes the invisible visible, creates things that do not yet exist and expands human potential almost ad infinitum – for every time something new is created, we increase our capacity to create something new once more.

4.3 The image as the portrayal and expression of imagination

Aristotle already saw that the imagination is oriented towards the senses as *phantasia aisthetike* and towards thought as *phantasia logistike*.[13] For Sartre too, the imagination bridges the senses and thought, so that a theory of the imagination has to explain how our perceptual images differ from those of the imagination and also clarify the role the images play in our thinking. Ever since Kant scholars have been concerned with the question of whether perception occurs without the aid of imagination or whether imagination is a prerequisite for perception and precedes it. According to Kant, imagination creates the preconditions for connecting pure receptivity and synthesis, for example what an animal looks like and how it moves, and the schema upon which our perception of the animal is based. Maurice Merleau-Ponty takes this still further.[14] In his view, our perception of things can be understood as a continuum in which the objective properties of things and what the subject experiences are inextricably interwoven. The reason for this is the chiasm between introjections and projection which does not permit us to distinguish between the inner and outer worlds.

For Gaston Bachelard, there is a fundamental difference between the image, the perception of the image and the image that the imagination creates. The perceived image and the imagined image are so fundamentally different that we really need two different terms to designate them adequately.[15] The imagined image influences the way we perceive the image; the perceived image influences the structures of the image in the imaginary that are in place before the individual act of perceiving. Gilbert Durand and his school were later to take up this view of perception.[16] They contended that mental images are subject to spontaneous change and symbolization processes in which they develop a dynamic of their own. Thus, there is no longer any point in relating them to perceptual images. On the contrary, these images develop a cultural autonomy which can be described as follows:

> The subject always moves within an iconosphere which is made up of his life experience and is composed of symbolic images, the sensory content of which is closely linked to an expressive and subjective meaning which goes beyond the meaning inherent in its conceptual verbalisation. In certain cases the imagination is not so much a re-portrayal of what is given in the percept or concept, but rather a prefiguration or a presentation of a reality that exists in an original mental space. This reality cannot be reduced either to the existential givens of the object itself via an extensional sensory impression or to the purified and unequivocal conceptual content of its abstract representation. This is why a daydream, or the anticipation of an event, a poem or a painting can therefore be considered to be more 'real' than the realities that serve as concrete subject matter or the idealities to which they refer.[17]

The imagination not only creates images but also modifies them. It organizes new associations between them and symbolizes. It creates dynamic collective and individual image networks with which we perceive the world, other people and ourselves. These networks structure our perceptions and are at the same time their outcome. The dynamic of the imagination is at work in them – it expresses itself in these images and becomes tangible in them. These images create an imaginary world in which we move, like nomads who move from place to place, from image sequence to image sequence, and have no place outside them. These chains of images are creative, because they create our worldview, our aberrations and confusions. These images are intangible, and yet at the same time have the power of reality, for they determine our perception, our memories and the way we anticipate the future. They are playful and attach themselves to other images in a continuous game into which we keep trying to put some kind of order. These images of the imaginary are the manifestation of energies which assume a concrete form in the images and their movements.

These images are not only visual – they have their origins in all the senses, they contain traces of sounds, smells, taste and touch. They intermingle with iconic images, linguistic images, metaphors, metonyms and oxymorons. They overlap and form hybrids and image chains; they duplicate and uncouple themselves. To begin with, mimetic processes take place which give rise to images – creative re-creations of cultural practices. Both representations and meanings are formed, and these are followed, in mimetic processes, by numerous symbolizations. Mental images arise which multiply in their search for animation and life. These images glide, form chains, seek meanings which emerge, break up and reconstitute themselves. They are polysemic; heterogenous energies cut across each other in them; they contain emotional values, are multidimensional and enigmatic. They resist any imperative to be unequivocal or pure. On the contrary, in images we find fuzziness, ambiguities and enigmas.[18]

Many images of the imaginary are collective images. Iconic images have their origins in the fields of religion and art, verbal images in literature. Other images are products of the activities that take place in rituals, institutions and the media. It is not only iconic and verbal images in a narrow sense that belong to the imaginary but also 'phenomena' of the imaginary which are linked to other senses, such as songs and pieces of music, movement images, dances, rituals and sporting activities. The intimate traces of smell, taste and touch likewise contribute to a culture's collective imaginary. The phenomena, traces and images that are associated with emotional and social judgements are handed down to the next generation. They become part of young people's individual imaginaries and are incorporated through their yearnings and habits. Children become familiar with many of these phenomena, which may come from different cultures, at an early age. Among the characteristics of these early processes of transmitting traces and images is the fact that as a rule they take place mimetically and unconsciously. In brain research, 'images' are also often called traces and 'entities' that come into being with the aid of other senses.[19] They have reciprocal relationships with each other, intermingle and complement each other and also repel each other. Studies conducted by French cultural scientists to date focus either on verbal images[20] or on iconic images.[21] The differences between the verbal images studied by Blumenberg[22] and Ricoeur, [23] for instance between metaphors and metonyms, are illuminating. As yet, very little research has been conducted into the relationship between iconic, auditory and verbal images in the arts and the influence the reciprocal relationships between them bring to bear on a culture's imaginary. It would be interesting also to make diachronic and synchronic comparisons.

According to a definition put forward by Bergson, images are both less and more than things. 'And by "image" we mean a certain existence which is more than that which the idealist calls a representation, but less than that which the realist calls a thing; – an existence placed half-way between the "thing" and the "representation".'[24] Mental images are described as being both 'more' and 'less' because they are not material and yet cannot be explained solely on the basis of their representational character. As mental images they are above all a part of the energy of the imaginary which creates images, relates them to other images and changes them, which in German is also referred to as 'Einbildungskraft'. The traces of these images can be seen today in various studies of the brain. However, neuroscientific imaging procedures cannot satisfactorily account for their content, although we know that they are very important for a theory of imagination. Unlike the images that are present as objects in the outside world, mental images are lively because they are connected to the energies present in the body, which allow us to make our mental images move, speed them up or slow them down. We can play with these images, and we can make them larger or smaller or zoom in on certain parts of them. We can handle them as if they were living monads in our mental world. Sometimes they appear, sometimes they disappear; then they resist our desire to become aware of them and make them appear in our mind's eye; they remain out of focus or do not take on form or shape. The images, sounds, smells and sensations have their own independent existence and identity, and yet at the same time they are part of our bodies, the image worlds inside us and our desire. Our imagination renews and reshapes these images. It can liberate us from the images of the real world and produce images for us that bring us joy and happiness, sometimes also by expelling images that represent reality or not permitting them access. The imagination is spontaneous and volatile; its configurations follow its own rhythms and laws, over which, although it has some influence, our consciousness cannot gain control. The imagination can acquire images from our worlds of experience, rearrange them in new contexts and provide them with new life and energy; here the imagination often acts in accordance with our desires. The images follow the impulses of pleasure and unpleasure, give expression to them and often change them. In these movements of the images, an important role is played by energies that are deeply embedded in the constitution of human life, of which we are often hardly conscious, but which the images continue to bring to our awareness. André Leroi-Gourhan believes that the images of the imaginary are determined predominantly by three 'organo-muscular' forms of behaviour relating to food, physical affectivity and spatiotemporal orientation.[25] Gilbert Durand has a similar view,[26] pointing out that the images of the imaginary contain traces of active postures of the body, of metabolic activities and actions based on rhythms, especially sexual ones; concluding from this, 'We shall assume as a working hypothesis that there is a close connection between bodily gestures, nerve centres and symbolic representations'.[27] The interplay between these three levels makes it possible for a mimetic relationship to develop between the outside world, the rhythms of the body and the human ability to speak and imagine.[28] Configurations of inner images come into being as a result of mimetic activities and neurobiological stimuli. Edgar Morin draws these strands together and concludes that two things happen simultaneously: the imaginary invades our perception of reality, and myth enters our vision of the world. From now on, myth and magic become both the products of and co-creators of human destiny.[29]

4.4 The image as form and expression of emotions

In his reflections on love, Stendhal compares the idealizing power of imagination to the process of crystallization in a salt mine, in the course of which many salt crystals attach themselves to the small twigs on a branch where they begin to sparkle and gleam like diamonds. In the same way, the power of imagination makes love more intense and more beautiful by adding to it countless glittering diamonds which make it shine with a fascinating beauty. This is also what happens in the case of the mental images that first arouse certain feelings inside us, then intensify them and give rise to the desire to act on them. This is clearly the case with those images that are linked to desire. However, even when it is a question of pleasure, fear and pain, the imagination plays an important role by creating images that we either try to live or to avoid. And yet images can sometimes become so strong that it becomes clear that it is not we who are invoking them but they that possess us and direct our feelings. This is how images of gloom and melancholy develop, that we are unable to defend against. In contrast, other images fill us with joy and happiness. Strangely these also leave us powerless. It is not we who determine them but they that determine how we feel and act. Sometimes they confront us with aspects of ourselves and the world that we would rather ignore, but they open our eyes to them without our being able to resist them. Images regulate our emotions without our knowing exactly how this happens.

Our imagination prompts us to feel, heighten or withstand feelings or run away from them. Sometimes these feelings also become imaginary themselves so that there is no way of using them to steady us or gain a sense of order. André Gide described this in a sceptical comment on psychoanalysis: 'Psychological analysis lost all interest for me from the moment I became aware that men feel what they imagine they feel. From that to thinking that they imagine they feel what they feel was a very short step. [. . .] In the domain of feeling, what is real is indistinguishable from what is imaginary'.[30]

Our emotional life depends, essentially, on the extent to which we believe in our inner images. These can sometimes become so intense that they persuade us to believe that they are more real than 'reality'. Then again we evaluate the mental pictures in terms of how well they match up with what is actually there in the outside world or with our memories. Whatever the case, the extent to which we believe in them determines their significance for us. We often think our mental images are real, knowing full well that we can always distance ourselves from them. We allow ourselves to enter into a game with the images, which also play a game with us (so long as we are willing). We can see our inner images *as* the outside world. We can see the outside world *in* the images, and we can see these images *in* the outside world *as* part of our 'inner world'. As long as we are in our right minds, we can break off this game at any time. In his *Confessions*, Rousseau describes this situation as follows:

> my restless imagination entered upon an occupation which saved me from myself and calmed my growing sensuality. This consisted in feeding myself upon the situations which had interested me in the course of my reading, in recalling them, in varying them, in combining them, in making them so truly my own that I became one of the persons who filled my imagination and always saw myself in the situations most agreeable to my taste; and that, finally, the fictitious state in which I succeeded in putting myself made me forget my actual state with which I was so dissatisfied.[31]

This situation becomes difficult the moment the individual succumbs to his or her inner images and is no longer able to resist them or adopt a critical stance towards them. There are many such examples in literature, such as Goethe's *Werther*, for example, where we know that in the years following its publication its effect on readers was such that many young men were inspired to commit suicide. In Flaubert's *Madame Bovary*, too, the influence of literary narratives and images on the desire, feelings and actions of the protagonist is a central theme. Where there is psychosis the situation is clearer still – the mentally ill cannot cross the boundary between their mental image world and the outside world. They are ultimately prisoners of the image worlds of delusion. These image worlds determine what they experience and how they are controlled by their feelings. They have lost control over the ego and its ability to create order in the eddying and reeling world of the images.

4.5 The dynamic of images

The dynamic of mental images follows the principles of both similarity and of contact. Thus, it is easy for us to associate water with rivers, lakes or the sea, or we make a link between water, birth and death. In both cases the images quickly multiply. 'This is why people sometimes seem to recollect from "places". The reason is that they proceed quickly from one to the other, for instance from milk to white, from white to air and from this to moist.'[32] Yet it is possible that the imagination obeys even stricter rules. Sigmund Freud believed it was responsible for what happens in dreams by differentiating between 'considerations of representability' or 'figurability', 'condensation', 'displacement' and 'secondary revision'. These rules are certainly still plausible to a certain extent today when it comes to understanding the dynamics of dreams. However, since then further advances have been made in the psychoanalytic interpretation of dreams. These rules are no longer considered paramount, and new ways of approaching the image world of dreams have been found. Carl Gustav Jung, in particular, developed new approaches which gave more weight to the anthropological nature of dreams. Jung's work raised an issue which is still an important focus for those who are attempting to systematically research the image world of dreams and the imaginary. The question is whether it is possible to discover images which become the starting point for other images or even chains of images or, alternatively, whether images are based on schemata which explain how they come into being and become combined with other images. Kant and Bergson, and also Jung and Durand, have postulated the existence of these schemata or underlying images which explain the development and spreading of certain images or chains of images far beyond the confines of the individual or even a single culture. Jung believed that there are such organizing principles for images, which he defined as archetypes: 'They are the *archetypes*, which direct all fantasy activity into its appointed paths [. . .] It is not [. . .] a question of inherited *ideas*, but of inherited *possibilities* of ideas.'[33] Freud was seeking for answers leading in the same direction when he identified complexes such as the Oedipus complex. Jacques Lacan also had similar ideas when he postulated the existence of an intruder complex which changes the relationship between brothers and sisters and thus also the relationship to the mother (and father).[34] Finally, Gaston Bachelard attempted to identify complexes with cultural causes, which he defines as spontaneous attitudes 'that govern the very process of reflection. [. . .] these are for example favourite images, thought to be derived from things seen in the world around us but that are nothing but projections of a hidden soul'.[35]

In these cases it is not merely a question of a 'contagious' spread of images, but rather more that the imagination develops the power to symbolize, which creates images, modifies them and puts them into new contexts and thus new contexts of meaning. Differing symbolic uses of the image of 'water' in the imaginary are a case in point. This image can have multiple meanings in different contexts within differing dynamics of time and space. Thus, the 'image, be it mental or material, cannot be grasped as a flat, homogenous idea; from the start it is the fruit of a complex inner construction'.[36]

In his work on the physics of dreams ('une physique onirique'), Gaston Bachelard attempted to show

> the degree to which the images of the elements (of water, fire, air and earth) develop their own semantic matrices according to a law of ambivalence (each large material image being capable of having a positive or negative pole, water evoking values of life or death) and also the degree to which the marriage of opposing elements (such as water and fire) has generated powerful poetic images.[37]

Gilbert Durand goes still further in his attempts to develop structures of the imaginary. In his view, what is at the root of the dynamics of the imagination are the two fundamentally opposite syntactical structures of the 'nocturnal order' and the 'diurnal order', where it is a question of schemata of separation and opposition in the latter and integration and intimacy in the former. In terms of space, in the first, above all, forms of distancing, breaches and tension are important; in the second, on the other hand, more forms of roundness and hollowness are important. In terms of time, both structures contain both unifying pinpointing in time and also suspension of time. The first tends to cover more heroic forms and the second more mystical and passionate forms. A third category of the imaginary leads to a synthesizing regime which links the two other regimes in a 'circle of reconciliation'. 'This is why in every work (literary or sculptural) we find dominant configurations which make it possible to personalise the imaginary of the creator and permit us to pick out among the repetitive figurative structures those which characterise it and endow it with the traits of an intimate world.'[38]

4.6 Image and pictoriality

All cultures have symbols in which they believe and with which they identify, and which play a role in creating a cultural community. In these symbols, there are various overlapping layers of meaning which are experienced in the symbol as a unit that cannot be dissolved. Even though we can work out these meanings by using a variety of ways to interpret them, for the believer they are all an integral part of the symbol itself which is what creates its mysterious quality. When we interpret symbols hermeneutically, it is important that we do so in full consciousness of the fact that our interpretations only capture part of a whole and are also provisional. We can thus avoid reducing rather than expanding the spiritual significance of the symbols. This may occur particularly where a symbol appears to elude the rational laws of everyday life and its otherness comes into play. The interpretation of symbols is dependent on the interpreter's engaging with and acknowledging them. If the symbol is not accepted, even provisionally or conditionally, then we are unlikely to grasp how it relates to other symbols, meanings and worlds and we fail to do justice to its complexity. We do nonetheless need to adopt a critical approach – this is essential, for example, if we are interpreting the political symbols of totalitarian states, where we must engage in a critique of their symbols and ideologies.

As we encounter the symbolic images of any culture, we experience its alterity, that is, an otherness that we can approach but we can never fully understand. If we could, we would be part of this culture and would have to give up our own cultural affiliation. However, many ethnographic studies have shown that this is not possible, demonstrating that our understanding of the Other is a relational process in which neither what is our own nor what belongs to the Other can be firmly established as an ontic quantity.[39] The hermeneutic process of understanding can only develop if both are able to allow their perspectives to become more flexible. René Char's comment about poems can also be applied to symbolic images – they know something about us that we do not know. They contain an element of surprise that cannot be foreseen, which often eludes the rationality of everyday life and which we often experience before the meaning of the images reveals itself to us.

The interpretation of the symbolic content of mental images brings to mind the processes developed by art historians for interpreting pictures, particularly where these pictures are part of the collective cultural images of a culture. It remains to be seen how suitable these procedures are for deciphering symbolic mental images. Although Erwin Panofsky's iconology was clearly a great advance for the history of art, today we can see the limitations of his method of interpretation, since its categories, which were developed for use on Renaissance art, are highly cognitive in nature and oriented towards the reading of texts, having only a limited feel for the sense of the pictorial nature of images.[40] If we try to use Panofsky's ideas to interpret mental images, we can conclude that in the first step of pre-iconographic understanding, the contours and colours of an imaginary image are initially grasped purely as such, that is, contours and colours. In the second, or iconographic, step, this is different. Here, to understand a mental image, for example, it is necessary to acquire additional information about its figurations, development and significance. Here it can also be important to gather information about the person's history. The third step is the iconological interpretation. Here the mental image must be grasped as the content and mode of expression of the given culture. In order to achieve this, it is necessary to carry out additional studies of the historical and cultural meanings of the mental image and to appreciate its historico-cultural significance. What is missing in Panofsky is sufficient consideration of the *iconic character of an image*, that is, the perception of its iconic qualities. If mental images portray narratives, iconicity must involve thinking about the relationship of the images to language, for instance about the difference that exists between the sequentiality of a narrative and the simultaneity of its mental portrayal as an image. As Panofsky's interpretive method does not help us to understand many mental images, we need to develop an iconic approach to their understanding. Such an approach

> creatively runs through the possibilities inherent in the image in a never-ending iteration. It is precisely as we run through the countervalences contained in the image that we, the onlookers [of the inner image] become aware of our own structuring activities and also of our own inability to gain control of them. This happens in the very special experience that any structure that we create is based on one and the same phenomenon, and also that none of the possible acts of structuring leads to our taking this identical image in, once and for all, and capturing it.[41]

This procedure gives the viewer of mental images a feeling of 'insurmountable powerlessness' vis-à-vis the image. It offers him or her the aesthetic experience that an 'image cannot be represented anything other than the image itself'.[42] In other words, images cannot be explained – they have to be looked at. Images have an irreducible quality inherent in their pictoriality, which keeps bringing us back to this very pictoriality.

4.7 Images and games of the imagination

Images play a central role in constituting the self. They mediate between the inner and outer worlds and enable individuals to develop themselves as unique persons. In our mental worlds, all human beings are unique – no one has the same internal images as anyone else. All human beings actively create their image worlds, whether these are composed of images of memory, perception or anticipation of the future. If it is a question of processing symbolic images from the collective stock of a culture, then the demands are still greater. The imaginary 'constitutes a veritable scaffolding of projection-identifications from which, at the same time as he masks himself, man knows and constructs himself'.[43] In order to make ourselves into human beings, we have to construct and shape ourselves, and this happens largely through the mental images that we have of ourselves. We use them to design and construct ourselves. In addition, there are also the images that other people have of us, which we accept as they are, modify or reject completely. However, inasmuch as these images determine the behaviour of other people towards us, they play a part in constructing us.

However, it is not only through images that imagination affects us. It also has a lasting effect on us in the performative nature of *games* which other people and institutions invite us to engage in, games in which we design ourselves, experience ourselves anew and change. Inasfar as playing games is a practice, imagination is revealed here as a cultural practice. We can identify many different forms of game. From Caillois' well-known division into four types of game, *agon, alea, mimicry and ilinx*, we can see that there are types of games, played in institutions, rituals and other social interactions.[44] A decisive characteristic of games, and where we see imagination come into play, is that people behave *as though the game were serious*, although of course it is not. Every action thus has a double meaning – it is meant seriously and at the same time it is not. It is only by using imagination that we can make this distinction and at the same time suspend it. At all events, this ambiguity is characteristic of games, and they cannot exist without this paradox. For a game to succeed, the players have to relate mimetically to the actions of their fellow players. In order to do this, all participants have to know what normally happens in the game; only then can they join in and enjoy it. Schiller also famously emphasized the special nature of games when he said that human beings have a special way of being free in games and that it is only in games that we really become human beings. Montaigne put our experience of playing games in a similar, if less idealized, way:

> Most of our occupations are farcical. The whole world is acting a part (*mundus universus exercet histrioniam*). We must play our role duly, but as the role of a borrowed personage. Masks and appearances must not be made into a real essence, nor that which is alien into that which is proper. We cannot distinguish the skin from the shirt. It is enough to make up our face without making up our heart.[45]

By meditating on symbolic images such as mandalas, the different religions have always used the power of the imagination to raise human spiritual development to a higher plane. Since Meister Eckart, using the power of the imagination to dissolve the image and achieve higher levels of spiritual experience has been an issue on the fringe of Christianity. In state-run schools in Germany, although the task of educating the imagination has always been important, it has rarely been expressly addressed. If we want to use our imagination to develop our personalities, then there are several ways of doing so. A good way to increase young people's productivity and creativity is to focus on the development of the faculty of contemplation. For this there is no need to idealize imagination in the style of Rousseau or the progressive educational theories, but we must simply consistently work hard to develop it. In other words, what we call 'rigorous thinking' is probably the ability to conjure up images that can be reprocessed in a second phase. This leads to the discovery of other things, so that the images end up having all the power.

II

Imagination and the imaginary

Collectivity and the dynamic of the imaginary

Since the 1980s, a considerable body of research on the collective imaginary has been established in the French humanities, inspired by the work of Gaston Bachelard and Gilbert Durand. In contrast to the studies influenced by Jacques Lacan which use the concept of the imaginary to analyse psychogenetic self-deception and enmeshment, in these studies the term 'imaginary' is used to refer to collective, cultural images. On the one hand, in these studies the term 'imaginary' is used as a synonym for the imagination and refers to the human capacity to create images and relate and link them to one another, while on the other it is understood to mean the results of the effects of imagination, that is, the images and their cultural meanings. This includes both the world of the images and the human capacity to generate them. The imaginary has effects on both of these forms, which permeate each other. It creates reality, and at the same time it uses reality to create its products. It can be compared to a map that we can use to read the world, although we know that this world is not accessible to us as a real world. And it is performative; it generates images and structures; at the same time, it is itself the result of images and social and cultural relationships that the body has internalized. Its images mediate between us, the world and other people. The concept of the imaginary appears to us as an image that opens up a perspective for us and leads the way into the depths. In a sense an image is only the visible tip of the iceberg and the imaginary the investigation of the relationships and organizational dynamic without which we would not gain access to the complex network of images or to the *mundus imaginalis*, the image world, to which it is connected. Thus, the term 'the imaginary' is also used to mean a system or network of invisible elements which leave their literary and iconic traces in various combinations, but in which the dynamic of the imaginary is not exhausted insofar as it repeatedly generates new combinations and hybrid mixtures.

Methodologically, Gaston Bachelard's studies on the four elements start from the assumption that in order to investigate images we need to use other images.[1] He was interested not only in literary studies but also in discovering by experimenting on himself how certain images affected him when he read attentively, what associations they triggered in his daydreams and how his imaginative processes unfolded. His studies focused particularly on poetic images. His mode of analysis differed from psychoanalytic approaches to image interpretation, which have too limited a perspective and involve aspects of interpretation that are too global and thus too superficial. There are no images without imagination, without a process that brings them to life. The imaginative faculty 'deforms what we perceive; it is above all, the faculty that frees us from immediate images and *changes* them'.[2] In this process, the imagination expands our inner worlds and frees them from becoming entrapped in our psychological development and the practices of our everyday lives. This process is supported by a willpower that is directed towards living, the relationship between the two being as follows: 'Imagination and Will are two aspects of a single profound force. [. . .] To the imagination that informs our will is coupled a will to imagine, a will to live what is imagined'.[3] The imagination influences the generation of the images even before they appear as representations of what we have perceived. It is understood as a transcendental force that is more than simply a mode of coping with the practical issues of daily life, but is associated with our passionate desire for beauty and the sacred. It wrests the world out of its lethargy and brings it alive. The imagination stands in opposition to and in tension with the real world that is the target of scientific investigation. Its subject matter is the unreal, the surreal, which has its own reality. The imagination permeates its images with energies that have strong attractive and repellent forces which transform a dreamed world into a world densely populated with emotions.

We can distinguish several different types of image. Our first images are unconscious and buried in the depths of our psyches. Only fragments of them are accessible to us in our nocturnal dreams. They are the wellspring of our feelings and meanings. These images are of a universal nature and not bound to the life histories of individual human beings; they are comparable to Carl Gustav Jung's archetypal images. These unconscious images are often organized in 'complexes', which have their own culture-specific links and forms. They constitute the earliest forms of organization of collective and individual life. The study of the imagination must therefore start systematically with the dream and reveal the true element and true movement of images.[4] The first images that are really available to us are accessible in spontaneous dream activity in which the control function of consciousness is disabled. These dream images evolve spontaneously, take shape and can prompt us to contemplate. They exist on a level that is prior to our thoughts and narratives. They do not age, and are thus timeless. They include, for example, images of trees, flowers, rocks, crystals and houses.

Images reveal their own creative dynamic when they are transformed into words and written down. The imagination is expressive. For Bachelard, this is vividly revealed in literary forms in which images can take on a new universality. Every literary image transforms or recreates images, and it is this that it endows it with its specific value. In Bachelard's view, an image can achieve its highest perfection as a metaphor. Literary images and metaphors can move and fulfil people psychologically.

The creativity of the imagination evolves through the exchange between the unconscious and the physicality of the body. Although these images arise in the unconscious, it would be too simplistic if we were to attribute them to our human drive structure in our attempts to understand the meaning of dream images. For these images to become literary or poetical images, sublimation is needed. In order to create a literary image in which archetypes are actuated, the image also needs some elements and substance from outside whose effects are needed for aesthetically valuable images to be produced. 'Basic images, especially those involving the way we imagine life, must be linked with elementary matters and fundamental movements.'[5] The imagination that develops as we interact with matter and things is complemented and permeated by the dynamic imagination. This dynamic imagination 'really creates only images of impulse, *élan*, and soaring; in short, images in which the *motion produced takes its direction from the force* that is imagined actively'.[6] Dynamic imagination is directed towards space and the future. Through the encounter with the elements and the other things in dreams and through the energies that the imagination has within the body, it enables us human beings to interact with the living world and to participate in the diversity of living things. We experience the spatiality and the temporality of consciousness and the rhythm of tension and relaxation in the movements of life.

The interweaving and interlinking of the images follow the dialectic and rhythmic movements of the imagination. While they have a certain autonomy, they are at the same time guided or even determined by rules. The imagination liberates us human beings from the constraints of reality. This process follows syntactical and semantic principles. The images do not remain isolated, but form clusters in which the dynamic images follow rules of composition and the material images are governed by rules of combination. The counterposing of, for example, the images of the elements of water and fire leads to an attraction and repulsion with the result that the images mutually enrich each other and the dynamic between them is intensified. The dialectic of the imagination unfolds in the back and forth between the opposing images.

In addition to the syntactical laws, there are also semantic laws. Thus, isomorphism, for instance, in which images remain constant when they are manifested in different forms (e.g. a cave, a house and a stomach), plays an important role in the use of literary images. It is one of the important rules of semantics that the relationship between images and metaphors, for example between blood and wine, is to a great extent reversible. The reversibility of subject and object and human and universe also plays a role.

Literature is an inexhaustible reservoir for the study of the imagination and the imaginary. This aspect of images may even eclipse their aesthetic aspects. Despite this critical objection, the attempt to make images the focus of the appraisal of literary works so as to use them to capture the imaginaries of writers and poets and thus to expand the reader's image world has led to many new perspectives for research on images in the humanities. Bachelard strove to work with the literary images, to keep the attention focused on their imagery and not to 'discard them' too fast by accepting the next best interpretation. He emphasized the importance of dwelling on the images, of experiencing them through the senses by reading the texts aloud, of tracing them back to the origins of creative dreams, of penetrating the dreams that form the ground of literary creation and of communicating with the poet's creative power. He also wanted to help people process their negative images and thus better handle their psychological inadequacies, anxieties and neuroses.

While Bachelard was more interested in finding out what significance images and imagination have for an epistemology of the humanities, Gilbert Durand, who had received much inspiration from Bachelard as a student, developed a mainly anthropological interest in images, the imaginary and the imagination. He was interested in the reciprocal exchange between the subjective and assimilatory drive impulses and the objective effects arising from cosmic and social constellations. 'The imaginary is merely the space of this dialectic whereby the representation of the object is assimilated and modelled by the drive-motivated imperatives of the subject, and reciprocally [. . .] subjective representations are influenced "by the previous adaptations of the subject" to the objective milieu.'[7] Thus this anthropological approach centred on the exchange between the human drive structure and the social world. This reciprocal relationship becomes visible and can be studied in the medium of images, in the structures of the imaginary and in the way in which the imagination functions.

The three main *gestures*, one of which is associated with the *posture*, another with the *digestion* and the third with *sexual intercourse*, constitute the starting point of this process. Due to its fundamental nature, each of these gestures becomes a schema which makes it possible to generate images that have to do with the posture, digestion or sexual intercourse in general and are affect-laden, and which accounts for the non-material character of the imaginary. The gesture of the posture comprises two schemata: one of rising verticalization and one of visual or manual separation; the gesture of digestion contains the schema of descent and the schema of 'nestling and snuggling'.[8] The gesture of sexual intercourse is a cyclical schema. These schemata do not constitute images, but they acquire form and shape in archetypal constellations and remain consistent across cultural boundaries:

> archetypes are remarkably stable. Thus, the archetypes of summit, head and light correspond immutably to schemata of ascent. [. . .] The schema of descent gives the archetype of the hollow, night, miniaturisation, etc., and the archetype of nestling and snuggling gives rise to archetypes of womb-like intimacy. What precisely differentiates the archetype from the simple symbol is its lack of ambivalence, its constant universality and its consonance with the schema: the wheel, for example, is the main archetype of the cyclical schema, for it is impossible to see what other imaginary significance one could give it.[9]

Thus, symbols are the historical and culture-specific manifestations of the archetypes.[10] They capture what is specific to each historical epoch and culture. It is at this level that cultural diversity re-emerges. Symbols tend to be manifested in narratives; this is how myths and other narratives come into being. Durand defines myths as 'a dynamic system of symbols, archetypes and schemata, which, under the impetus of a schema, tends to be composed into a story'.[11] Normative protocols for imaginary representation grouped around the original schemata, which Durand also called structures, also develop under the influence of the schemata. There are 'well-defined and relatively stable normative protocols *grouped around the original schemata. We shall call these structures*'.[12] These structures are modifiable and organize how the images are grouped. When these structures organize themselves in larger units, they are termed 'regimes'.

Gilbert Durand distinguished the two regimes of 'day' and 'night'. The 'diurnal' regime corresponds to the images that are connected to the postural gesture and its two schemata of ascendant 'verticalization' and visual and manual division.

The 'nocturnal' regime corresponds to the images connected to the gesture of digestion and its schemata 'descent' and 'nestling and snuggling' in intimacy and to the gesture of sexual intercourse and its cyclical schemata. The structures of the 'day' are 'schizomorphous', that is, characterized by splitting; they are concerned with separation, measurement and so on. Two different types of the 'night' regime can be distinguished: the mystical structures with the images of intimacy and the synthetic structures with the cyclical images.

The link between image and imagination is determined by the simultaneous appearance and intermeshing of the basic gestures of the body, the nervous centres and the symbolic representations. The gestures of the body lead to the development of the symbolic representations of the imaginary. Unlike signs in semiotics, which are arbitrary, as symbolic representations images carry meanings that are not arbitrary and originate in the gestures of the body, its effects on the world and, in turn, their repercussions on the imaginary. This function of the fundamental gestures that link the body with the world can be described as follows. The gesture of the upright stance of the body creates visual things and produces techniques of separation for which weapons, arrows and swords, for example, are the symbols. The second gesture of 'descent', which is linked to the digesting of food, creates matter of the depths. Thus, water or underground hollows or cavities generate images of containers such as bowls and chests and stimulate reveries about food and drinks. The rhythmical gestures, whose model is sexuality, have parallels in the rhythms of the seasons and are transferred to the wheel, spinning wheel and churn. This three-part classification 'is therefore in agreement with, among other things, the technological classification which distinguishes: a) striking and bludgeoning tools, b) containers and recipients linked to the techniques of digging, c) the principal technological extensions of that exceptional tool, the wheel – both a means of transport and the basis of the textile and fire-based industries'.[13] From these gestures, schemata evolve, out of which, in turn, the most basic images, the archetypal images, arise, which, because they remain semantically constant, create a link between the imaginary and the processes of rational thinking.

Durand focused particularly on the myths, which he saw as models that can be used to investigate how schemata and archetypes affect narratives. From his reflections on myth criticism, he developed a procedure for analysing literary and artistic texts in which societies express their identities. *Repetition* and *redundancy* play an important role in the analysis of myths. No myth becomes part of the imaginary if it is not repeated, even if this is in different forms.[14] Repetition and redundancy can lead to a kind of synchrony in the diachrony of mythological narrative and can become important for discerning the mythical structure at work in the background. In Durand's view, the analysis of a myth should begin with a myth-critical interpretation of the texts of a particular time or culture, which can provide some important insights into the myths of the society in question.

People can neither produce nor think anything without images playing a pivotal role, and it is therefore of central importance for anthropology to have a knowledge of and investigate those images that structure human beings and their works. Durand believed that the importance attached to myths has declined and that this is partly due to the Aristotelian understanding of the possibilities of direct realism and Descartes's low regard for images. Only since German Idealism and the Romantic era has this situation gradually begun to change, leading to anthropologists becoming increasingly interested in images, the imaginary and imagination. Subject and object, world and human being, one human being and another meet in images. The difficult question arises as to how invariant elements such as the three fundamental gestures, the schemata that evolve from them and the archetypal images that in turn develop from the schemata, are connected with the changes that take place in human societies and cultures in the course of history and to their effects on the imaginary.

The research carried out by Durand and his followers has placed great emphasis on the significance of the invariant elements of the imaginary. While this does not mean that these authors did not appreciate the historicity of the imaginary, they did not link it strongly enough to all aspects of the imaginary. In their system the three fundamental human bodily gestures are invariant components which are not enduringly shaped by historical or cultural conditions. The historical and cultural aspects of the two regimes and the schemata and structures that arise from them and the archetypal images that are produced by their effects are also not taken into account. Historical and cultural differences are only assumed and accepted for symbols. This conception of the invariant or constant character of the bodily gestures, structures, schemata and archetypes must be seen within the context of structuralism, which was dominant in the humanities at that time and led to a relative neglect of the historicity of the body and its gestures. It was believed that there was a constant element that was determined by the attributes of the human body and included the structures and archetypal images of the imaginary. It was also thought that there was a second part of the imaginary that was produced by the interaction between the part that remained constant and the external world and in which historical and cultural modifications and shaping take place. This distinction is not very convincing. It is more likely that the bodily gestures and the structures of the imaginary already come to differ from each other historically and culturally as they develop. Even if the three fundamental gestures of the body are common to all human beings, the way in which they are practised differs depending on the historical and cultural conditions. The same also applies to the two 'diurnal' and 'nocturnal' regimes and the structures and schemata associated with them. Only if we view them more or less in isolation from their respective contexts do they appear to be universal. On closer analysis we see from the start – and not only on a second, less abstract level – that 'night' and 'day' have had different meanings in different cultures and at different times. Thus, for example, since the use of electricity has become widespread the night has become a quite different phenomenon from what it was before.

Wittgenstein's thoughts on language games are also helpful in solving this dilemma.[15] There are language games pertaining to 'day' and 'night' in all cultures. However, no unchanging knowledge about the differences between 'day' and 'night' emerges in these language games. Rather, the respective language games are bound to differences in activities of daily living, which are different at night from during the day. Many different action and language games evolve. As they are repeated again and again, a diversified body of practical knowledge associated with the respective games develops. The societal conditions prevailing in the various cultures and at the different points in history are incorporated as this knowledge is accumulated. What develops is not an abstract, invariable knowledge about the differences between 'day' and 'night', but a practical knowledge that is based on the different action games and language games. This knowledge is linked across cultural divides by a certain 'family resemblance' or 'family likeness' (Wittgenstein) between the different forms of knowledge. In none of these cultures is this knowledge identical to the knowledge in a different culture; it is only similar. For example, in one action or language game there may be a similarity between two cultures whose action and language games differ in other areas. It cannot therefore be assumed that they are identical, but rather that there is a family resemblance between these cultures as, for example, there is a family likeness between the shapes of the mouths of a father and his son or between the shapes of the eyes of a mother and her son or between those of the chins of a brother and sister. The language and action games associated with day and night are thus not the same in different cultures and in different times, only similar in the way that a family likeness is. This similarity is enough for people to be able to gain a practical knowledge of what the language and action games 'day' and 'night' mean. In this view, the historical and cultural character of the bodily gestures is present from the start. The same applies to the 'diurnal' and 'nocturnal' regimes, which are now understood as ensembles of different action and language games whose commonality is their family resemblance. Since these concepts are associated with different practices of everyday living, the concrete societal conditions in which these practices are performed are also incorporated, together with the various areas of knowledge.

This also applies to the structures and the schemata. They develop from the start in various different action and language games which are not the same but show family resemblances. Not only do the schemata and structures result from action and language games, they also in turn structure actions and speech. Thus, they are structures that are both structured and structuring. It is precisely this dual action of structuring and being structured that takes place in language and action games. It is therefore these structures which are considered to be historical and cultural from the start, and which also create ensembles of images of the imaginary. Such basic images or archetypal patterns develop in language and action games. The wheel is a good example. How a wheel works is experienced very early on in action and language games in which a practical knowledge of how a wheel is used is acquired. This practical knowledge can be experienced differently in different cultures and in different historical times, for example in the use of a cart, a scooter, a bicycle or an express train. Due to the family likeness between these experiences, a generalizable knowledge develops so that even children grasp that the wheel is what these objects have in common and that it has a similar function in all of them. On this basis, it is not necessary to assume the existence of an archetypal image of the wheel in order to be able to show that there is a knowledge of the wheel and its use in different cultures and at different points in history. The above is not, however, sufficient to explain innovative uses of the wheel or how symbols such as that of wheel of fortune come into being. In order to understand these processes, it is necessary investigate the symbolizing power of the imagination, which often creates something new.

5.1 Historicity and the symbolic character of the imaginary

The fact that the structures of the imaginary were not thought of in historical terms led to a heated debate between Le Goff and Durand. The question arose as to whether the structures identified do not become a straitjacket that only allows the dynamic of the imagination to become the focus of attention in a limited way, since it is the logical consistency of a structure that is the most salient aspect, and less the dynamic of the imagination, to whose vegetative and mimetic bodily contortions and convolutions such a coherent and rational system does not do justice.

Rather than attempt to identify structures of the imagination in this way, there would seem to me to be more to be gained by taking a closer look at its symbolizing function. Ricoeur defined symbol as 'any structure of signification in which a direct, primary, literal meaning designates, in addition, another meaning which is indirect, secondary, and figurative and which can be apprehended only through the first'.[16] There can be no doubt that the imagination does not create only images whose meanings do not go beyond the image that precedes symbolization. On the contrary, it creates images with symbolic meanings. The figurative content of such images cannot be reduced to a single meaning but to many, some of which are hidden and can only be rendered accessible through interpretation. An interpretation can only be developed in a relationship between the image and the interpreter in which the historical and cultural contexts of the image and the interpreter are related to each other. The idea that the meaning of an image is contained within the image alone and that nothing or very little has to do with the viewer is not very convincing. Since the interpretation depends on this relationship, it cannot be ignored. Without it there can be no horizon of meaning within which the interpretation of an image would be possible.

For Durand, the symbol is paradoxical in that it transcends its meaning and carries a passion towards a being that is objectively absent. The symbol is experienced both as insufficient, since it is only a signifier, and at the same time as the only possible approximation insofar as the signified is never given alone. Thus, the symbol highly intensifies what is represented, transforming the image into a sacred icon, concealing its meaning and embodying the possibility of multiple interpretations.[17]

The imagination symbolizes. It thus modifies unequivocal, linear, pictorial representations that are tied to pragmatic contexts of meaning and discovers contexts of meaning, which are both distant and yet also close. They go beyond everyday consciousness and open us up to transcendent issues. 'The essence of cosmic life, the origin of evil and the experience of death are thus important sources of symbol production across all cosmogonic and eschatological myths, since their meaning, which is existentially decisive, eludes discourse, but allows the imagination to unveil it figuratively.'[18] Symbols have a further important function in the different religions where they are intended to provide human beings with an orientation for their further development, for example in the symbol of the cross or a sitting Buddha. They also point towards the sacred and its promotion of spiritual development in human beings. In many cultures, symbols show believers the way out of everyday life into the sacred world. Many of them are closely related to transitional rituals such as those carried out on the occasion of births and deaths and open up our eyes to a transcendental world.

The imaginary, the symbolic and the real

Dedicated to Dietmar Kamper

In this section, I examine the relationship between the three orders of the imaginary, the symbolic and the real, the analysis of which was the focus of Dietmar Kamper's research on the theory of imagination.[1] Taking Lacan's differentiation between the three orders as a starting point, I propose that the relationship between them is not harmonious. On the contrary, the subject is split. However, it is capable

> neither of resisting this split, nor of repressing or permanently forgetting it. This is at the root of the turmoil of its shock at itself. On the other hand in contrast to the suspension of the subject in surrealism and post-structuralism, Lacan continues to claim that in the dramatic movement of desire and under the dictate of deprivation the subject begins to extricate itself, that is, it transcends itself in language, which is wiser than all speakers. Furthermore, it overcomes, in the name of the dead father, the omnipotent delusion of imaginary obsessions.[2]

The concept of need is replaced by the concept of desire, which is excentric, paradoxical and unconscious, but, as the unconscious, it is structured like a language that consists of chains of signifiers. It functions only as a desire for the Other in the sense that it emanates from the Other and is thus desired by the subject. The desire stems from the wound caused by the separation of the individual at birth and from the search in the imaginary for the lost oneness. In the triangulation of the Oedipus complex, the incestuous wishes of the individual are displaced and brought under the aegis of the law of the father or the symbolic order. The wishes are displaced and the individual thus enters the 'structure of the social'. This oedipal situation contains within it the disaster 'that the subject's misconception of itself (as being or wanting to be the centre of the world and master of its desire) is both the cause and the pitfall of all wishes and vicissitudes of bodily impulses'.[3] The displacement of the wishes makes it clear that there can be no satisfaction of wishes and that the wound that arises from the loss of the original oneness cannot be healed. All attempts to insist that one's needs be satisfied rather than accept that one's desire will remain unrequited can only meet with partial success. Efforts to construct an ego identity that individuals can use to calm the diverging impulses at work within them are inadequate. In the view of the human being developed here, there is no reconciliation. In their unavailing attempts to restore oneness in the imaginary and hampered by their oedipal self-deceptions, individuals cannot escape becoming embroiled in their own wishes and the structures of the order of the father. There is still something beyond this that is elusive and never seen for what it is: the real. For Kant, it is the thing in itself, for psychoanalysis the unconscious. Both of these, by their very nature, present human cognition and self-knowledge with an insurmountable challenge. For us human beings, it is the mysterious recognition of our mirror image that plays the central role in our becoming enmeshed in the images of the imaginary, 'which appears to bring to an end the early infantile experience of being a fragmented body; however, the fantasy is simply superimposed on the trauma of the original separation and functions as a screen that protects us from the incommensurable and thus constitutes the beginning of the chain of diverted and displaced wishes'.[4]

From this point onwards, desire pursues two strategies:

> either it takes the 'real' to be what is undeniable and indisputable and ends up with the disastrous consequences of the coercive power of the 'imaginary', or it experiences the real as the impossible per se and takes an endless detour via the 'symbolic', well aware that in practical everyday living the theoretical difference is associated with a multitude of tears, ruptures, bends, niches and chasms, etc.[5]

The only choice left to the subject is the one between distorting itself in fantasies of omnipotence and relativising itself by integrating itself into the symbolic order, an endeavour that will, however, not be permanently successful. What is needed is a shift from a subject that is the centre of power to a subject that is a 'disempowered, constituted element of a trans-subjective structure (desire, language, symbolic order)'.[6] The question that arises is to what extent the symbolic can compensate for the impossibility of accessing the real. However, here doubts are in order. 'Where the word is, there is no room for the real. There language prevails, acting as proxy for the body and things.'[7]

Since we have no direct relationship to the real, the only way that we humans as speaking creatures can free ourselves from the constraints of the imaginary, of our misconceptions ('méconnaissance') of ourselves and of our delusional objects is by fitting into the symbolic order. For Lacan, this human dilemma is expressed in the formula 'the closer to the real [we get], the deeper in the imaginary we are', which captures the hopelessness of the situation. This definition abandons the historical differentiation between reproductive and productive imagination. Reproductive imagination, according to Lacan, recreates something that already exists and inserts what has been produced into our habits. In contrast, in productive imagination something that did not previously exist is created. Here the imagination is seen as a force that creates something novel, a paradigmatic 'productive force', that is, as being capable of engendering, rendering visible, presenting and bringing to light. Thus, in analogy to the creative power of God, which brings forth by thinking, the task that falls to human beings is to 'create' their world in images by means of their imagination. Using their imagination, ('*Einbildungskraft*' or the power of imagination), human beings have powers that they can use to liberate themselves from the structures that are occupied by the imaginary. As these powers develop, they are interlinked with social conditions and the psychogenesis of the individual.

> As sleep keeps our memories of life in the womb alive, narcissism keeps the image of a oneness alive that takes the place of an unbearable experience, one of life-threatening fragmentation. The fruit of an imaginary death is extraordinarily productive. Together with our dreams it constitutes the driving force of human survival – a kind of primeval fantasy. Thus seen, it functions as a scar out of which the delusion of identity gradually evolves by means of its synthetic power. The imaginary has a monadic structure and henceforth represents the real, in the sense that it is superimposed over a traumatic and irreparable injury, a lack.[8]

This is the source of human productivity; it is the attempt to deal with the wounds and scars of human existence.

Since the Renaissance, with its belief in rendering the world visible, the production of images has reached a scale that is hardly conceivable. These images inscribe themselves into the human imaginary, which becomes superimposed on our memories of the lost oneness and serves to protect us against our fear of death. As the images have become hypertrophic, new constellations have arisen which affect the human body and our experience of time and language. The human body has long been exposed to increasing levels of abstraction and representation in images. This development is evident in the growing predominance of instrumental thinking that affects all areas of human life. Only what is functional, rational and generally valid is valued. Anything complex, polymorphic and fragmentary is accorded little attention and is repressed and suppressed. The relationship between sense and the senses is a good example.

> Sense in the singular is understood to refer to the overall, unified body of the meanings with which we invest events and processes, and which are based on a common ground of diversified relationships [. . .]. This used to be called the objective mind, later it came to be known as manageable instrumental reason, which can be for any purpose. The senses, in the plural, i.e., the eyes, the ears, the nose, the mouth and the skin are the bodily organs that are oriented towards the outside world. Not to forget the sense of balance, which is linked to the *sensus communis* in a way that still remains a riddle. These senses guarantee our receptiveness for complex information. How they interact remains mysterious and sometimes wonderful.[9]

All of this gives us a different perspective on the conflict between 'Logic and Passion'.[10] While in the first case human consciousness is seen as a multilayered system of defence, negation, denial and repression, in the second the other side of consciousness is addressed with 'the senses': the body and desire, wishes and passions, and sensory perception. *Mainstream* science is dedicated to the logic of the general with its control and power mechanisms, within which there are only a few openings for the other side of consciousness.

In these debates, instrumental reason and imagination are interwoven. Imagination is defined as 'imagination and fantasy in their basic forms, as a transcendental synthesis of the different sensory channels, the internal sense of time and, in its split-off form, as media imaginary, as currently obsessively structured by the audiovisual pictorial media' (ibid, p. 29). The imaginary is described as follows:

> The imaginary that has an effect on society is an 'inner-world-space'[11] in which the world is depicted and which has a strong tendency to close itself off and create an immanence that is virtually infinite. In contrast, human fantasy and imagination are the only powers that have the capacity to force open closed spaces and temporarily to transcend them because they are identical to the discontinuous experience of time itself.[12]

This makes it clear that the imaginary creates an 'inner-world-space' that contains a world but which is in fact illusory. In this space more and more people are, in the final analysis, living under the influence of the new media. It is inhabited by the images in such a way that it becomes a prison that can only be broken out of with the aid of fantasy. This differentiates between the imaginary and fantasy, whereby the imaginary is seen as negative, and imagination and fantasy as positive. This distinction allows us to evaluate certain cultural development processes in different ways. With this in mind, we can take a different perspective on certain cultural development processes. The imaginary is associated with 'the sensory', instrumental reason, the humanities and economic rationality, whereas the imagination is associated with the 'senses', the body and resistance to abstraction and the process of transformation into images. 'Thus, images and the products of fantasy are of a dual nature. They are reflections and at the same time they provide bridges to the other. The culmination of reflection is the imaginary. The power to build bridges, to open windows, is the imagination.'[13]

The European Renaissance saw the beginning of a shift from a religious-aesthetic, ascetic portrayal of the body to 'rendering the materiality of the body visible in images', that is, to a transformation of the material world and bodily aspects of life into images. Since Leonardo da Vinci, the real has been increasingly understood as that which is visible. The goal at the time was therefore to render anything and everything visible. 'Since then, rendering things visible and revealing them have been the main objectives of the most important human activity, i.e. producing. Producing is presenting, representing and exhibiting.'[14]

> European panel painting did not describe the world but constructed it. Like the science of observation, it laid down how the world is to be seen. The subject's desire was organised in such a way that it contented itself with the world as an image. What people call their reality is thus actually constructed as a result of implicit norms. Without the iconic mode and the ingenious invention, 500 years ago, of a new visibility we would not have standardised perception today.[15]

This passion for the visible has become stronger over time, as a result of the invention of both the telescope and the microscope and has also been fuelled by voyages to distant shores where there was something new, something hitherto unknown that was discovered and brought under control. The discovery of the 'New World' resulted from a search for an earthly paradise, which was driven by longing and greed. 'In their rebellion against the old order of the 1500s it was imagination, not reason, that was used as the guiding principle in constructing a human world. The origins of the modern era and the Enlightenment were heretical; they were founded on imagination, i.e. on an "imagination fondatrice".'[16]This trend has continued. The boundaries of the imaginary have expanded, and this limits our opportunities to have experiences. The eye has been enthroned as the 'guiding sense of orientation in the world'. The arts and sciences have participated in this development. The circle of the visible has been further expanded. Today it also includes the inner spaces of the body. The image has become a bearer of insights that it would be difficult to show or convey in any other way. However, it has also become evident that the more the sphere of the visible grows, the greater the sphere of the invisible becomes. The more the light increases, the more the shadow also grows. 'The optical era has demonstrated it *ex negativo*. Its motto "Render visible all that is invisible" was doubly deceptive. It failed to capture what used to be invisible and it has also produced a new realm of invisibility. There is a specific blindness inherent in seeing – the more is visible, the more is invisible.'[17]

Things can only be identified if we immobilize them. 'To grasp the world through the viewfinder of visual perception is to take the life out of it. Images are corpses of things. Unrestrained, the imaginary wields the power of death.'[18] The gaze is capable of killing, and where it does not kill, it controls. Foucault demonstrated this in his studies on the 'medical gaze' and Bentham's Panopticon. In the first case, it is the gaze that captures things in the way that it needs to have them for its investigations, and in that way alone. For example, in order to be able to examine the reactions of the muscles to certain stimulations in dissection experiments, the living body must be (gradually) killed. Only if the body is transformed into a dead 'object' can the experiment be carried out with a scientific gaze. In the case of Bentham's Panopticon, it was the gaze that had been internalized by the prisoners that led to the shift from external to internal control.

When photography was invented, there were also extensive discussions about the fact that photographs kill the reality that they depict. This view of the relationship between reality and photographs is still widespread today in some cultures. Roland Barthes also drew attention to the close link between photographs and the past and also decay and death.[19] Photographs record a moment in time that has already passed when they are looked at. They are thus images of something that no longer exists. This moment is also not reproduced as a living moment in the photograph. The photograph merely alludes to the moment and its aliveness. If the moment recorded by the photograph is to come 'alive' again when it is looked at, it must be reanimated by the viewer, which is why the cult of photographs and images has much to do with animism. However, it is not that there is life in the images, but that the people who look at them bring them to life. Copying images is another way to rob them of their fascination. Walter Benjamin described this mechanism and its effects as a loss of the aura of the images resulting from copying.

When images are reproduced, there is a risk that the desire for the one and only image, that of a non-existent and unattainable oneness glimpsed at the mirror stage, will be lost. What looks like infinite expansion is simply the obliteration of the traces of the desire. People will therefore lose the pleasure of seeing, because the gaze has become technified. Today technically produced images have already lost most of their evidential value and their aura. They are no longer images *of* something to which they refer and thus they lose their bearings. There is no longer a clear answer to the question, "Where are the images? Inside or outside?" When prohibitions on images are transgressed, we are forced to participate against our will in the attempt to shift the power of the imaginary to the inside, not by means of prohibitions, but by means of excessive release, by means of metastases.[20] From this perspective, even the Enlightenment can be seen as an attempt to 'transform the real, the weighty and the body into a brightened image and to dematerialise, which unexpectedly ended in a transparent nihilism'.[21]

The images of the imaginary are no longer images that provide bridges to the Other, about whom they help us to discover something through mimetic appropriation. They are not windows through which we can look and perceive an impression of otherness, with which we can get to grips. These images have become mirrors in which we see not otherness but ourselves and in which we cannot gain an experience of otherness, but only of ourselves. These images become prison walls that permit no escape. As little as these images convey to us of an outside that is other, they do still protect us from fear, from the *horror vacui*, even if they do restrict our gaze and, functioning as a mirror, turn us back on ourselves. The gaze is now forced to 'act in a world of pure surfaces in which only outlines, sketches and drawings, at best with the illusion of space, but without the bodily experience of the world, predominate. The life space is then literally the screen or display, which does not become spatial simply because it is situated in a space or opens up virtual spaces by means of the appropriate connections'.[22] Movement and perception are accelerated, leading to an increase in what can be seen and in the images of the imaginary. Insofar as the images no longer make reference to external worlds, but rather to one another, accelerating them also expands the imaginary. More and more institutions are producing more and more images of more and more things. With the aid of new technologies, even the murky inner spaces of the body can be transformed into images that are stored for comparison and follow-up examinations. Enormous image archives are being built up in which digital images are stored in such a way that they can potentially be retrieved at any time. The computer technologies produce virtual spaces that simulate space and time. Whole universes of digital data are forming, the abstract quality of which stands in contrast to the materiality of the human bodies that are being captured by floods of images which are becoming ever faster and larger. Only images count, be they of politicians, commodities or bodies. The pictorial nature of images makes politicians, commodities and bodies reproducible. As images, they are no longer bound to locations and points in time and are almost ubiquitous. People and things are meaningful in the form of images. The images promise to overcome ageing, frailty and death. Images do not age or decay, and unlike the bodies from which they are derived, they are not mortal. Images lead a life of their own in the imaginary cosmos of the media, the collective consciousness of society and the individual memories of individual people.

The images generate a pressure to make everything visible, to dissolve the boundaries between the private and the public spheres and to create new forms of intimate public life. On the television screen, people and things lose their three-dimensionality and their materiality. As images they can be linked together in next to no time. What has previously been hidden is dragged into visibility. It is 'no longer the obscenity of the hidden, the repressed, the obscured, but that of the visible, the all-too-visible, the more-visible-than-visible; it is the obscenity of that which no longer contains a secret and is entirely soluble in information and communication'.[23]

Associated with the loss of the mystery of the images is also the loss of their resilience. This is because most images allude to something that they are not, that is, to an alterity that lies outside of them. The moment that images only reproduce what is known, that is, they are reduced to being mirrors, this resilience, which is tied to their allusion to alterity, is diminished. The images become commodities, and as such they can be consumed easily and rapidly. Some have called this iconophagy, which is an apt description for the phenomenon. References to the gobbling up and consuming of images are also illustrative of the addictive nature of iconophagy. Instead of consumption of commodities, we have consumption of images, for which equivalents are sought in reality. Floods of images have taken the place of the consumption of commodities and are gobbled up like commodities.

The mirror metaphor may not be sufficiently broad to cover these new digital images. These images are not surfaces and no longer consist of lines.

On computer screens and in digital cameras there is only the 0-1 binary code that directs the streams of energy according to algorithms that were developed at some point in the past and which allows us to perceive image structures. The binary system, this '0-1' of the media (on, off) is gradually replacing all ternary structures, not to mention the quaternary structures, and reduces the

whole world to a sequence of energies. It is thus no longer the mirror image that
ensures the primacy of the imaginary, but a time machine that depicts the flow
of dots on a surface, whereas the mirror image still suggested a visual presence,
a presence of the self, which was organised in a way that matched with the true
presence of the Other.[24]

Many of the images perceived by people today come into being on the television
screen, which therefore plays a special role in forming the imaginary. We can see
it as a 'place of fear' and interpret the image processes that take place there in
terms of early forms of physical fear responses present in the imaginary.

> The original meaning of screen was not a component of a television set, but
> a component of mental apparatuses in the infant psyche. Their purpose is to
> regulate fear. Excessive stimuli that are strong enough to cause injury are
> incorporated in images and rendered harmless. We need phantasms in order
> to prevent traumatisation. At the same time both the true injuries and the
> potential ones are lost in the images. They become inaccessible to recall. The
> screen is halfway between trauma and phantasm. On the one hand it provides
> protection against too much reality, while on the other it gives shape and form
> to experience.[25]

The floods of images perceived on the screen meet together with the viewer's
individual imaginary, which has already formed, and contains individual
and collective receptive patterns which select, take in and process the images
perceived. In this process, early experiences of fear and also of happiness are
reshaped. Later there are no pure perceptions, since all perceptions coalesce
with the individual and collective structures of the human imaginary which
co-determine how images are perceived, experienced and processed.

As a result of the floods of images and the aestheticization of reality and
iconophagy, images no longer promote oneness and security. There are now
new possibilities for simulation, in addition to extensive mimetic processes.
'Simulation replaces a reality with images that are deceptively similar. Mimesis
creates a reality by means of bodily gestures that give expression to wishes.'[26] As
a result of simulation, images are disseminated irrespective of their origin and
allude, as images, to other images, giving rise to a promiscuity of images that
can no longer be stopped. Thus, images cite other images, play with them and
content themselves with doing this. They want no more than to be themselves
and to be received as such. Recently, there has been talk of the self-referentiality
of images. Here again there is a risk that the outside and the allusion to alterity
will be lost. Only self-referential images which allude only to other self-referential

images – if they orient themselves towards anything at all – are transformed. In this way, chains and spirals of simulation are formed, within which the images are permanently altered. Citing Baudrillard, Kamper sharpens the concept of simulation even further.

> To start with [for Baudrillard] it is a deceptively authentic imitation of the genuine thing. Secondly, it is the 'more genuine' substitute for the genuine thing. Thirdly, it is the claim that there never has been anything genuine. Fourthly, it is a calm, pleasant awareness that is able to defend itself so successfully against all negative impacts from outside because at the height of its expansion it knows no alternative. The indifferent, allusionless form of simulation is thus attained, a delusion of omnipotence that invests all its strength in the effort it requires to function smoothly and without disturbances.[27]

A level of escalation is thus reached that is expressed in the dimensions of simulation, substitution, dissolution and the extinguishing of reality. The imaginary is involved in all four dimensions,[28] unfolding its entire power above all the dissolution and substitution of reality. This can only be countered by the imagination of the writer. Since accession to this constantly expanding world of the imaginary is collective, even imagination can only exert its influence here and there.

These thoughts on the relationship between the imaginary, the symbolic and the real and thus on the situation of human beings today are based on anthropological assumptions that are related to historical developments which have taken place specifically in the European cultures. They claim to provide evidence and plausibility for a diagnosis of important aspects of contemporary life in Western cultures. The question as to the extent to which these analyses are also valid for the situations of people in other cultures remains open and requires further research and clarification.

The performativity of the imagination

7.1 Performativity and mimesis

For several decades, images have been a major research topic in anthropology and cultural science. The interest in this field began with the question 'What is an image?'[1] The starting point was the omnipresence of images in linguistic metaphors, artworks and the new media. Images have become ubiquitous, and it was time to develop a new understanding of the image as a cultural figuration. Taking as our point of departure the idea that the metaphor is a bridge between the subject and the world and that thought is dependent on metaphors, it was considered necessary to gain a better understanding of the central performative role of images in culture, the sciences and philosophy. The 'discovery' of the gaze and the crossing over that occurs in it between things and the eyes, which are attached to the body, opened up a new understanding of the relationship between image, gaze and body. The chiastic model of crossing gazes in which there is an intertwining of seeing and being seen makes clear how images are created by the gaze, deposited in the memory and then revived in recall. In the phenomenological view of seeing and the reading of images, seeing is considered to be an independent and irreplaceable cultural act which plays a constitutive role in the performativity of the imagination.

Images play a central role in the performative character of language, the staging and performance of social actions (e.g. rituals) and in the aisthesis of social acts and artistic acts (such as performances). In the linguistic dimension of the performative, metaphors have a special significance. In social practices, the mental images of the protagonists contribute substantially to the results of performative arrangements. Group-specific and/or collective images mingle with images of individuals and produce specific stagings and performances. Images of social scenes from the past are brought into the present by means of recall and converted into actions by mimetic processes. Cultural activities arise out of the performativity of the imagination. At the same time, these stagings and performances become the starting point for new mental images in the protagonists and their audiences, which are superimposed on earlier images and generate future actions, whose staging and performance they co-create. Stagings and performances become models which the imagination uses to produce mental images which it integrates into the imaginary. Finally, the social and cultural performances also have an aesthetic dimension in the form of images, sound and taste, smell and touch sensation, and it is only these that can be perceived. Human performances cannot be transformed into symbolic language without reducing their quality and complexity.

The mimetic processing of artistic images leads to iconic experiences, since mimetic processes are aimed at 'recreating' images through seeing and at incorporating them into our inner world of images through imagination. The recreation of images through seeing is a process of appropriation which absorbs their imagery into the inner worlds of the imagination and memory, where their performative effects unfold. The mimetic processing of the images is aimed at appropriating their imagery, which is present before, during, after and outside of any interpretation. When images are absorbed into the inner world of images, they serve as reference points for interpretations that undergo repeated changes in the course of a person's life. Irrespective of how they may be interpreted in the individual case, when we reprocess images by mimesis on repeated occasions, each time we engage in a renewed act of appropriation, of insight, even. Each time we concentrate on and surrender ourselves to the recreation of the imaginary images once more, needing to be 'refresh' them again and again through visual encounters with the real images or their reproductions. Reconstructing their shapes and colours in the act of seeing requires us as beholders to suppress the inner images and thoughts that arise in our minds and to hold on to the external image as we contemplate it, to open ourselves up to its imagery and abandon ourselves to it. The mimetic process consists in our 'making ourselves similar' to the image through visual recreation, absorbing it and using it to expand our inner image worlds.

In the mimetic-performative assimilation of an image, we can distinguish two phases that merge into each other. The first phase is concerned with overcoming the mechanical form of seeing in which images of art and other objects are perceived merely as objects, and deals with them simply by 'knowing about' them. This kind of seeing that is focused on orienting ourselves and gaining control often serves as protection against becoming overtaxed by the images. However, it also reduces the potentials inherent in seeing. In acts of conscious seeing, the goal is to develop the capacity to see. This includes lingering over the object, overcoming what is familiar and discovering what is not familiar. From this perspective, we can say that when we assimilate images and objects mimetically, we are forced to slow down, which permits us to take something in by allowing ourselves to be affected by it. In the second phase, the image has already become part of our internal image world as a result of the mimetic seeing. Only in this phase does the mimetic assimilation take place. It is of necessity incomplete and can attain new levels of intensity through repetition. Holding an image that has been assimilated in this way in our imagination trains our capacity to concentrate and thus also our imaginative powers. To reproduce an image in the imagination, we must constantly resist its inherent tendency to disappear and hold on to it in spite of the stream of 'interfering images' that arise internally. This activity of the imagination is involved every time an image is creatively produced. The fact that its intensity and the results that it produces must by nature remain open-ended challenges the imagination to keep on producing.

Mimetic processes are processes that are sensorily oriented towards images as images and which both assimilate and expand the world. In these processes, the imagination, which is rooted in the vegetative system of the human body, forges a link with the world and turns the outside world into the internal world and the internal world into the outside world. In these processes, the desire to assimilate the world plays a constitutive role. In this desire, it is not only we ourselves who produce the images but the images that produce us. Due to the desire structure of our bodies and our perception, the things look at us before our conscious perception is directed towards the things. Today iconology must take on the additional task of further elucidating these relationships.

7.2 The interplay of image, body and medium

When we speak of the performative nature of images, the question arises as to whether we are referring to external or internal images. The fact that the concept of the 'image' includes both possibilities is indicative of something that is characteristic of images. External images hark back to internal images and internal images to external ones. Both have a determining effect on human behaviour. All images are products of the human imaging power that is rooted in the vegetative system of the human body and is highly performative.

We have only limited control over the images we perceive and the internal images that we create out of them. Where our gaze dwells and what it excludes, what we absorb into our memories so that we can remember it is a process that is only partly conscious. It is no less important to make human desire, other people, situations and things part of us in the form of images. Our mental images guide our perception and determine what we see, fail to see, remember or forget. Not only do our inner streams of images determine which people or external things become images because we focus our attention on them, they also regulate which images become internalized without our being aware of it. We are at the mercy of our internal images, even if we constantly try to gain control over them. These images fluctuate and change over the course of our lives. Images that were once important lose their meaning and are replaced by new ones. All images allow human beings to experience themselves in them and can use them to assure themselves of who they are.

Mental images usually result from the external images that are brought to our attention. As products of our culture, they are an expression of this culture and differ from the images of other cultures and other historical epochs. On their way from the objectified forms in the external world to the 'interior' of the human body and through their superimposition on the images that are already there, the collective character of these images assumes its individualized shape. Some of these images are part of the collective imagery that have been produced and disseminated by various media.[2]

Images exist as a result of their links to the *media* in which they are objectified. This is true of the early cave paintings in which the stone is the medium to which they owe their existence. It also applies to the death masks of antiquity in which the face of the short-lived body is transferred to a different medium, thus surviving the mortal body. In photography, films and videos, we have a similar situation. In photos, a light imprint of the human body is made on a negative through light-sensitive processes and is then transferred on to and preserved on photographic paper. The image can have a quite different history from the body from which it originates. The situation with films and videos, in which there is also movement as an additional factor, is similar. In each case, the media are not external to the images, but a constitutive element of them. Without the medium there would be no image that we could perceive, transfer and incorporate into our internal image worlds. The images only exist because they are tied to a medium, that is, because they appear in a medium that enables us to perceive them, inscribe them into our bodies and experience their effects through our senses. The media in which the images are conveyed to us have a decisive influence on the way in which we experience them. As media they affect the way in which we perceive the images, irrespective of the image itself. There is a qualitative difference between looking at an image that has been painted, photographed or digitally produced. This difference is overlooked in visual semiotics, for example, where images are reduced to signs.

Space and time also serve as important reference points for how we experience images. Bodies that become images escape mortality in image form. The early death masks are also evidence of this. Even photographic images produced on paper suggest to the human body that it can overcome its temporality. Photos prompt us to remember and allow us to survive in a social community as images. Because they exist in a medium, images can be stored and are available at all times, that is, they can be perceived at a time that is different from the time of their creation.

The fact that images are transmitted through a medium renders them independent of the space in which they were created and makes it possible to introduce them into various spatial contexts. Images can be presented anywhere. The image on the television screen shows viewers in their homes places that are somewhere else, which they 'enter' in their imaginations. Where are the viewers? Are they still at home or are they in some faraway place to which the camera has led them? Despite their lack of dependence on space and time, since they are conveyed by media, *as* images images are not independent of context. Rather, not only their meaning but also their image character changes in relation to the context. The fact that the images are conveyed by a specific medium determines the criteria that guide how they are used, or applied performatively, and provide instructions as to how they are to be perceived. In any possible use of an image, different times and spaces are superimposed on each other, making it possible to distinguish between the time at which the image was created, the time to which its representations refer and the time at which it was perceived. The same applies to space.

Cultural anthropology can quote many examples of the violent changes in the imaginaries of human beings.[3] Such a change took place with the colonization and Christianization of Mexico, for instance. The Spanish conquerors concentrated all their efforts on destroying the collective imaginary of the indigenous peoples and on replacing it with the Christian imaginary so as to ensure that the *colonization* would endure.[4] In complex mimetic processes, the Indios' imaginary world was permanently altered and an amalgamation of imaginary 'heathen' and Christian figures evolved. The incorporation of the new Christian points of identification in the imaginary of the Indios made their subjugation final.

The body is accessible to human beings in its concrete objective forms in images, languages and cultural stagings. Like other objectifications, historically and culturally images have been and are different kinds of expression and representation of the body. The relationship between the human body and the images changes, this transformation often being brought about by changes in medium. Even mirrors allow us to see our bodies where they are not, in glass or in metal. With mirrors, as also with paintings, we have a translation of a three-dimensional body into a flat surface. The medium likewise alters the nature of the image in photography, where a light imprint of the body is created that makes it appear on a flat surface. If we conceive of the new media as prostheses of the body even digital images assume a relationship to the body, albeit a more abstract one. There currently seems to be a general increase in interest in the mediated character of images and how media are involved in the relationship between human beings and the world. This development also includes the imaging procedures (e.g. X-ray, electron microscopy and computed tomography) which are now indispensable in the natural sciences and whose importance for epistemology and the cultural sciences is only slowly becoming apparent. The performativity of the images varies depending on the media employed.[5]

In images, the presence and absence of human beings and objects are inextricably intertwined. While a body is present in the medium of photography, a photograph of it also refers to the absent body. The image always has a mental property and the medium always a material one, even if both are linked in the sensory impression.[6] The photograph becomes an image when people look at it and make it come alive with their gazes. Here the fact that photography uses a medium recedes into the background. This is even more the case with films and television. In both cases, the viewer is drawn into the world of images presented to him or her in the medium. Even if we are basically aware of the fact that images exist in or on media, we 'forget' it in the process of looking, in which the images created by media join together with our own mental images and produce the television and film images as images of human experience. In this process, the images conveyed in the present by the media superimpose themselves on those associated or remembered by the viewer. Both the television and film images that we are currently viewing and our own mental images have a deeper level in the imaginaries of the culture and society. This deeper level is repeatedly 'alluded to' and is what gives meaning to many of the 'current' images.

Unlike film and television images, *digital images* have a matrix that is no longer an image. However, both their image character and the fact that they are transmitted by a medium have become a problem in that the mathematically generated electronic processes only a few people are able to apply them, while at the same time they guarantee a high level of manipulability. In synthetic images, the traditional 'link between image, subject, and object' is dissolved.[7] Even if this is the case, there is always a link between the synthetic image and what it represents, although the nature of the link may be new and different. Also, the synthetic image needs a screen in order to be represented and thus become an 'image'. As such, it bears reference to the mental images of its viewers and, like all other images, is superimposed on and interwoven with them. The appearance of the images on a screen suggests that they we can gain access to them in a clear and controllable framework. The relatively small size of the screen, the ephemeral nature of the moving images that appear on it and the standardization of how we look at them add to this illusion. As moving images, synthetic images convey a double illusion to the viewer that includes both the image and the movement, the latter being all the more sustainable because the body is motionless and in a sitting position. If the increasing dissemination of synthetic images helps to dispel the belief in the representative nature of the images, this may lead to lasting changes in attitudes towards images and their cultural use.

Vilém Flusser has described the evolution of this situation as follows:

> First, man took a step back from his life-world, to imagine it. Then, man stepped back from the imagination, to describe it. Then, man took a step back from the linear, written critique, to analyze it. And finally, owing to a new imagination, man projected synthetic images out of analysis. [. . .] But what concerns us right now in an existential sense is the burdensome, but necessary, leap out of the linear into the zero-dimensional (into the realm of "quanta").[8]

7.3 The performative energy of fantasy and imagination

Fantasy has a chiastic structure in which there is a crossover between inside and outside. Both Maurice Merleau-Ponty and Jacques Lacan have drawn attention to this structure that is so important for the production of images. A conception of seeing that assumes that objects that are identical with themselves stand opposite to who see and who are 'empty' to begin with fails to take this structure into account. Rather, seeing contains something that we can only grasp more accurately by feeling it with our gaze.

> The look, we said, envelops, palpates, espouses the visible things. As though it were in a relation of pre-established harmony with them, as though it knew them before knowing them, it moves in its own way with its abrupt and imperious style, and yet the views taken are not desultory – I do not look at chaos, but at things – so that finally one cannot say if it is the look or if it is the things that command.[9]

Such a crossover or chiasmus takes place between the senses and the outer world that they perceive not only in vision, but also when we touch and hear, and in principle also when we smell and taste something.

Thus, human perception is not without preconditions. To start with, we perceive the world in an anthropomorphous way, that is, based on the physiological givens of our bodies. Secondly, our perception is influenced by historical anthropological and cultural factors. For example, following the discovery and dissemination of writing, there was a change in visual perception in cultures that used writing as compared to vision in oral cultures. The new media and the acceleration of images associated with them are having a similarly pronounced effect on our perceptual processes.[10] As research in gestalt psychology has shown, our fantasy is involved even at the level of pure perception, for example when we complete the gaps in the figure we are perceiving. Similarly, the things we perceive only assume meaning in conjunction with our cultural frame of reference. History and culture both enable us to see and constrain what we see. Thus, as a process of seeing is modifiable, contingent and forward-looking.

A closer look at the bodily basis of fantasy brings us to an assumption of Arnold Gehlen, according to which we

> find the concept of the 'primal imagination' (. . .) manifested in the detritus of our dreams, or in the periods of concentrated vegetative processes, in childhood, or in the contact between the sexes; in other words, wherever the forces of developing life announce themselves. There are, amid ever-changing images, certain primal visions or images of the overall purpose of life, which senses within itself a tendency toward a higher form, a greater intensity of current, so to speak. An immediate vital *ideality* exists, a tendency in the *substantia vegetans* toward a higher quality or quantity (whereby it should be noted that the right to make this distinction remains questionable).[11]

Gehlen interprets fantasy as a projection of excess drive so that the urge to live can create images of its satisfaction in it.[12] For Gehlen, fantasy is tied to the status of human beings as 'deficient beings' and to their residual instincts and the hiatus between stimulus and response. It is thus connected to needs, drive impulses and wishes for satisfaction. But fantasy is much more than this. The plasticity and openness of human beings to the world need for structuring through culture. Fantasy plays such a large role in this that human beings might justifiably be defined as both 'being[s] of imagination *(Phantasiewesen)*' [and] 'being[s] of reason *(Vernunftwesen)*'.[13]

Clearly, fantasy is opposed to understanding. Even images can only be understood as manifestations of this elementary force that eludes us and cannot be objectified. We can distinguish four aspects of fantasy that relate to different historical periods and cultural contexts. One aspect of fantasy has to do with the possibility of human beings participating in the perfection of (classical) art. Another is involved in the understanding of the alterity of cultural and human worlds, which can only be 'recreated' with the aid of fantasy in such a way that they can be understood. A third aspect draws attention to the association between the unconscious and fantasy. Here fantasy is the force that contributes to the structuring of the human image world outside of consciousness, which is articulated in dreams and fantasies, the currents of desire and the vital forces. Finally, a fourth aspect relates to the wish and the ability to realize what one wishes in defiance of reality. In all four cases, the goal of fantasy is to change the world, but spontaneously, eventfully and in a meandering way, rather than strategically.[14]

Adorno went right to the crux of the cultural debate on the role of fantasy in the sciences and academic disciplines, art and culture, when he wrote,

> It would be worthwhile to write an intellectual history of fantasy, since the latter is the actual goal of positivist prohibitions. In the eighteenth century, both in Saint-Simon's work and in d'Alembert's *Discours préliminaire*, fantasy along with art is included in productive labour and participates in the notion of the unleashing of the forces of production. Comte, whose sociology reveals an apologetic, static orientation, is the first enemy of both metaphysics and fantasy simultaneously. The defamation of fantasy or its relegation to a special domain, marked off by the division of labour, is the original phenomenon of the regression of the bourgeois spirit. However, it does not appear as an avoidable error of this spirit, but rather as a consequence of a fatality which instrumental reason – required by society – couples with this taboo. The fact that fantasy is only tolerated when it is reified and set in abstract opposition to reality, makes it no less of a burden to science than to art.[15]

The concepts of imagination and '*Einbildungskraft*' (see Chapter 1, this volume) have been further differentiated in various ways over the course of time. A glance at the English history of ideas reveals that for Locke the imagination was the 'power of mind', while for Hume it was a 'kind of magical faculty in the soul which [. . .] is however inexplicable by the utmost efforts of human understanding'.[16] Coleridge saw imagination as being a human faculty or capacity and distinguished two forms of imagination.

The IMAGINATION then, I consider either as primary, or secondary. The primary IMAGINATION I hold to be living Power and prime Agent of all human Perception, and as a repetition in the finite mind of the eternal act of creation in the infinite I AM. The secondary Imagination I consider as an echo of the former, coexisting with the conscious will, yet still as identical with the primary in the *kind* of its agency, and differing only in *degree*, and in the *mode* of its operation. It dissolves, diffuses, dissipates, in order to re-create; or where this process is rendered impossible, yet still at all events it struggles to idealize and to unify. It is essentially *vital,* even as all objects (*as* objects) are essentially fixed and dead.[17]

In this view, the imagination is part of the subject, in whom it operates and with which the subject makes the world come alive. For Coleridge, the imagination also includes the ability to dissolve and destroy existing connections and thus to create new ones. While he considered the first form of imagination to be more analogous to the force of nature, *natura naturans*, he saw the second form of imagination as relating to the world of things, which it destroys and recreates. He also added a third force, fantasy, which he referred to as '*fancy*', and he saw as creating and combining things and relationships. He conceptualized these three aspects of the imaginative capacity as acting together in a playful way, creating and destroying images and linking their elements into new images in an oscillating to-and-fro movement.

Sartre and Lacan emphasize the performative nature of the imaginary. Sartre defines the imaginary as the 'irrealising' function of consciousness, within which consciousness creates absent objects, rendering them present and developing an imaginary relationship to them.[18] For Lacan, the imaginary belongs to a prelinguistic bodily state in which the individual is not yet aware of its boundaries, its lack.[19] Thus seen, the imaginary has its origin in the toddler's identification with her mother, who is so strong that she does not yet experience her mother as 'different' from herself. The child is fascinated because she is impressed by the wholeness of her mother's body. She experiences this wholeness of her mother's body as her own unfragmented intactness and power, as in a mirror. And yet at the same time, the experience of the mother's wholeness threatens the child's own 'completeness', and she experiences herself as incomplete and dependent on others. The experience of her own incompleteness and finiteness is also the birth of the subject as a sexual being. For Lacan, the imaginary with its world of images precedes the symbolic with its world of language.

Cornelius Castoriadis also takes up this position, defining the relationship between the two worlds as follows:

> the imaginary has to use the symbolic not only to 'express' itself (this is self-evident), but to 'exist', to pass from the virtual to anything more than this. The most elaborate delirium, just as the most secret and vaguest phantasy, are composed of 'images', but these 'images' are there to represent something else and so have a symbolic function. But, conversely, symbolism too presupposes an imaginary capacity. For it presupposes the capacity to see in a thing what it is not, to see it other than it is. However, to the extent that the imaginary ultimately stems from the originary faculty of positing or presenting oneself with things and relations that do not exist, in the form of representation (things and relations that are not or have never been given in perception), we shall speak of a final or radical imaginary as the common root of the actual imaginary and of the symbolic. This is, finally, the elementary and irreducible capacity of evoking images.[20]

Fantasy or imagination, the capacity to imagine (*Einbildungskraft*) and the imaginary are energies that create images when they become performative. These images are embodied. In order to be seen, these images require a medium. In the interplay between fantasy, which has its roots in the body, and a medium, mental images become external images that can in turn once more become internal through mimetic processes. Performativity plays a role twice, the first time when the images are created in a medium, since mental images are manifested not only in other images but also in the medium of enactment and arrangement of cultural presentations. These cultural presentations can then become performative by virtue of their aesthetic or aisthetic aspects. They then stimulate the fantasies of the actors and their 'audiences', who absorb the images of these acts into their imaginary worlds, that is, into their imaginaries.

8

Images as actions

Images have a performative dimension. This is particularly true of images of social life, which develop when social actions, including rituals and ritualizations, are staged and performed. They have an ostentatious character, the purpose of which is to create a specific image of the ritual arrangement which is directed at both the participants and the audience of the ritual acts. This image contains the community's portrayal of itself staged in a ritual act in a condensed form. The goal of many rituals is to create an image of belonging and thus to strengthen the social coherence of the community. There is a *magical intention* associated with these images, the aim of which is to use the performative character of social images to 'convince' the participants and audience that they belong together. Rituals are arranged in such a way that images of social life are created that reinforce the participants' confidence in their community. These images therefore contribute substantially to the effects of the rituals.

These images create a *collective and individual imaginary* which connects the participants of ritual acts with each other. The imaginary contains both elements that are common to all and others that vary widely from one individual to another. Central elements of the rituals are remembered by all involved, while others are remembered by only a few, possibly also very differently. The conditions that these images of social action come up against differ depending on the class, gender, ethnic or field affiliations and individual characteristics of the participants. They thus become linked together in different configurations, leading to the development of diverse combinations of images in which different memories and different projections of the future are formed. The relationships between the collective and individual imaginaries can best be described by Wittgenstein's concept of *family resemblance*. There are correspondences and similarities between individuals' differing images, and thus there are also commonalities which reveal a 'family resemblance', despite the differences between the images.

These images of social life account for a large part of the mental image worlds of human beings. It is these historically and culturally shaped mental images that we have acquired and developed and had impressed upon us since our early childhood that make it possible for us to see. Without these images, we would not be capable of seeing. This view is supported by the fact that some people who were blind in their childhood and youth report that when they later became able to perceive the world, they were unable to see or grasp what they were seeing. There are three important aspects to this. Firstly, we have to learn to see social constellations and arrangements. Secondly, this capacity to see, which we acquire in early childhood, enables us to grasp the world in the act of seeing. Thirdly, previous visual experiences and the images that resulted from them play a central, indispensable role in how we comprehend things in the act of seeing them. If we are to be able to grasp social acts in the process of seeing them, we must already have accumulated historical and cultural schemata and mental images. Without them it would not be possible to grasp as we see.

Without mental images, which are part of the imaginary, social acts remain external to the person perceiving them and cannot be comprehended. Thus, our mental image world must already exist in order for us to understand social actions and to relate our own actions to those that we perceive. This process of perception and comprehension and the actions that are related to them do not usually take place on a conscious level. They only become conscious when we experience difficulties. We then assess our perceptions on the basis of our mental schemata and images. Differences and congruences between the expectations expressed in rudimentary images and the social actions that we are perceiving become conscious, and we need to weigh them up and come to decisions.

As a rule, the perception of social actions takes place in processes of practical mimesis. We see social actions and relate to them in our perception, and thus the actions of other people become meaningful for us. When their actions are directed towards us, the impulse to relate is kindled by them, but it requires us to respond. Perception of social actions always leads to the establishment of a relationship in whose development our mental images play an important role. Many perceptions of social actions are also mimetic in the sense that they implicitly prompt us to join in, to participate in the game, and we respond accordingly. We enter into the action game and act in accordance with what is expected of us in this social arrangement, either by responding to or by modifying the expectations or acting in opposition to them. What makes our actions mimetic is not so much similarity as reciprocation. Once we have become engaged in an action game, we perceive the actions of the other participants and relate our own actions to them. In order for us to be able to do this, several conditions must be fulfilled.

To begin with, we must understand the implications of other people's social actions and the expectations of responses implicit in them. Our previous social experiences and the mental images associated with them are important preconditions for this. Secondly, we must have practical knowledge that makes it possible for us to act. Important components of this practical knowledge are the experiences of actions that we have acquired in previous mimetic processes and our mental images and schemata. However, we need more than this if we are to grasp the performative significance of the action. In the staging and performance of social actions, spontaneity and ludic elements are important modes of expressing the imagination. These processes of practical mimesis are also physical, sensory processes. The physical presence of another person, a person who is carrying out social actions, is required for mimetic processes to be triggered. The sensory presence of that person's actions initiates the mimetic processes, which take on a reciprocal character in the joint social actions. Finally, reciprocal desire plays a role in these processes and frequently becomes the motor of mimetic processes. We want to understand the other person and be understood by them. We want to relate to them or be invited by them to enter into a relationship. Images from the past and also of our wishes for the future are involved in the development of this desire. They influence our perceptions of the social actions of other people and also guide social actions without the participants becoming aware of it.[1]

There is a close relationship between mimetic reference to the actions of another person, and the fact that when we perceive social actions, images of desire and internal images that we have acquired at an early age interact and affect how we understand other people's social actions and also how we perceive, absorb, classify and process the images that we perceive. Clearly, both collective and highly individual schemata and images become superimposed on one another in this process. The interactions between them form the human imaginary and link them together. Since these schemata and images form in historical and cultural contexts, they can only be understood if we take their historical and cultural significance into account. When they are represented as a concrete image, something becomes visible that would otherwise remain invisible. In this respect, the power of the imagination becomes concrete in them even though we cannot grasp the imagination itself.

Since the conditions into which human beings are born are historically and culturally shaped, their mental schemata and images are also shaped by these contexts. These conditions are determined by many factors, the most important of which are *social class, gender, ethnicity* and *social environment*. Each of these factors makes it possible for certain schemata and images to form and in so doing excludes others. These processes lead to the development of a habitus which can be understood as a system 'of durable, transposable dispositions, structured structures, predisposed to function as structuring structures'.[2] As a product of history and culture, the *habitus* gives rise to individual and collective practices, the scope of which is both made possible and restricted by the aforementioned factors, that is, class, gender, ethnicity and social environment. It is the habitus that ensures that we are actively conscious of previous experiences and the mental schemata and images associated with them. Alongside our perceptions and actions, it also influences the forms in which we feel and think. It consists of an incorporated, practical knowledge that has been acquired mimetically in social situations. The dispositions acquired in the images and schemata that constitute this knowledge determine our social actions. The habitus incorporates, or embodies, the values and norms, images and schemata that we acquire through our affiliations to a social class, gender, ethnic group and our social environment and thus also become the starting point for further actions.

Rituals play a particularly important role in the incorporation of the dispositions that make up the habitus and the values and norms, images and schemata that belong to it. The performativity of rituals initiates mimetic processes of embodiment. The repetitive character of the performativity results in the incorporation of both the action sequences generated in their staging and performance and the associated schemata and images, while its ludic quality leads to their being absorbed into the habitus. The power relations expressed in the ritual actions are also assimilated into the habitus through mimetic processes. Rituals serve to embody the values, norms and dispositions contained in institutions, organizations and social fields in the habitus through the medium of mimetic processes and to place them at our disposal for future actions. This generates social and cultural reality, not only in institutions and social fields but also in people's bodies, in a way that is also restricted by their affiliations to their respective class, gender, and ethnic and social groups.

When patterns of social action are incorporated into a habitus in rituals and ritualized activities, dispositions are formed which enable us to participate in social actions. The spectrum of social actions ranges from the actions of everyday life which are conditioned by our habits and which we carry out with the help of our practical knowledge and the dispositions contained in it, to a great extent without reflecting upon it, to actions with a high level of complexity, which are associated with insecurity and uncertainty and whose outcome is uncertain. Such actions can only be conceived of and guided with the aid of the imagination, particularly when they are carried out under unknown conditions. When spontaneity and ludic elements become important for social actions, the imagination comes into play. With the imagination novelty, that is, alternatives and innovations, can develop. Now is the time to restructure and relearn. With the aid of the imagination, social actions are freed from the shackles of the previously formed habitus. These processes involve projections and images oriented towards the future and change, the unknown and the novel.

If learning processes associated with *class, gender and ethnic affiliation* and *social field* are especially important for the development of a habitus and a social identity, this must also apply to the schemata and images that evolve. Class is manifested by the fact that human beings assume differing positions in social space, which is a space of *differences*, depending on the availability of economic and social capital. However, this space is not only a space of differences but also a space in which there are *relationships* between people. The distances between the positions that people assume in social space have an influence on the *how they lead their lives*. They are manifested in differences in perspectives on the social world and social practices in which differentiations are made and differences judged, which is what endows them with their social significance.

> The classifications and principles of differentiation and the evaluative and cognitive schemata embedded in the habitus are reflected in our everyday practices. The habitus mediates things (homes, books, cars, clothing, objects of art, tenures, etc.) and activities (sporting activities, cultural activities, trips, social occasions), transforming them into 'distinct and distinctive signs', while continuous distributions [. . .] become discontinuous opposites [. . .] – the differences in the physical order of things enter into the *symbolic* order of significant differentiations.[3]

These processes of distinction and transformation take place mainly through *taste* and the differences in taste that exist between the classes. The decisive difference between the dominant classes and the lower classes consists in the 'primacy of form over function, which leads to the denial of function'.[4] Whereas a taste for luxury is characteristic of the upper classes, for the lower classes it is a taste for necessity (*goût de nécessité*) that is typical, which has an effect on all aspects of how people lead their lives. 'Every field of primary tastes is organized according to the primary opposition, with the antithesis between quantity and quality, belly and palate, matter and manners, substance and form.'[5]

Bourdieu described these differences in detail in his work *Distinction*, making clear how differences in our style of speaking and eating become features that differentiate between classes.

> Plain speaking, plain eating: the working-class meal is characterized by plenty (which does not exclude restrictions and limits) and above all by freedom. 'Elastic' and 'abundant' dishes are brought to the table – soups or sauces, pasta or potatoes [. . .] and served with a ladle or spoon, to avoid too much measuring and counting, in contrast to everything that has to be cut and divided, such as roasts [. . .]. Strict sequencing of the meal tends to be ignored. Everything may be put on the table at much the same time [. . .], so that the women may have reached the dessert, and also the children, who will take their plates and watch television, while the men are still eating the main dish and the 'lad', who has arrived late, is swallowing his soup.[6]

In contrast, the bourgeoisie insists on eating 'with all due form',[7] that is, in regulated processes revolving around an order of meals that prescribes what dishes are permitted to be put on the table together and provides a framework in which each and every one has to eat each dish together.

In addition to these different customs and lifestyles, the differences between the classes are also partly engendered by differing schemata and images. The class-specific differences in taste lead to differing preferences for images and arrays of images. In mimetic processes, these images and the aesthetic values underlying the ways in which they are positioned are incorporated and contribute to the consolidation and differentiation of taste and the differences that taste helps to create. The images of the various different lifeworlds also become vehicles for characteristics that define class difference. In this way, class-specific experiences and feelings are tied to the images of the different ways of eating meals described earlier. These experiences and feelings are expressed in images and can be communicated by them. Since these images are bound to lifeworlds of different classes, certain image combinations suggest themselves, while others are closed off or even excluded. And finally, these images guide the imagination and determine how it can be expressed, while at the same time limiting its richness and variation.

Images that are created as a result of *gender and ethnic and generational affiliation* have a similar significance for how we conceive of ourselves and interpret our identity. We perceive other people as young or old, male or female,

Indian, Turkish or Asian the moment we see them. Existing mental images are activated, particularly stereotypes, which are often not engendered by our own experiences. Many of these images are linked to the collective imaginary of a culture. Its images are related to historical experiences and social value judgements deriving from societal conditions which have become entrenched 'inside us' as individual human beings. On the level of attitudes and sensation as individuals, we are relatively powerless in the face of these images. The only way we can gain some appreciation of their effects on social actions is to confront them consciously. This relative powerlessness vis-à-vis such attitudes is partly due to the fact that they are diffuse, which makes it difficult to deal with them constructively on the level of emotions and attitudes. It is easier to confront these schemata, images and stereotypes on a rational level in an attempt to become aware of their effects and in the hope that we will gradually be able to replace them with other attitudes. It has become clear from recent intensive discussions on stereotypes in regard to gender, racism and ageism that it is frequently not possible to alter these attitudes through insight. The resistance of these images to change results from the fact that they can be used to reduce the complexity of social relationships. If these images that guide our attitudes towards the other sex and members of other ethnic groups are rendered more flexible, we become able to modify and differentiate them with the help of new images that are linked to different experiences. That such transformations are possible is evident from the changes in the relationship between the sexes and our attitudes towards other countries that have taken place over the past few decades.

Our schemata and images that are based on gender and ethnicity are resistant because these images are incorporated and connected to the habitus, and thus they are not easy to change. Judith Butler also made this clear by drawing attention to the fact that we are 'made into' girls and boys.[8] Recent research on the development of gender identity has shown that the effect of being referred to as a girl or a boy, a man or a woman, and thus gender ascription, becomes firmly established in the body through repetition in everyday life and through processes of 'doing gender'.[9] The relationship between the sexes is one of the earliest schemata of social differentiation. Human beings start to develop a gender-specific habitus right from birth. The development of both gender and the identity are strongly influenced by the gender-specific character of the division of labour and the differentiations associated with it. 'Gender is a very fundamental dimension of the habitus which, like the sharps or flats or the key signatures in music, modifies all the social characteristics that are related to the fundamental social factors.'[10] It is characteristic of the relationship between the sexes in most societies that it is constructed as being a relationship of polar opposition. Thus, gender identity usually results from differentiation and distinction and the associated simplifications and exclusions which are used to construct distinct genders. This differentiation is based on the body, which becomes the starting point for putting people into social categories and how they are embodied. It is in this way that the relationship between the sexes and the identity patterns that go along with it become embodied.

> It is the habitus that determines the social construction of the relationship between the sexes, how the body is imagined and experienced, sensory perception and how joy and suffering can be felt and expressed. What is associated with the body has a direct effect on a person's identity, even if these are things that are apparently banal and completely 'external' to us.[11]

Mental images of gender identity arise through the perception of social actions with a gender-specific connotation, and they support and uphold the aforementioned processes of the development of gender affiliation. The perceived images are superimposed on previously existing mental images, coalesce with them, reinforce or modify them and support the development of a gender-specific habitus.

In addition to experiences with class, gender and ethnicity, human beings undergo important experiences in *social fields* which contribute to the development of their habitus and in which schemata and mental images are formed which promote these processes. The concept of social field defines those sectors of social life which arise as a result of the division of labour and the differentiation of social systems and whose mode of functioning is marked by relative autonomy and an intrinsic logic. In these sectors, an interaction occurs between the acting subjects and the conditions in the social fields which is mediated by the habitus. Social fields can be understood as ensembles of societal interactions. They include fields of forces whose mode of functioning cannot be reduced to money and power, although money and power play an important role in their dynamics and logic. The social fields include, for example, politics, the economy, academic institutions and also religion, education and art. They are characterized by five attributes.[12]

Firstly, all social fields are characterized by their own specific intrinsic dynamics and logic. The professional activities of the people who work in schools, for example, are characterized by specific conditions. The learning processes that take place at school are partly due to the intergenerational difference between the teachers and the children and to the functions that schools have, that is, provision of qualifications, selection and social placement. These conditions influence the dynamics and logic of the learning processes without fully determining them. Despite their significance as factors that structure the social field, they still leave enough leeway for individual teachers to make their own decisions. Teachers use these opportunities in different ways, depending on their habitus. However, the differences in the way they act do not pose a threat to the educational mandate of school as an institution. The images and schemata they incorporate into their worlds of mental images in the course of their daily work influence their worldviews, their understanding of society and their social actions, but do not determine them. The dynamics of this social field allow individual teachers to make their own decisions without compromising the meaning of the institution.

A *second* characteristic consists in the fact that, as in the case of school, people are active as professionals in this social field. This involves a division of labour that also serves to help people develop different occupational skills in the real worlds in which they move. This, in turn, is associated with an increase in the complexity of their occupations and a further differentiation of their skills. A teacher who works at a primary school will develop a different habitus from a teacher who works at a secondary school. The mental images that arise in connection with the teachers' everyday practice in these two different professional fields of activity also differ, and accordingly also their self-images

Since the social field is understood as a system of forces, a *third* characteristic consists in moving away from the idea that a social sector is homogeneous. This gives the individual actor more room for individual actions while staying within the framework of the concept of the 'social field'. This has been demonstrated by studies on the differences between teachers' images of themselves as teachers and their self-images. Their personal habitus and the actions that are structured by them lead to a wide range of diverse actions in which the meaning and values of the social field and the personal characteristics of the person acting are related to each other. Even although the teachers' actions differ on the individual level, they are still oriented towards implementing the purpose of school as an institution. The teaching staff of any one institution may include teachers with very different individual approaches, without this threatening the social function of the institution. On the contrary, the differences between their actions ensure a varied distribution of the social positions within the given social field and its dynamics. Thus, for example, in one team there may be positions such as the strict but fair teacher, a friendly but unassuming teacher, a somewhat indolent teacher who just manages to do the minimum and the committed teacher who does lots of extracurricular activities with the children, etc., without these personal differences jeopardizing the teachers' task as educators or the meaning of the institution. The mental images that teachers have of their work determine their self-images and become the drive behind what they do, and also vary in accordance with these differing modes of behaviour. In short, teachers' professional imaginaries vary depending on the work they are doing and prefigure their perceptions of how they are going to act in the future.

Thus, *fourthly*, the actors in a social field are not restricted to any one direction of action, but rather their actions are determined by the scope available to them for their action games within the specific framework to which they are subject. Here the word 'game' is not meant in a metaphorical sense. Rather it is understood in the sense that there are different '*action games*' in social fields that determine professional activities. In the action games in schools, the goal is to get the students to join in the action games. If this is successful, the students are successful in the institution; if it is not successful, they become excluded and are burdened with substantial disadvantages as they embark on their future lives. One important way to integrate the students in the action games of an institution is to enact and perform rituals through which they learn to participate in the various action games of the school. Rituals impart institutional modes of action and the values and norms of school life to the children and ensure that all that is associated with them becomes established. Although from an existential perspective this game is very serious for the children, the concept of game also includes the notion of the freedom of action of all the actors in the school, whose ways of enacting and performing the action games of school also change the practice of the game and thus likewise the teaching and learning processes. As with the rituals, what is decisive for the action games of a social field is that all participants believe in the game and join in with it. This is ensured by rituals and action games and the habitus produced in them. The habitus both results from 'successful' rituals and action games and helps to make the rituals and action games successful, so that the objective meaning of the institution or the social field are absorbed into the children's subjective image worlds. The mental images incorporated in the action games promote the interconnectedness of institutional social actions and help to ensure that all of the actors are able to grasp the expectations of the social field

Fifthly, the social field as a unit forms as a result of a homology between the different actors in the social field and the different approaches associated with their respective positions. For instance, there are both negative and positive homologies between heads of schools and their teachers and between the teachers and the students, also including their parents. It is important for the functioning of the social field that the people occupying the different positions both believe in the appropriateness of their different positions and recognize that of the positions of the other actors and their actions. This also includes recognizing the differences between the actions of the holders of the different positions, which is of major significance for the development of a professional image and for sustaining the homology in the social field.

Space and time play an important role in the development of mental images of social life and their effects on the habitus and the structuring of social actions. Like social actions, the mental images associated with them are tied to space and time. Since historically and culturally shaped images of social action can be brought into the present with the aid of the imagination, the action potential implicit in them can be applied to present and future actions. This implicit action potential lies in the feelings, wishes and action impulses associated with these images. It serves to devise actions and to adapt them to the specific situation. Mental images brought into the present with the aid of the imagination provide different angles on the situation, construct possible modes of action and render the action coherent. They assume special importance when people do not know how to act or when the social situation is so complex that they seek alternatives that fit the social situation better than the actions they initially intended. The decisive contribution of the imagination to actions consists in adapting experiences gained in previous situations in the form of schemata or mental images to the new situation and suggesting alternative actions. The difference in time between the earlier actions and their circumstances and the present is overcome and the images are adapted to the present or future circumstances. It may be decisive that it is not the first alternative solution suggested by the mental images that is put into action, but that the situation is kept open and in suspense until better – or worse – alternatives present themselves and a decision can be made. It is especially in more complex action processes that these mental images play a role. They are less important when actions are needed that have become automatized, where the habitus generates plans of action that the person follows without further reflection. But even in these situations where the images do not become conscious, they play a role when we make a choice and act accordingly.

Since these mental schemata and images are intangible, they are flexible and can be adapted to new situations. The imagination creates new relationships between existing and newly emerging images. This is its productive aspect. It is less a matter of 'applying' existing schemata than one of creating new relationships between differing mental images and 'inventing' new ways of acting in complex social situations. In these situations, there is an interplay between the mental images acquired in the past, current alternatives put forward by the imagination as possibilities for action and projected images that anticipate future situations.

Social images produce mental schemata and images that are memories of actions previously carried out and have potential for actions in the present or future. Insofar as these images help to stage and perform actions, they have a performative force that is bound to the imagination and leads to new actions. Since images play a *transitional role* between past, present and future realities, they can stimulate and invent actions. As images they retain their difference from reality and can never coincide with it. This becomes particularly evident in the case of images of desire and wishes which have originated in the past and whose imaginary nature thus renders it impossible for them to be fulfilled.

The intensity of the mental images and their relevance for social actions depend on the intensity of the mimetic processes in the course of which they become integrated into the world of mental images. The spectrum is wide. At the one end there are images that evolve through perception in processes of practical mimesis and images that arise from the desire to become similar to the other and which therefore have a strong motivational and action potential. At the other end we find imaginary iconic and linguistic images that develop as people turn towards such images and use mimetic processes to make them into their own mental images.

III

Imagination and practices
of the body

The world of play and games

'What giants?' said Sancho Panza.

'Those thou seest there', answered his master, 'with the long arms, and some have them nearly two leagues long'.

'Look, your worship', said Sancho; 'what we see there are not giants but windmills, and what seem to be their arms are the sails that turned by the wind make the millstone go.'

'It is easy to see', replied Don Quixote, 'that thou art not used to this business of adventures; those are giants; and if thou art afraid, away with thee out of this and betake thyself to prayer while I engage them in fierce and unequal combat'.[1]

Imagination, evidently, is already in play as soon as we perceive something.[2] We would not be able to see or absorb anything if we did not have our imagination to transform the outside world into images and ideas. On the one hand these processes are universal, and yet at the same time they conform to historical and cultural norms, and they are also unique. The aforementioned scene is a good example. Of course, these are windmills with sails that everyone in this region recognizes and knows the function of. Thus, our perception of the world, different as it may be from one person to the next, follows historical and cultural codes. This is what makes a common understanding possible, despite all differences.

Don Quixote objects to this customary view of the world. He sees the windmills as giants and the sails of the windmill as the long arms of the giants, and rather than his being on a journey with a specific purpose, he sees it as an adventure and a 'fierce and unequal combat' in which he must prove himself. He manages this by using the *world-creating power of his imagination*, which brings a new world into being and transforms the world of real things into a fantasmatic world. The real world of windmills loses its reality, and a different world is created – one of adventures and combat. Don Quixote's adventure world would not be possible without Sancho Panza's real world. If we are to be able to create a fantasy world which transforms and reinterprets the real world, a real world must already exist. As implied by the original Greek meaning of the word 'fantasy', we need to use it to make Don Quixote's world of adventure and play appear; world is a happening. As an aesthetic event, this world is fictitious, and, thus, for the readers who allow themselves to be drawn into it, it is a real world that they experience in their imaginaries.

We are only able to enter the world of fiction and play if we believe in it. It is only if we *believe in the world of play* that we can play in it. If we do not believe in it, it will be impossible for us to take part in the 'as if' nature of the game. Don Quixote views the windmills 'as if' they were giants. This 'as if' perspective permits him to do battle and survive adventures. One function of the 'as if' is to create space and time (essential elements of the game) so that the game can take place. If the elements of space and time are not established, then there can be no actions in the game.

If we believe, as did Buytendijk, Huizinga and Fink,[3] that *games are completely disconnected from the constraints of the world we live in* and therefore offer us a space where we can be free and a chance for us to develop our human potential, then we must also, following Wittgenstein, see that games are regulated social actions which shape our social world.[4] In the view of Gebauer and myself, there is a mimetic relationship between the internal rules of the game and the rules of the society in which it is staged and performed. 'In the actions of games we see the way in which a society is organised, makes decisions, constructs its hierarchies, distributes power and structures its thinking.'[5] The actions of the game pick up elements and structures of the social order, render these visible in the staging and performance of the game, alter them and influence them in turn.

In play the body is duplicated. On the one hand, there is our own individual body that enters into a world of play, and on the other hand there is a second body that superimposes itself on the first one, as dictated by the rules of the game. In a game of Cowboys and Indians, the body of a ten-year-old boy becomes that of a Red Indian chief, but only for as long as the game lasts and he and his friends believe in it. In this *duplication*, a *play body* comes into being which moves in accordance with the rules and criteria of the particular game without being seriously limited by them. Thus, the boy has *his own* body and *that of a* Red Indian chief. With his own child's body, he performs the gestures and actions that he thinks would be right for a chief. If something unforeseen happens that forces him to leave his play world, he will quickly make every effort to reimmerse himself in it and make his body go on playing the duplicate body required by the game.

With the aid of imagination, games create *play worlds which have a relative autonomy* and at the same time forge a link with one or several worlds outside the game. When the boy plays Cowboys and Indians, he is forging a link with the world of the Indians, the structure of which was in place, temporally speaking, before his game. This does not mean that the boy's world is a simple copy of the Indians' world. The link is more complex than that. No statements are made about the world of the Indians. What does happen, however, is that, driven by the desire to become an Indian for as long as the game lasts, the boy's mental images or conceptions of the world become similar to those of the Indians. In this process, fantasy comes into play.

The child uses fantasy to create internal images of a world that is long gone but that is accessible to him from fiction and films. What is important is not that the images are absolutely historically correct but that he creates images which fulfil his desire to leave the everyday world and become *someone else* through play. Certain gestures and props such as smoking a peace pipe or wearing a feathered headdress are the means he uses to effect this transformation. He employs ritual actions to 'switch identity', to fulfil his wish to become someone else. This wish creates images of a different life and enables the child to assume different roles and identities. The child turns into a wild Red Indian chief, the leader of other Indians, who seeks battles with enemy tribes or with the evil 'palefaces'. It is *his* imagination that creates *his* Red Indian world, the shape of which is formed by his desire for new experiences. If he manages to live out this desire, then the game becomes intense and intoxicating. In terms of the typology of play established by Caillois,[6] aspects of *agon* (or competition), *mimicry* and *ilinx* (whirling) come into play here – agon in the fights with other Indians, mimicry in the copying of the Indians' appearance, ilinx in the intoxication of being different. In many games, the interplay of these completely heterogeneous aspects creates their excitement and intensity.

In such a game, *a paradoxical situation* emerges – the child is the Red Indian chief and at the same time he is not. His actions and words are those of a chief and at the same time they are not. The claim that the boy is a Red Indian chief is true and at the same time it is not. It is only true as long as all the players and the world around them believe in the game and the fictional or imaginary conditions laid down in it.

In the game, there is *a mimetic reference to previous situations in other games or worlds*. The game must be *believed* in for players to be able to *mimic* imagined images and ideas and for the game to be *staged and performed*. A *real unreality* is created which makes it possible to step beyond the limits of our everyday lives and to live new moments of *intensity*, thus *going beyond ourselves*, in the process of which we become *someone else*. In this example, the child playing the Red Indian develops new gestures and ways of behaving. He learns to lead other children, to remain unperturbed in the face of all dangers and to make up again after playful battles, only to fall out again and test his strength in a new game. He also practises his ability to construct an imaginary world, immerse himself in it, hold fast to it in the face of opposition and to shape it himself. Games are secondary worlds which can certainly have an effect on our everyday worlds. In an essay that has been much discussed and also provoked some controversy, Clifford Geertz demonstrated that in Bali cockfights are a portrayal of *driving societal forces*, that is, the dependency relationships which find expression in mutual obligation, in 'prestige and the 'necessity' to affirm it, defend it, celebrate it, justify it and just plain bask in it'.[7] In the cockfight, the Balinese hierarchy of status and the network of social obligations are transposed into a game, where they are staged, performed and put on show. This fight simulates the social matrix of the complicated system of interlocking and overlapping groups to which supporters in the cockfight belong. Every participant in the game believes in this social hierarchy and the necessity of showing it publicly and of staging and performing the honour and prestige of their group and their lack of regard and disdain for other groups that do not belong to their own. These principles are also applied to the way they act in everyday life. They are displayed in the cockfight. In the cockfight and in the passionate support of the ' participants' in the fight who place bets on the cocks, social conflicts are staged and performed by proxy. This is not imitation but in the cockfight something is rendered visible and portrayed in a differentiated way that would not be expressed elsewhere. In these fights the Balinese men are either completely triumphant or completely defeated. Even if we do not agree with every one of Geertz's interpretations, his attempt to analyse the social and cultural dimension of the game has exemplary significance.

It is true of the cockfight and of all games that *every staging is unique*. Although it may relate to a previous staging or the same or a similar game, every staging is different because it differs in its participants and the place or the time period in which it is played. Games are *repetitive*, yet they are never mere repeats.[8] Each time the world is staged in a new and different way. What happens in a game is never the same as something that has happened before; often *similarities and contingencies* take shape or perhaps *complementary actions and situations*. As Bateson has shown,[9] due to the differences between individual persons and positions, that is, due to schismogenesis the different positions become more similar or complementary to each other. In both cases people make reference to the other person, who is different, by mimesis, which leads either to their *becoming more similar* or to the *difference becoming more pronounced*, which leads to a complementary relationship.

Games are staged and performed. They are *performative*. As such they are *inseparably linked to the body, they are expressive and also displays*. In many cases they are a consequence of the staging of mental images which are given a new context every time they are staged and offer the chance to display inner images in bodily performances. Games are created, and they make something visible. They happen. In games, emotions are expressed and made public. Many games have a demonstrative aspect. They not only portray something; they aim to make what they express also be seen. To do this, they require a creative space that allows for differences in staging and performance. The expressive character of games also goes hand in hand with the fact that they are displays. In a period of relative order, our everyday lives tend to become boring and lacking in excitement. In such situations, the stimulating and expressive components of many games take on a new significance. In games, individuals are able to sense who they are, their emotions and their passions. Elias and Dunning[10] speak of a *quest for excitement*. Games produce the *moments of intensified life* for which we strive because of their physicality and the performativity associated with this.

The *performativity of games* embraces the following aspects.

Firstly, a game involves the transition between what we have in our imaginations and performance, thus creating a world of play, where the movements of the protagonists can be perceived aisthetically. Secondly, the performativity of the game includes the historic and cultural dimension of the staging and performance of the game, which will show similarities with other games and which become comprehensible when the players or onlookers know what it means to play a game. Furthermore, there is a symbolic aspect which defines the framework of the game. Finally, the performative aspect of the game includes the creation and application of rules and other elements of play. It is only through playing a game that it becomes possible to determine what a game is. This cannot be done by simply attempting to define it, but only by acting the game out, in short by playing it.

Wittgenstein drew attention to the fact that we can only understand games by playing them and that explanations and instructions are only aids. *Play is only learnt in play*. We need *practical knowledge* to be able to play. It takes more than verbal explanations to learn how to play a game. The necessary practical knowledge is acquired mimetically. We gain practical knowledge if we draw mimetically on existing games and game worlds and if we take an 'impression' of these which we transfer to our world of ideas and then translate these mental images into the movements the game requires. A continuous realignment back and forth between internal images, our own body movements, and external scenarios and movements of the game has to take place. We acquire the *practical knowledge of the game* that we need through this to-ing and fro-ing, which is characteristic for mimetic movements. This is *knowledge acquired by the body*, which needs the imagination of movement of our bodies to be translated into stagings and performances.

By acquiring practical knowledge of the game mimetically, we are able to grow by acquiring new skills.

Players use their bodies, language and feelings to perform and portray *their* version of a game, and in so doing they turn their own individual commitment into a public performance that everyone can see. In a game we face outwards and expand our repertoires of actions. Our sensations and feelings, skills and potentials are expanded. The organizing principles of the game become certainties as they become the immovable foundations of game in the form of subjective inner states and are also externalized and objectivized in the activity of the game. The models which help to structure our internal workings also demonstrate organizing principles that are analogous to those of social practice. Seen in this way, games are mimesis not only of our social world but also of the way we process this world internally. They are a *medium* that links our inner world and the language we use to talk about our inner world. We cannot express in words what a game shows, and therefore this cannot be replaced by language. All we can do is show it in a different way, in a new game.[11]

In games, individuals become part of an extensive relationship network. What they do in the game connects them to other players, onlookers and past and future games. It has to do with the material requirements of the game and concrete spaces and processes taking place over periods of time. Players carry out their practical actions and take part in stagings and performances in reference to these conditions. Alongside the certainty that comes from experience, there are also the ways in which the experiences are regulated and structured, in particular in terms of space, time and social stratifications. These are *practical interpretations* of the world, which provide a solid basis for the social actions.[12]

Play is a form of social action that is based on practical knowledge and takes place in a framework which constitutes its 'as if' character, the structure of which is influenced by the organisztional principles of society. These in turn are learned in mimetic processes in the game, practised and incorporated. The agonal (or competitive) aspect, the combination of individual and collective performances, the demand for top performance stretching oneself to one's limits, as we see, for example, in football, correspond in many ways to the values and organizational principles of capitalist bourgeois society. These values and organizational principles are staged and performed in every football game – they are learned, practised and endorsed in mimetic processes. Since work has become a central organizational principle of society, Bateson believes that it is the principles of work that structure the behaviour of players and spectators. Like language, the *game becomes a medium*, in which principles of labour, the division of labour and the community are staged, performed and endorsed.

As children and young people acquire a practical knowledge that enables them to join in games, they also acquire the values and organizational principles which they then incorporate through mimetic acts. As this happens, *trans-world elements* emerge. These are to be found in the social world and in many games that are connected with each other through a *family similarity*. These elements, which are repeatedly acquired in different games, rituals and other social actions, are inscribed in the body which is at the same time actively processing them and, thus, also inscribed in the body memory.

The gender roles prevalent in society are one of the many trans-world elements that are learned in games. These can be seen in the different way boys and girls behave in games. It can be seen that boys' games use a substantial amount of space; they are public, have a strong physical element and are organized in a hierarchical, competitive way. Girls' games, on the other hand, take up less space and tend to be private and cooperative, with a focus on relationships and intimacy.[13] For reasons of societal and gender politics, we may well deny that such a difference exists. It does, however, have firm social and cultural roots and is reproduced and reinforced again and again in games and rituals, even though deviations from these stereotypes are becoming increasingly frequent.

As different as games are from one society or one culture to another, and as much as they differ from a historical point of view, from an anthropological viewpoint they are indispensable for societies, communities and individuals. This applies equally to language games, games with rules and games without rules. Furthermore, many human activities, such as liturgies, ceremonies, celebrations and interactive rituals contain ludic elements. Games create continuity between past, present and future and lead to change within society and the individual through their potential for innovation. Fantasy and imagination are rendered visible in games; what is invisible is made apparent, often by means of a performative gesture. Games are paradoxical; they stage 'as if' actions and create a duplicate body in the body playing the game. In games we expand into other worlds; foreign horizons and structures become visible. We have new experiences, in which chance and contingency play an important part. We need knowledge of a game in order to be able to play. This knowledge is not theoretical, but a performative, practical, embodied knowledge which is acquired, remembered and shaped in processes of mimesis.

10

The anthropology of dance

Dance is one of the most important ways for human beings to portray and express themselves. Dances express our cultural identity and our relationship to ourselves and the world. Dances can be seen as 'windows' on a culture, which enable us to understand what makes it what it is. Dances are productive and create their own sphere of cultural praxis, which is a synthesis of many characteristic elements.[1] They form part of our human cultural heritage that is passed down to us in a practical way and is therefore difficult to grasp and access. Although dances are not intangible *practices*, they are designated by UNESCO as ' *intangible*' cultural *heritage*, and it is upon this aspect that I shall be focusing here.

The body is central to dance. Dances display moving bodies and present corporeality and the way it is determined by history and culture. The forms and figures of the dance emerge out of the movements and rhythms of the body and are therefore subject to the laws of time and space to which the movements of the body are adapted. Specific dance figures arise from the dance movements that are executed in space and which form over the course of time.

Many dances take place not only in the medium of the body and the movement in time and space but also in the medium of sounds, that can be very different. Dances alter our relationship to the world; they cannot be completely translated into language, even if this helps us to understand their meaning better. They arise from the movements of the body, from rhythms and sounds, and not from language. Nevertheless, if we are to understand and do research on dances, it is important to find a way of describing and interpreting them.

Dances affect us synaesthetically though our various senses, particularly those of kinaesthesia, hearing, touch and sight. Dances play a key role in the forming of communities. The synaesthesia and performativity of the dance create an emotional and social closeness between people who are dancing together, which can help to establish a community. The synaesthetic and performative aspects of dances lend them an extra dimension which contributes to their social dynamic and significance. They are historical and cultural in nature, which can be addressed with a historical anthropological approach, in which the historicity and culturality of the dances is seen in relation to the historical and cultural situation of the spectators. It is this dual historicity and culturality that is the focus of anthropological research into dances.[2]

Dances are physical, performative, expressive, symbolic, follow rules and are non-instrumental. They are repetitive, homogenous, ludic and public. They form patterns in which collectively shared knowledge and dance practices are staged and performed and which reveal how a community portrays and interprets its own rules. They have a beginning and an end and thus also a structure for communication and interaction within time. They take place in social spaces which they shape. Dances have something that sets them apart. At the same time, they are determined by the frame within which they take place.[3]

10.1 Anthropological structural features

From an anthropological point of view, it is possible to differentiate between several structural features that are important in dance.

Space and time in dance. Dances are tied to the spatiality and temporality of the human body, and they develop their formations within space and time. They are linked together by movements in which the human body moves in space in temporal sequences, either on its own or together with other bodies. The context and the framing of time and space play an important role in this process. There are also historical and cultural, collective and individual elements involved which determine the atmosphere of the dance and how it is portrayed and expressed. The image scenarios, the virtual spaces and the multidimensional time structures of contemporary avant-garde dance create conditions of time and space which expand the potential of the dance.

Dance and movement. In the movements of the dance, the body experiences itself, the music and the movements of fellow dancers. In its movements, the body develops the ability to be creative – it creates its own form and becomes an instrument that is used without being simply functional. The dance movements acquire an extra dimension through their presentation and expression. Formations are imagined and acted out. Dance movements shape the body that produces them. They create imaginative scenarios and give them substance by staging and performing them over and over again. They have regularity and are an expression of order. In dance movements we see how easily the body learns – this is seen in exercises and the repetition of movements. In dance movements there is an implicit knowledge whose spectrum is vast. The movements of each dance are embedded in social power structures to a greater or lesser extent or, as in contemporary avant-garde dance, are largely free of these.

Dance and community. It is impossible to conceive of communities which do not have dances. Dances contribute to the formation of communities partly through the symbolic content of the forms of interaction contained within them, and especially through the performative processes of interaction and generation of meaning. The techniques used in dance make it possible to repeat the necessary figures and to direct and control them. Informal communities formed around dances are distinguished not only by the space of knowledge that is shared on a symbolical level, but above all by the forms of interaction in the dance with which the communities display and perform this knowledge. These stagings can be seen as an attempt by the community to portray and reproduce itself and its existence as an integral body. On an emotional, symbolic and performative level, dances create communities – they are performative and expressive. However, it is impossible for us to agree completely about the ambiguity in the symbolism of dances.

Dance and structure. In dance, movements undergo a rhythmic dynamization, and there is a playful approach to the creation, modification and dissolution of structures. As interactive action patterns, dances develop a specific structure and regularity. It is possible to identify and analyse similarities between the dances and the culture that produced them. This becomes clear if we compare the dances of the French court and those of bourgeois society at the beginning of the twentieth century along with their social structures at these two times. Dances can provide ways for us to analyse social structural and power relationships, which in turn can give us clues as to how to understand the structures of dances.

In dance, movements become rhythmically dynamic, and we find a playful treatment of the creation, modification and dissolving of structures.

Dance and identification. Through processes of mimesis, we identify with the dancers and the dances and also with the body movements and body images that are implicit in the dances and the feelings that these trigger in us and the values and norms inherent in them. Processes of inclusion and exclusion are not uncommonly tied up with this. By identifying with certain dances, we also identify with lifestyles, milieus and groups and this is embodied in the dance.

Dance and memory. Dancing creates memories, which include movements, rhythms and sounds. These memories become the starting point for atmospheres, erotic experiences, feelings of 'flow', intoxication and sometimes even ecstasy, memories of moments of intensity and rhythms in which we feel both ourselves and others. These memories are synaesthetic and embrace several senses. Some are memories shared by the collective, while others are highly individual. Some memories are tied primarily to mental images, others to movements.

Dance as the processing of differences. In many dances, differences are processed. These include, for example, gender, age or ethnic differences. When different people dance together, differences that would otherwise exist between them are pushed into the background. They can only manage to execute the movements of the dance together if they cooperate and tune into each other. They process the differences that separate them by relating to each other mimetically in the dance and adjusting their movements to make them more similar to those of the other. By temporarily putting differences aside, they create a feel of togetherness in rhythmic movements. In dance, where feelings of being a community are created, consolidated and changed, ritualized forms of enactment, physical action and play practices and mimetic response become central. A performative community of people dancing can therefore be seen as providing a space in which people act and have experiences and which has performative, mimetic and ludic elements.

Dance and transcendence. In many cultures, dances are connected with the cosmic order, with gods, spirits, the dead and the unborn. Dances are an attempt to gain influence over the powers of the Beyond. In many cases, these dances are part of sacrificial rituals whose purpose is to gain the goodwill of the gods and spirits. This happens mostly with magical dances in which people use masks and other 'props' to lend themselves supernatural powers with which they can then drive out and banish the evil gods and spirits. It is not unusual for the intoxication and ecstasy in these dances to release 'superhuman' forces which are intended to ward off threats and dangers to the world. In these dances, people use exclusion and inclusion to establish order and power. By so doing, they also aim to establish the cosmic order.

Dance and practical knowledge. Anyone who dances learns far more than just how to dance. When we dance, we develop a physical skill which is important not only for dance but also for other life contexts. It goes hand in hand with a sensitivity to movements and rhythm, to space and time, and sounds and atmospheres. In dance we develop a practical body-based knowledge that is acquired in processes of mimesis.[4] In these processes, we absorb images, rhythms, schemata and movements into our image world, and in so doing we acquire a practical knowledge that we can transfer to other situations. This practical knowledge is practised, developed and modified through repetition. The knowledge that is incorporated into our bodies in this way has historical and cultural roots and as such is open to change.[5]

Dance and aesthetics. Because they portray, express and perform, all dances have an aesthetic dimension. Thus, dances are human forms of expression which makes them valuable components of our human cultural heritage and quite unique. All dances have aesthetic elements – the dances at the court of Louis XIV, avant-garde contemporary dance art, magical dances conjuring up gods and spirits, twentieth-century folk dances and society dances, and also the dance forms danced by young people today. Dances from a great variety of different cultures have different implicit aesthetics. Here there are a number of similarities but also major differences.

10.2 Future directions

If dances are ways in which cultures represent themselves, then they must also reflect the cultural diversity which defines cultural life in the world, despite all the levelling tendencies of globalization. If we accept that it is more necessary than ever to be able to manage cultural diversity for the sake of the further development of human co-existence, then dances, as practices that form part of our intangible cultural heritage, enable us to open ourselves up to strangers and to experience dealing with cultural diversity. They also bring challenges and offer opportunities for the field of education.[6]

Dances are ways for us to portray and express ourselves that enable us to experience something that we could not experience without them. In many dances, people experiment – with themselves, their history and their culture. They try to express something that cannot be enacted or performed in any other way. For this reason, many dances, and above all those that are classed as dance art, are conceived as being experimental. This encourages the dancers to use the methods of staging and performing the body to invent something and explore, which contributes to our knowledge of ourselves as human beings. If we look at this knowledge today from an anthropological angle, we find many paradigms of anthropological research which can guide anthropological research on dance. These are firstly the evolution and hominization of *Homo sapiens*, or philosophical anthropology, as developed in Germany, which stresses the fact that human history is fundamentally open-ended and that it is possible for humankind to perfect itself. Secondly, we have historical anthropology which began in the 'Annales School' which emphasizes the historical nature of human culture and focuses on the investigation of mentalities. Thirdly, there is Anglo-American cultural anthropology or ethnology with its interest in cultural diversity and heterogeneity, and then, finally, our attempts to develop a historical-cultural anthropology.[7] The next step is to develop a branch of research on dance, based on these paradigms, that is informed by historical anthropology. It should not be restricted to certain cultures and eras and be capable of overcoming the Eurocentric stance of large sections of the humanities and aesthetics by reflecting on its own historicity and culturality. This type of research requires a transdisciplinary and transcultural approach and also reflective self-criticism.

The human need for rituals

Rituals are among the forces that constitute the imaginary. They stage and portray social life and play an important role in processes of education and learning. Since rituals are processes that generate continuity and change, they can take on many different forms, depending on their purpose, content and context. Because they involve the body and are rooted in a historical and cultural context, they have an extra dimension of meaning that is impossible to capture. As well as having a tendency towards conformity and even oppression, rituals and ritualizations can also have a productive aspect, of which we are often less aware. This productive aspect creates communities and enables them to process their problems and conflicts. Rituals are social performances, experienced by the senses, in which relations and facts and circumstances are portrayed, which themselves affect, shape and change this portrayal in turn. Like dances, as cultural performances they are also physical, performative, expressive and symbolic; they follow rules and are efficient. They are also repetitive, homogenous, liminoid, public and operational. They create social arrangements, which are perceived as images of social relationships. They become inscribed into the individual and collective imaginary as memory images and shape this by means of repetition in a variety of forms. Rituals are institutional patterns in which collective knowledge and collective forms of praxis are staged. Rituals also confirm the way the structure of an institution or community portrays and interprets itself. Their scenic arrangements contain elements of reproduction, construction and innovation.[1] Ritual acts have a beginning and an end and thus a time structure. They take place in social spaces that they themselves shape. Ritual processes embody institutions and organizations and give them a concrete form. They stand apart from everyday life. They are performative and are defined by however they may be framed. They lend shape to the transitions between social situations and institutions and process the differences between people and situations. Rituals are involved in power relations and structure social reality. They create and change social orders and hierarchies. People need to have knowledge of a ritual in order to stage and perform it. The knowledge required is practical knowledge,[2] which is acquired by means of mimesis when we participate in ritual situations.[3] Since it is practical knowledge, it is also a sensory, mimetic knowledge, which gives it performative power.[4]

Since the staging and performing of the human body play a central role in rituals, rituals are among the most effective forms of human communication. They help to create communities and to organize transitions within and between them. As opposed to purely linguistic forms of communication, rituals are social arrangements which create orders and hierarchies through common social action and the way this is interpreted. Ritual acts include liturgies, ceremonies, celebrations, ritualizations and conventions. They can be religious rituals, the transitional ceremonies that take place at weddings, births and deaths and also the interactional rituals of everyday life. Rituals are complex social phenomena and as such are studied by many academic disciplines. However, since the differences between the positions of the various academic branches are pronounced, there is no generally or internationally accepted theory or definition of ritual.[5] Different aspects are emphasized, depending on the field, discipline and methodological approach. Nevertheless, today there is widespread agreement that there is nothing to be gained by limiting the breadth and wealth of views in favour of individual theories. On the contrary, the general consensus is that the discussion should focus on the diversity of different viewpoints, thus revealing the complexity of rituals and research on them.

In view of the increasing importance of individualization and self-determination in modern societies, we sometimes come across the view that in today's world rituals are superfluous and can be replaced by other social practices. Such a view is unsustainable even if we apply a very traditional concept of the ritual. It remains impossible to have communal life without rituals and ritualizations, because every change in or reform of institutions and organizations also requires a change in the rituals. Rituals are historical and cultural products, and when we perceive them we see the culturality of the social phenomena and the historicity of the research on rituals superimposed on each other.[6] Rituals are, however, also research constructions in which social practices are considered to be rituals and are analysed as such.

Rituals play a central role in all areas of socialization and child-raising and education, and they also contribute to the creation of the cultural imaginary. They are especially important in *the family, school, youth culture* and *the media*.[7] It is not possible to have family life without rituals and ritualizations. These include, for example, rituals connected with mealtimes, Christmas, children's birthday parties, first communions or confirmations and holiday trips. School, too, is a ritual 'event' in which teachers have to have a level of professional skill in performing rituals, without which they cannot do their job properly. In school, rituals and ritualizations play an important role in the structuring of the teaching. They create a framework for the learning process, without which institutionalized learning cannot take place. They are also important in structuring rituals of starting or leaving school, or rituals for Christmas celebrations or summer parties, for example, and therefore they play an important role in creating the culture of the school or the class a child is in. Similarly, in youth culture rituals are important in determining whether adolescents are included or excluded in peer groups, in the learning of breakdance and at LAN parties, for instance (see the following paragraphs). For education and learning processes where electronic media, television and computers are used, they are particularly important. Rituals connected with watching television, and how children and young people process them, play an important role in the forming of an imaginary which transcends their cultural backgrounds.[8] Also, online communities of adolescents are formed as a result of new rituals, and these accordingly demand a new form of ritual knowledge without which children and young people are unable to act appropriately in these communities. Before we analyse the importance of rituals for education and socialization, I will first give an overview of important positions in the history of research on rituals and the role of rituals in our modern culture.

11.1 A historical perspective

It is possible to distinguish four historical approaches in international research on rituals from which we can see how far research on rituals is determined by the conditions under which it is carried out and the basic assumptions on which it is based. The first approach focuses on rituals linked with religion, myth and culture.[9] The second approach sees rituals as a means of analysing social structures and values. Here the focus is on the connection between rituals and the structure of society.[10] In the third approach, rituals are read as text. The aim is to decode the cultural and social dynamic of the society in question and also to investigate the meaning of ritual practices for cultural symbolizations and social communication.[11] This is the starting point for many research projects on the practice of rituals and ritualization,[12] which prepared the way for the fourth approach. This fourth approach emphasizes above all the practical, staged and performative aspect of rituals. The main focus is the forms of ritual action that enable communities to generate and restore themselves and process their differences.[13] The field of international research on rituals could, of course, be further differentiated,[14] but it is the aforementioned four that are of interest here.

11.2 Rituals in modern culture

In the current political situation where there are many discussions about the breaking down of social life, the loss of values and the search for a cultural identity, rituals and ritualizations are becoming increasingly important. For a long time, discussions on rituals were mainly concerned with stereotypy, rigidity and violence. Now they are seen as serving as a bridge between individuals, communities and cultures. Today rituals are regarded more as ways of creating social coherence, the ethical and aesthetic aspects of which provides security in times of confusion. Rituals promise to offer compensation for the experiences of loss of community, identity and authenticity, order and stability associated with the modern era, all of which are connected with tendencies towards individualism, abstraction and virtualization and the erosion of social and cultural systems.

Rituals are indispensable for the creation and practices of religion, society and community, politics and economics, art and culture, child-rearing and education. They are used to structure and interpret the world and human relations, which are experienced and constructed in rituals. Ritual actions create a connection between past, present and future. Through them continuity and change, structure and community and also experiences of transition and transcendence become possible.

Ritual performances differ depending on the particular social field, institution or organization. The aforementioned differentiation between *convention, ritualization, ceremony, liturgy and celebration* makes it clear that we are talking about different ritual performances or practices, between which the boundaries are fluid, but which do have to meet different structural requirements depending on the cultural practices involved. This also applies to the following *types of ritual*:

- Rituals of transition (birth and childhood, initiation and adolescence, marriage, death);

- Rituals of institution and induction (taking on new tasks and positions);
- Seasonal rituals (Christmas, birthdays, days of remembrance, public holidays);
- Rituals of intensification (celebrating, love, sexuality);
- Rituals of rebellion (peace and ecological movements, rituals of youth);
- Rituals of interaction (greetings, taking leave, conflicts).

The cultural conditions under which these rituals are performed vary widely from one culture to another, which determines their quality as cultural performances.[15] Here too it is true that the concrete conditions under which rituals are performed have a considerable influence on the way they are performed. This is evident in ritual celebrations, for example, such as Christmas, weddings and baptisms.

In many cases, the cultural nature of ritual performances depends on the symbolic capital of those acting out the rituals. What do the people acting out the rituals have in terms of economic, social and cultural capital and how is their contribution expressed in the scenes of rituals? There can be no doubt that the symbolic capital of the people who act out the rituals has an influence on the nature of their cultural performances. Many rituals even have the task of expressing these various different symbolic capitals. They are a way of portraying different degrees of availability of social and cultural capital in the ritual and of processing the differences in such a way that the social or cultural hierarchies become acceptable. In the ritual arrangements, this is frequently done, making them appear natural, rather than conditioned by society and history and therefore open to change. These connections are obscured by the magic of many rituals, which causes the participants to believe that they are unchangeable and fitting and upholds the illusion that they are natural.

Since rituals are embodied stagings and performances, they usually have more social weight than mere discourse. By using their corporeality, the people acting in the rituals bring 'more' than simply linguistic communication into the social situation. This 'more' is rooted in the materiality of the body and in the existential nature of human life to which this gives rise, our bodily presence and vulnerability. The staging and execution of rituals processes differences and creates shared realities. This is achieved not only through linguistic communication but also on a bodily, physical level. People stage and perform themselves and their relationships with other people and create social life by performing it. By staging and performing social life, they create it. They create structures, which are often hierarchical. The hierarchies are an expression of power relationships – between the members of different classes, between the generations and between the sexes. By performing and expressing these power structures physically, people find themselves viewing the structures and power relations as being natural and generally accepted. Anyone who refuses the invitation to 'play along' will find themselves excluded from a community – they are excluded and can become a scapegoat upon whom people can project their negativity and violence.[16]

11.3 The Berlin Study on Rituals and Gestures

Rituals play a larger part in modern societies than was long thought to be the case. It is in the fields of education and socialization, however, that they are most important. This was shown in a large-scale empirical study on the significance of rituals and ritualizations in the major fields of education and socialization, that is, *family, school, child and youth culture and the media.* The study focuses on the importance of rituals and ritualizations in the development of social skills in communities,[17] in child-rearing and education[18] and for learning processes in children and young people.[19] The importance of gestures is also discussed, an area that had previously been largely overlooked.[20] The main study participants were children and young people from an elementary school in an inner-city area of Berlin. This is a school with 300 children from twenty-five different ethnic backgrounds which typifies the conditions in today's inner-city schools. This school is a UNESCO model school, with progressive educational principles, an outstanding head teacher and highly committed teachers.

At this school, we also found *families* who were prepared to work with us and whose rituals we were able to study. These included the small rituals of the family breakfast, which helped the family members to reconsolidate their feeling of belonging. There were also the children's birthday parties. Here the children, who make a family rather than a couple, are at the centre of the celebrations. At the same time, a child's birthday party is an important celebration for the peer group and their feeling of community, which is staged at the birthday party. The most important of the repetitive cycle of family rituals in Christian families is the celebration of Christmas. This is when the families stage and perform themselves in relation to the birth of Christ and the unity of the 'Holy Family'. Another of these rituals that sustain the family and reinforce the feeling of belonging is the family holiday, repeated every year, when family members leave their everyday lives and have new experiences together that are reminiscent of the dream of paradise.

Clearly, *school* is a ritual event in which fundamental insights can be gained into the connection between the institution and ritual and also into hierarchical and power structures. We see this in the ceremonies surrounding the first day at school and the last day at school, in which a time of transition is staged and performed in a ritual. In the ceremony marking the first day at school, that takes place in Germany, the progressive school in our study staged itself as the 'school family' with the aim of making it easier for the new pupils to experience the transition from the world of family and kindergarten to the world of school. Many different rituals are employed to create the class community, which is the main part of the children's everyday school environment, as well the school community. Thus, ritual Summer, Advent and Carnival celebrations form part of everyday school life in which dialogue, work, play and celebration are pillars upon which teaching and school life are built. As well as these rituals, there are also many micro-rituals in which the interactions between the children and also between teachers and children are staged and performed. For instance, every Monday morning lessons begin with the ritual of the 'morning circle' where the children spend a few minutes telling each other what they did at the weekend. For the children, this ritual is a way of mastering the transition between the world of family life at the weekend and the social and academic demands of the school. Another ritual, which teachers often announce with a gong, involves maintaining a meditative silence for five minutes, a task which many children like although they do not find it easy. Teachers and pupils perform processes of learning and education in rituals and ritualizations in which they process the differences between the agendas of the children and those of the school institution.

The social element in *child and youth culture* also develops by means of and in rituals. This is evident in the breaks between lessons when the children are playing in the playground and different groups are formed which either include or exclude. Important criteria here are the type of game and the children's *gender* and ethnic backgrounds. In the playground performances, social groupings are formed that are sustained for extended time periods and vary in how open they are to new children wanting to join them. Breakdance groups with all the rituals that go along with them are particularly popular among young people at youth centres. The aforementioned LAN parties, where many young people come together in large halls to play computer games with each other, also have set ritual game and group structures. In our investigation of rituals inspired by the media, we initially looked at ritual media performances. That is, we analysed the influence of media items such as advertisements, news programmes, talk shows and crime thrillers, on the children's worlds of ideas, that is, on their imaginary. In order to ascertain the influence of these ritualized TV sequences on the behaviour and actions of the children and young people, we invited them to form groups of their own choosing and then use a camera to make a film. Some of them took on the roles of actors and others directors and cameramen or women. In these 'film shoots', it was fascinating to see how the ritual structures present in German television shape the collective worlds of ideas, the collective imaginary of the children and young people, regardless of ethnic background. We then looked at the learning processes that take place through the use of computers in teaching, in both the official and the unofficial school curricula and also the rituals that young people develop in online communities.

Methodology. In the field of investigation that we set up as described earlier, we used qualitative methods, which enabled us to reconstruct and evaluate the empirical material and to process our research questions in a way that remained close to the phenomena under investigation. The investigation was inspired by *Grounded Theory*, which sees theory as a process, with its recommendations to collect, code and analyse information.[21] Because our focus was very much on the performative nature of the processes of learning and education in rituals and ritual activities, we selected investigative methods which enabled us on the one hand to learn something about the staging and the performative character of ritual acts and on the other hand also to gain information about the meanings the participants attributed to the rituals and how they understood and interpreted the learning processes inherent in the ritual. For the first of these objectives, we used both *participant observation* and video-aided *participant observation*. For the second objective, we also used *group discussions* and *interviews*. Each method gave us different information, which was encoded and interpreted in a different way. Since all research methods have their limitations as well as their well-known advantages and disadvantages, in many cases we tried to use overlapping methods to observe the same ritual actions.[22] In the various parts of our study, the previously mentioned procedures were weighted differently. The reasons for this lay in the different research questions and in the structure of the field of investigation.

11.4 Rituals as performative acts

The results of the research done by the Berlin Study on Rituals in the fields of child-rearing and socialization, education and learning have shown that the sustainability of rituals is linked to their performative nature, that is, to the corporeality of the scenic stagings and performances. When they use their bodies in portrayals in rituals and ritual scenes, people show who they are and how they grasp their relationships with other people and the world. Ritual processes can be viewed as *scenic stagings of performative acts*, in which members of an institution assume different roles. Some ritual performances are spontaneous; in these cases, it is often hard to identify why they have emerged or are emerging at a particular point in time. Other ritual performances can be understood from the context in which they are taking place and the history that has gone before, insofar as this can be ascertained. In ritual arrangements, the contingencies in the philosophical sense are important. Although scenic performances consist of specific individual elements that are linked together, this does not mean that each individual element can be replaced by a similar or new one. Because ritual performances are of a ludic nature, the relationship between the scenic elements is one of contingency, which is what constitutes the dynamic of the rituals.[23]

Rituals are among the most important forms of performative action. They take effect first and foremost via the *staging and performing of the bodies* of those taking part. Even if these people interpret the ritual differently, the very fact that they are carrying out the ritual has the *effect of creating a sense of community* between them. The celebration of Christmas is a good example of this. Regardless of the differences between the way people perceive Christmas – young children still expecting the Christ Child or Father Christmas to come, their parents taking pleasure in the happiness of their children, adolescents finding the whole event of Christmas stale and empty, the granny remembering the celebrations of her childhood – the staging and performance of the Christmas ritual has the effect of drawing all the participants together. This effect consists above all in the fact that the *differences* between those taking part are *processed* in the performance of the ritual itself. Despite different situations, different states of mind and different interpretations, the ritual act leads to a sense of (festive) *community*. This becomes particularly evident if the ritual goes wrong and tensions or feelings of aggression come to predominate, thus completely destroying the community-enhancing effect of the Christmas celebrations.[24]

Choosing the right *frame* is also an integral part of the staging and performance of rituals.[25] The frame enables us to recognize how the ritual relates to actions that have gone before and helps us to understand what the ritual is about. The frame makes it different from everyday actions, *sets* the ritual *apart* and ensures the *magical nature* of the ritual procedures. This results from the fact that all those taking part believe in the ritual, whether it creates a sense of *community*, as with Christmas, or whether, as with investiture rites, it draws a dividing line in whose existence and legitimacy the participants believe, regardless of whether they are among those who stand to gain from it or those whom it excludes. However, even in rituals that create a sense of community a line is drawn between those taking part and those who are excluded. This demarcation can happen spontaneously; it can also allow some permeability, or it can permanently exclude.

Many rituals require *performative statements and props* which are part of the way they are staged and performed. In the case of Christmas in Germany, these include certain verses from the Bible and religious carols, as well as the Christmas tree, the presents and the Christmas meal. In rituals, performative acts produce scenes and sequences. These include not only the staging of human bodies but also the *arrangement of the surroundings that are part and parcel of the ritual*, which also need to be organized in such a way that the ritual comes together *as a whole*. The *ritual structure* emerges out of this 'Gesamtkunstwerk' or artistic synthesis.

Ritual performances require *movements* of the body, which are used to stage closeness and distance between the participants of the ritual. These body movements express social attitudes and social relationships. For example, hierarchical relationships that are determined by power differences require different body movements from friendly or even intimate relationships. When body movements are used to master social situations, our bodies are also controlled by these social situations – they are civilized by them. *Social situations* are created by movements of the body. Such situations are particularly memorable because of their figurative and pictorial quality and they therefore lend themselves to being performed over and over again. Ritual enactments contain an important *performative quality* – the participants want their actions to be seen and appreciated as befits them. The movements of the body are intended to portray and express this wish.

When we speak of the performative, performance and performativity, we are stressing the aspect of the body that constitutes the world. This is evident in language and in social action. When we speak of the performative nature of the body, we mean language as action and social action as staging and performing. If we view human action as performative cultural action, this necessitates changes in our understanding of social processes. In this case, the participants' corporeality and also the fact that the actions are staged and a special event require greater attention. What now becomes evident is that social action is more than simply fulfilling intentions. This extra dimension of meaning is partly due to the way the actors pursue and try to fulfil their aims. Unconscious wishes and early experiences and feelings enter into this process. Despite the fact that two or more people can have the same intentions in carrying out an action, considerable differences can arise in how it is physically performed, with the emphasis on the word *how*.

The character and quality of social relations depends essentially on how people use their bodies in ritual acts, the space they put between their bodies, the bodily stances they adopt and the gestures they develop. People use these means to convey a great deal about themselves to other people. They tell them something about their attitude to life and their way of seeing, feeling and experiencing the world. Despite the fact that this is of central importance for the effects of social action, these aspects of bodily performativity are overlooked in many theories of action in which the sensory and contextual conditions of people's actions are ignored and the actors are still reduced simply to their conscious minds. If this impoverishment is to be avoided, it is necessary to examine how ritual acts arise, how they are linked to language and imagination, how social and cultural patterns make them possible and in what relationship their event character stands to the fact that they are also repeated. We must also analyse the extent to which speaking and communication can be seen as action and also the role that forms of address and repetition play in the development of gender, social and ethnic identity. Thus seen, action is understood as imitation, participation and shaping of cultural practices by the body and the senses. In this view, artistic and social actions are seen as *performances*, speaking as *performative action* and *performativity* as an overarching concept that is derived from and addresses all these relationships. We can differentiate between at least three aspects of the performativity of rituals.

Firstly, rituals can be seen as communicative *cultural performances*. As such, they are the result of stagings and processes of corporeal portrayal in the course of which ritual scenes are arranged whose participants fulfil various different tasks. By making reference to each other by means of speech and actions, they create ritual scenes together. Like works of art and literature, these rituals can be seen as resulting from cultural action, in the course of which the heterogeneous forces of society are brought into an acceptable structure.

Secondly, the performative character of *language* acquires considerable importance in ritual acts. This is evident in the rituals of Baptism and First Communion, for example, and in rituals of transition and inauguration, in which the words spoken in the course of the ritual play a considerable role in creating a new social reality.[26] The same is also true of those rituals in which the relationship between the sexes is organized and where repeatedly addressing a child as a 'boy' or a 'girl' helps to shape sexual identity.[27]

Finally, the performativity of rituals also includes an *aesthetic dimension* that is an essential element of artistic *performances*. This aspect reminds us of the limitations of viewing the performativity of ritual acts in purely functional terms. We view artistic performances from an aesthetic angle, which means that we do not view them purely in terms of their intentions. Similarly, an aesthetic approach to rituals reminds us that the meaning of rituals is more than simply the realization of intentions. The way in which the actors realize their aims is no less important.

Despite the participants having the same intentions, there are often considerable differences in the way the body is used in the performance of rituals. Among the reasons for this are general, historical, cultural and social conditions and also specific conditions connected with the uniqueness of the participants. It is the interplay of these two groups of factors that creates the performative character of linguistic, social and aesthetic action in stagings and performances of rituals. The event and process nature of rituals clearly limits the extent to which they can be planned and predicted. The importance of the style of ritual performances becomes evident when we take into account the aesthetic dimension. The difference between what is consciously intended and the many dimensions of meaning that become discernible in the scenic arrangements of people's bodies is obvious. The performative character of ritual action gives rise to various interpretations without the ritual arrangements losing their impact. On the contrary – part of their impact is due to the fact the same ritual actions can be interpreted differently without losing any of the rituals' social magic.

Social communication depends to a large extent on how people deploy their bodies in ritual actions. Despite the central importance of the performance of the body for social action, this aspect is ignored in many traditional theories of ritual, where the cognitive aspects of the actions are stressed at the expense of the sensory and contextual conditions of the participant actors. If we wish to avoid this simplification, we must examine how ritual action comes about, how it is linked with language and communication, how social and cultural patterns make its uniqueness possible and how its event character relates to the fact that it is also repeated.

11.5 How practical knowledge is learned mimetically in rituals

To acquire the practical knowledge required to stage and perform rituals, which is learned in mimetic processes, the rituals must be performative.

Practical knowledge of rituals is necessary if children and young people are to learn what they have to do in rituals, what actions are expected of them and what options they have to shape their actions in an individual way without endangering the integrity of the ritual as a whole. Current efforts to improve the quality of learning in school greatly underestimate the importance of implicit practical knowledge in learning and education. Only the UNESCO report: *Learning, The Treasure within* has highlighted its central importance. This report identifies 'learning to know', 'learning to do', 'learning to be' and 'learning to live together' as important pillars of education.[28] Rituals and the practical knowledge taught by them play an important role in the acquisition of these forms of knowledge.[29]

The practical knowledge learned in ritual actions is not theoretical or reflexive knowledge which can simply be put into practice in social praxis. Practical knowledge is acquired in mimetic processes.[30] Mimetic learning takes place when children and young people participate in the scenic performances of social actions and perceive how other people behave in ritual scenes. Since people grasp how social actions are performed via their senses, the *how* becomes very important when it comes to being on the receiving end of and processing actions mimetically. It is only by using *aisthesis* (perceiving via the senses) that the scenic arrangements that constitute and concretize the social actions can be perceived and processed.[31] The mimetic incorporation of ritual actions that takes place here is an active, productive process, during which the rituals and ritualizations that have been perceived are individually processed and reworked. In mimetic references to other people, a scenic performance of ritual actions or an imaginary world, something different happens every time because everyone who behaves mimetically has a different starting point. Mimetic processes involve *becoming similar*, which focuses on the way in which people stage themselves both physically and socially, how they behave towards the world, other people and themselves. The mimetic process is oriented towards the uniqueness of other people and leads to our incorporating 'likenesses of them and their social actions into our mental image worlds'. Mimetic processes turn the outside world into the inner world and lead to an expansion of our inner worlds.

The acquisition, in mimetic processes, of practical knowledge which generates social actions does not have to be based on similarity. If, for example, mimetic knowledge of ritual acts or performances is acquired through referring back to a previous world, then it is only possible to determine from which standpoint the mimetic reference was made by comparing the two worlds. Similarity is only one, albeit frequent, trigger for the mimetic impulse. However, the creation of a *magical contact* can also be the starting point for a mimetic action.[32] A mimetic relationship is even necessary for differentiating the current ritual from other, existing rituals and performances. Without this, it would not be possible to accept, deviate from or reject of previous rituals and other social actions.

A disciplined and controlled form of practical knowledge arises from disciplining and controlling the movements of the body. This practical knowledge, which is stored in our body memory, enables us to stage the corresponding forms of symbolic, scenic action. It relates to the forms of social action and performance that have emerged through the process of civilization, and thus, although it is clearly a performative knowledge, has limited historical and cultural potential. The practical knowledge that is relevant for performative actions is body based, ludic, ritualistic and at the same time historical and cultural. It is formed in face-to-face situations and is semantically ambiguous. It has imaginary components, cannot be reduced to intentionality, has an added dimension of meaning and reveals itself in the stagings and performances of everyday life, literature and art.[33]

11.6 Key functions of rituals

Rituals have many different functions, which, however, do not capture their essence entirely. Their importance in child-rearing and socialization, in education and learning, can be summed up under ten points, which form the basis of the theory of rituals.[34]

1. Social life as ritual. Without rituals, communities would be unthinkable, since it is in and by ritual processes and practices that they form and undergo change. Through the symbolic content of the forms of interaction and communication and above all through the performative processes which generate interaction and meaning, rituals preserve and stabilize the community itself. The community is the cause, process and effect of ritual action. Rituals frame specific everyday practices, with the result that unstructured behaviour becomes structured through the restrictions imposed. Thus, rituals create a procedure that is relatively safe and homogenized. The associated techniques and practices ensure that the necessary actions can be repeated, that they can be directed and controlled and also that effects and problems can be identified.

Social, institutionalized and informal communities are characterized not only by the common space of a symbolic knowledge shared by all, but above all by ritualized forms of interaction and communication in which and by means of which they stage this knowledge. These stagings can be understood as an attempt to establish and sustain the self-presentation and reproduction of social order and integrity, to build symbolic knowledge through communication and above all to create spaces for interactions and fields in which expressive actions can be dramatized. Rituals create communities in an emotional, symbolic and performative way. They are fields in which actions are staged and expressed and the participants tune in to each other's worlds of perception and ideas through mimetic processes, despite the impossibility of reaching complete agreement about the ambiguity of the ritual symbolism. By bringing people together and the way they interact, rituals fulfil a community-building function.

2. *The ritual as a force for order.* In their role as communicative action patterns, rituals create a specific form of rule-bound activity, conventionality and 'correctness', which assumes that communities share a certain practical knowledge and way of perceiving things. Here it is not possible to determine whether the ritual has emerged from the social order or whether it is the social order that is generated by the ritual. Rituals are embodied practices which reduce and expand, channel and reshape the form and content of experiences, thought and memory. Thus, rituals create a particular form of reality. They are not concerned with truth but with acting correctly. The joint action needs to be correct so that the participants can decode the symbolism of the situation, using certain rules that have been created by ritual. Rituals are oriented towards correctness and therefore the structure of joint action that is compulsory for all participants. If the shared reality of ritual actions arises from an underlying structural asymmetry, then rituals can also be used as tools of conformity, manipulation and oppression. In this case, they degenerate into mere stereotypical modes of behaviour and staging.

3. *Identity building through rituals.* If rituals mark a transition in a spatial, temporal or social sense, then we speak of *rites of passage*.[35] This refers to the function that rituals have of promoting identification and enabling transformation. Their potential to transform and innovate lies in their symbolic and performative character, in their creative, reality-generating side. They serve as rites of initiation where, as, for example, in the case of circumcision or starting school, it is evident that the crucial aspect is the removal or processing of difference. In rites of identification and initiation the attempt is made to make people into what they already are. Rites of passage therefore have a paradoxical structure. They create a new order, establish a new state of affairs and facilitate the emergence of a new social reality that has the appearance of being natural, which makes it hard to distance oneself from it and resist it. In many of these rituals,

it is a question of 'invoking' or attributing to people a particular skill or ability. Rituals of identification are performative acts, which produce what they describe by challenging people to demonstrate an ability that they do not yet possess, thus recognizing them as the people they are yet to become. In this process, people become social beings through attribution, naming and categorization.

4. *The ritual as recall and projection of the future.* Rituals have the function of consolidating a community's present life over and over again, of confirming through repetition that its order is timeless and has immutable validity while at the same time endowing its potential for transformation with permanence.[36] They also have the task of staging continuity, timelessness and constancy and the process quality of communities and their orientation towards making plans for and orienting themselves towards the future. Rituals form a synthesis between social memory and a community's vision of its future. Our ritualized handling of time engenders ways of dealing with time and social skills. Ritualizations of time are a medium of social coexistence, considering that in industrial societies the ritual order of time structures our whole lives. The time of the ritual itself is that of the shared presence of the members in a community whose time is subdivided once more into time sequences by the ritual itself. Thus, ritual acts promote certain memories and condemn others to oblivion. Their repetitive structure suggests permanency and immutability and performing them produces and exercises control over our social memory. Ritual performances bring past events into the present, enabling us to experience them as present events. The work of reminiscence involved in rituals forges a link between the present, which is liable to be forgotten, and that part of the past that has importance for communities, constituting their tradition and history. Rituals continually evolve because they can never be performed in exactly the same way twice, but are always mimetic, and because creative potential is already introduced into these mimetic processes through repetition.

5. *The ritual as a means of overcoming crises.* Rituals are needed when communities experience differences and are undergoing crisis situations. This is because rituals provide a relatively safe, homogenous process in the course of which communities can negotiate the experiences of integration or segregation involved in making the transition to a different status, for example. Rituals can help to achieve an understanding through communication about a new situation which presents a challenge to everyday life and is perceived as a threat. However, they are not a kind of instrumental arrangement for action and cannot be deployed as a technical means of solving concrete problems. The energy produced by joint ritual action is stronger than that which can be produced by

individuals on their own and leads to the creation of community and solidarity. Crisis rituals, such as the identification and sacrifice of scapegoats, offer an opportunity to channel social violence and shift it away from the community.

6. *The ritual as an act of magic.* In rituals, by performing practices together, situations that cannot be completely overcome or brought under control in 'real'-life contexts are practised and rehearsed. For this reason, rituals can be considered to be arrangements that serve to simplify complexity, helping us to develop a relationship with the 'outside', inasmuch as participants draw dividing lines, bridge distances and believe that the mimetic and performative energies that unfold in the ritual have an effect on 'reality' not only internally but also externally. Thus, in rituals we become an 'Other', or behave as such towards the 'absolute Other'. On the one hand, this seeing others in terms of their otherness is reinforced by the symbolism which makes it possible to transform experiences, raising them to a level where they have social or religious meaning, and on the other hand it is evoked by the communal performative acts that can generate new realities. Thus, the sacred in ritual interactions ensures that there is a solidarity that has an organizing tendency, and, as a principle that makes distinctions, it brings about divisions and taboos that cause us to attach a heightened meaningfulness to experiences of time, space, objects and actions. The sacred can be seen as the idea of a specific form of transcendent efficacy and powerfulness, which relates to objects, actions, writings, people and communities and so on and is surrounded by feelings of reverence and awe as well as a code of rules, norms and taboos. The community appears to be dependent on the sacred, the ritual relationship to the sacred adopting the function of shaping integration, differentiation and exchange within a community. To this extent, the basis of the ritual is the specific belief in the transcendental or what a community holds sacred, endowing the community with a certain security and familiarity. This is why sacred festivals are important for communities.

7. *The ritual as a means of processing difference.* Rituals are action systems for processing differences. By guaranteeing the integration of an interactive context of action, they are oriented towards integration and the creation of community. The concept of the performative community does not refer to pre-existing, organic or natural unit, emotional togetherness, a symbolic system of meaning or a collective consensus on values, but rather to the ritual patterns of interaction. The answer to the question as to how communities are created, reconfirmed and modified is through ritual forms of performance, physical and verbal practices, spatial and temporal framing and also mimetic exchange. Community thus appears to be not so much an intimate, homogenous and

integrative environment, but more a precarious experiential space with tensions, divisions and negotiating processes. By performative community, we mean a space in which actions and experiences take place and which is characterized by enactive, mimetic, ludic and power elements.[37]

8. *The ritual as initiator of mimetic processes.* As already indicated earlier, ritual action does not merely produce a copy of rituals that have been previously performed. Each staging of a ritual is a new performance which leads to the modification of previous ritual actions. There is a mimetic relationship between past, present and future ritual actions in which new actions are produced by referring to or reconnecting with previous ones. In mimetic processes, a relationship to a ritual world is forged. This relationship is often based on similarities, for example the similarities in occasions, the people involved and the social functions of the rituals. What is crucial, however, is not the similarity but the forging of a relationship with the other world. If a ritual action reconnects with an earlier one and is carried out in a similar way, then we are inspired with the wish to do something like those performing the ritual with whom we are connecting and to adjust ourselves to become similar to them. This wish derives from our desire to become like the others while at the same time differentiating ourselves from them. Despite our desire to become similar, we want to be different and independent. The dynamic of rituals pushes towards both repetition and differentiation at one and the same time, thus generating energies that drive the staging and performance of ritual actions. The repetition in mimetic processes involves taking a kind of 'impression' of ritual actions that have gone before, and then applying it in new contexts. The repetition of ritual actions never leads to an exact reproduction of the previous situation, but always to the creation of a new ritual situation in which the difference from previous situations is a constitutive element. This dynamic is why ritual actions are so productive. By preserving continuity, ritual actions offer us space for lack of continuity. Ritual arrangements make it possible to negotiate the relationship between continuity and lack of continuity. The particular conditions in which individuals and groups, organizations and institutions find themselves are important in the different ways they deal with ritual patterns and schemata.

9. *The ritual as a generator of practical knowledge.* If we are to be able to act competently on a social level, theoretical knowledge is less important for us than practical knowledge. Practical knowledge enables people to behave appropriately in different social spheres, institutions and organizations. A large amount of this practical knowledge is acquired in ritualized mimetic processes. In these processes, the performers absorb images, rhythms, schemata and the

movements of ritual elements into their imaginative worlds and use them to stage and perform the required ritual acts in new contexts. It is by appropriating these processes mimetically that performers develop a practical knowledge that can be applied to new situations. Due to the ritual nature of the appropriation, this mimetically acquired practical knowledge can be practised, developed and altered as it is repeated. The practical knowledge thus becomes embodied: it is historical and cultural in character and as such open to change.[38]

10. The ritual as a generator of subjectivity. For a long time, rituality and individuality (or subjectivity) were regarded as being opposed to each other. It has only recently been recognized that this is not the case in modern societies. The way in which people act results from practical social knowledge, which they can only acquire through rituals. This does not, of course, mean that no tensions or conflicts exist between the community and the individual. The real difference between them is too marked. However, the two are interdependent. Individuals can only lead fulfilled lives if they are capable of acting and communicating competently. In the same way, a community needs a variety of individuals who are able to behave in a socially competent way and who acquire this competence in ritual mimetic actions.

Gestures as language

Gestures are portrayals that contain complex cultural and social actions in a condensed form. Despite the fact that their meanings are contradictory and by no means explicit, as bodily portrayals and non-verbal forms of expression they can be partially understood. Because of their iconic character, gestures play an important role in the imaginaries of societies, communities and individual subjects. They lend themselves to being remembered and reproduced in mimetic processes. In every staging and performance, they have a scope of action which makes it possible and allows them to be adapted to the respective context.

In the course of the 'The Berlin Study on Rituals and Gestures', we found that not only rituals and ritualizations but also gestures play a central role in child-rearing, education and socialization.[1] We therefore investigated in detail how they appear and are used in the areas of the family, school, peer groups and use of the media as fields of socialization, thus establishing an anthropologically oriented branch of research on gestures. While some studies which helped to demonstrate the relevance of this research had already been published previously,[2] before we began our study there had been no comprehensive ethnographic research that investigated the context of the effects of gestures in the areas of education and socialization. We also analysed their potential to convey power, for instance the changes between commitment and distancing in learning situations which gestures render visible,[3] and the processes of recognition, exclusion and authorization that are effected by gestures, and the forms of social positioning in educational contexts that are accentuated by gestures. The differences between the institutional settings of the various actions that are executed in the areas of family, school, peer groups and media use provide a valuable context for comparison.

It is also important to study the practical and reflexive potential of gestures used in a learning context, since gestures not only stabilize social relationships, but also have a role to play in teaching and learning processes. To this end, we can draw on Bertolt Brecht and Walter Benjamin's concepts of the gestural, which stress that gestures are memorable and thus make it possible for us to distance ourselves and interrupt the flow of a situation. Reflecting on gestures, we can discern not only the specific medium employed in the gesture but also its potential. Thus, our study not only focuses on gestures but also examines a concept of the gestural in order to expand the scope of our investigation and the ethnographic methods employed. It is only in the observation of body movements in a learning situation that the gesture is isolated and becomes significant as part of a *tableau of learning*. Analysing how such gestures achieve their effect adds to our insight into the importance of the meaning of performative bodily behaviours and inspires us to revive educational traditions that include this.

Anthropological research into gesture must begin with a discussion of the different concepts of gesture. Agamben, for example, describes the gesture as something in between acting or performing (*agere*) and making or creating (*facere*).[4] Brecht required actors to render the 'in between' character of the gesture clearly visible as a dialectical (or performative) phenomenon. With his concept of the gestural, Brecht showed the complexity of gestures and the way they relate to each other and to the context in which they are performed. They work through the principle of interruption which makes situations visible. For an empirical study, we must start with a broad concept of gesture, since this is the only way to grasp the spectrum of empirical phenomena. George H. Mead's understanding of gesture is a good point of departure.[5] He sees gesture as a phase of bodily movement which, because of the body's social sensors, functions as a basic unit of mutual adaptation for social interaction. The comprehensive gesture research results presented previously by Kendon and McNeill[6] also make important contributions to this field.[7]

The ethnographic approach to the study of gestures in the field of educational sciences differs from the experimental research conducted by other disciplines which attempts to gain insight into the effects of gestures by comparing several experimental and control groups.[8] For example, some research on linguistic gesture looks at the effects on listeners of verbal statements accompanied either by gestures, with no gestures or with mismatching gestures. Important as these studies are, many of them measure the role and significance of gestures only against semiotic and semantic criteria, and thus the pragmatic aspect of the gestures is lost. Moreover, they have all the well-known advantages and disadvantages of experimental research, namely that their experimental designs create conditions that differ widely from those in the field, that is, in our case that of educational practice.

My main goal in my ethnographic research into gestures is to investigate *the embodied, mimetic and performative characteristics of gestures*. I aim to show in various fields and contexts of the education of adults and children *how* people develop gestures in order to be able to express themselves and portray something that would otherwise remain invisible. The focus is on the *how* of the gestural portrayal and expression. Since gestures are largely dependent on context, we need to study the social framework in which they arise and show how they display the very essence of intentions and feelings and thus the significance gestures have for child-rearing and education. This is based on our assumption that gestures are influenced firstly by *collective ideas and practices*, secondly by the *circumstances and traditions of institutions*, and thirdly by *individual circumstances*. All of these need to be explored.

In order to carry out this research successfully, we need to develop a *frame of reference* (see the following text) for the *participant observation*, the *video-aided observation*, the *interviews* and the *group discussions*, so that these can be interpreted and communicatively validated. The following areas are key for the formation of gestures as a focus of anthropological research:

- Gestures as movements of the body
- Gestures as forms of expression and portrayal
- Gestures as forms of child-rearing and education
- Gestures as ways of endowing things with meaning

In these four aspects, we find a number of anthropological characteristics that have received very little attention in previous research on gestures. They provide a basis for a new anthropological field of research on gestures since they suggest important aspects that expand previous discourses and categories. What they have in common is the fact that gestures can be grasped as a language in which feelings are expressed and portrayed.

12.1 Gestures as movements of the body

Gestures can be understood as *movements of the body*. They are some of its most important forms of self-portrayal and expression. Since human bodies are always shaped by their place in history and culture, their gestures must also be read in the context in which they appear. The attempt to view gestures as a universal body language has not been as successful as was hoped. Historical and cultural anthropological studies show how differently gestures have been understood in different cultures and periods of history.[9] Gestures are significant movements of the body, whose modes of portrayal and expression cannot be fully explained by the intentions that prompt them. There is an obvious difference between gestures as bodily forms of portrayal and expression and the linguistic meaning of gestures determined by interpretation. *Gestures have a content that transcends their intentionality and can only be experienced through mimetic recreation.*

Gestures play a central role in all verbal communications and social interactions. Their function is to impart something. This is also discussed by social psychologists and ethnologists. Studies on proxemics show how individuals create symbolic spaces around themselves by using their bodies and gesture. In kinesics, the study of body movements, Birdwhistell has analysed codes of nonverbal communication.[10] Ethology examines the similarities between human and animal behaviour and forms of expression. Darwin's study *The Expression of the Emotions in Man and Animals* is a seminal work in this field and is also well worth reading.[11] Morris[12] studied the origins and distribution of gestures in Europe and carried out an empirical identification, comparison and analysis of the similarities and differences between them. Following on from this, Calbris published her *Semiotics of French Gestures*, which contains detailed information about how gestures are treated.[13] Linguistics, too, has long since discovered the significance of body gestures and stressed their importance for speech. Several authors have proposed that the gestures of the body are early forms of language which were important for the development of speech and remain indispensable for the development of thoughts and sentences and how these are understood. All of these studies have demonstrated how central gestures are for the portrayal, expression and understanding of social action and speech. At the same time, they show that we only use and control gestures consciously to a very limited extent. In the grey area between gesture and mimicry, many gestures fail to become conscious and are therefore beyond our control.

Gestures that we use consciously, using different parts of our bodies, are attempts to escape situations where we are simply in-our-bodies and to take charge of our bodies.[14] We can do this because of the excentric position that we have as human beings. Excentricity means that, unlike animals, human beings can step outside of themselves and view themselves objectively. Imagination, language and actions become possible through the 'mediated immediacy' of the excentric position.[15] We can make a distinction between, gestures that are intentional, on the one hand, which require us to be in charge of our bodies so that we can use them as we wish, and forms of mimetic bodily expression and forms of gestural expression over which we have no control, on the other hand.

These include, for example, the facial expressions of joy and laughter, of pain and crying, and also less clear expressions such as frowning, shaking our heads and holding our heads high or bowing them (which often turn into gesture). For this reason, it is not sufficient to say that gestures express intentions but that feelings are articulated in facial expressions and take this as a basis for differentiating between facial expression and gesture. Although facial expressions are often immediate and involuntary, this does not mean that on the facial expression side of the gesture spectrum there are not also gestures that are involuntary and uncontrolled. These have often been called *'beat' gestures*, that is, gestures that show beat or rhythm timing. At the other end of the gesture spectrum, we find the more intentional gestures, that is, *iconic* and, above all, *metaphoric* gestures.[16] These gestures shape the facial expression material and use it for a language of gestures that is not universal but specific to a culture, time or situation.

Unlike facial expressions, apart from the rather unspecific beat or rhythm gestures, gestures can be detached from their immediate contexts, shaped and learned. Whereas in facial expressions form and content, expression and feeling, spiritual content and bodily expression concur, in conscious gestures we see differences between these aspects which make it possible to construct them. Perfect gestures attain a high degree of artificial naturalness and give the impression that psychological content and bodily expression are interlocked. To the extent that we can perceive gestures as being the expression of our inner and outer selves, gestures are among the most important ways in which we can express ourselves and experience ourselves and the world. We embody ourselves in gestures, and it is in this embodiment that we experience ourselves. As we use gestures in social interactions, we can transform our bodily 'being' into 'having'. This transformation process makes human existence possible. The performing and constructing of rituals requires specific gestures. Especially in religious and political rituals in which the portrayal element is important, the staging and arrangement of gestures becomes highly significant.

12.2 The gesture as expression and portrayal

Although human beings 'are', without 'having' themselves, and gestures are ways of expressing what is inside us, we can gradually learn to use gestures to acquire a relationship to our bodies and to our own inner worlds. By developing a mimetic relationship to our gestures, we experience ourselves in their portrayals. In our facial expressions and gestures, we express ourselves and learn about how other people react to what we are expressing, we learn who we are or rather how other people see us. The image and body language of gestures is a cultural product which moulds children and which they themselves help to elaborate. When we acquire gestures mimetically, we are assimilated into cultural body and image traditions that are updated as the gestures are used and related to current conditions. *Gestures are expressions of a bodily configuration, an inner intention and a mediated relationship to the world.* Physical sensations and psychological feelings come together in the gesture. This makes it impossible to determine which aspects of a gesture of joy, for example, are physical and which aspects are psychological. The inseparability of the two aspects is expressed in the corporeality of the gesture.

Many gestures are the products of culturally shaped facial and gestural expressions that may be either flowing or indistinct. Researchers have kept returning to the question of how this raw material of facial expressions develops. There have been various attempts to explain it. In analogy to the fact that certain organs, such as the appendix, no longer have a function and that they are consequently 'useless vestiges', Darwin explains facial expression as being what remains of something that once had a purpose.[17] On the basis of this theorem, it is also possible to explain the fact we draw our lips into a grimace and bare our canines when angry as being because the early human beings had very pronounced teeth that they could use as a threatening gesture when attacked or defending themselves. It is thought that the movement of the mouth persisted after the canines had regressed. By drawing an analogy between facial expressions today and their archaic function, we can explain certain human aspects of facial expression.

Independently of Darwin, one could also say that a facial expression is an action with a fictitious objective. This relates to the importance of imagination and mimesis in facial mimicry and gesture. In this view, facial expression relates to something fictitious and evolves in relation to this fiction. The fictitious thing can be something in the past, present or future. Facial expressions and gestural expressions that are initially indistinct are mimetic reactions to a fiction. In the theatre, facial expression and gesture are mimetically related to the imaginary plot and how it is staged. The facial expression, which remains largely unconscious, and indistinct gestures are transformed and stylized into a gesture that is consciously articulated. This becomes an element in a scenic arrangement which is of central importance for the mimetic processing of the performance by the audience. The same is true of the social performances and the gestures employed in them that are staged in other institutions such as school and the family, and the use of media.

Many gestures are not forms of direct expression. Feelings and sensations are only directly articulated in facial expression and in some gestures. The feelings that are shown here can only be concealed with difficulty. The body's signs, its symptoms and its 'language' are considered to be unadulterated expressions of the world inside us, of the human psyche. Lavater and his successors' notion of 'physiognomy' was an attempt to understand these relationships. However, it is almost impossible to identify them, although they are still of interest to us. *Facial expressions and gestures in everyday life point to there being a body knowledge that produces them, shapes them and renders them comprehensible. We do not acquire this knowledge through the analysis and explanation of gestures. We acquire it mimetically through social processes.*

12.3 Gestures as forms of child-rearing and education

Gestures play an important role in the processes of human education. In gestures, the inner and outer coincide. They arise out of our human openness to the world, but at the same time, they place limitations on this condition of human existence by making things concrete. This restriction of the permitted modes of gestural expression through culture and historical tradition creates social togetherness and security. By becoming familiar with certain gestures, we become familiar with individual people and groups. Children and young people know what certain gestures mean, how to assess them and how to respond to them. Gestures make it possible for us to predict human behaviour. They are a part of the body language that tells the members of a community a great deal about each other. Even if these messages are part of our unconscious perceptions of ourselves and others rather than conscious knowledge about others, their feelings and intentions, they are highly socially significant. These messages become part of the social knowledge that individuals acquire as they become part of society, and they play a major role in the way individuals learn to regulate their social actions in an appropriate way.

The meaning of gestures changes *depending on time and space*. We can also observe differences relating to gender and social class. Some gestures are gender- or class-specific, and others do not seem to show any such differences. Others again are tied to social spaces, times and institutions. Institutions such as churches, law courts, hospitals and schools insist upon certain gestures being used and sanction any neglect of them. Institutions assert their claim to power by means of this insistence on using the gestures specific to them. Using these gestures imprints the institutional values and views on the bodies of the members of the institutions and also on those to whom the gestures are addressed, and they are confirmed and revalidated by repeat 'performances'. Examples of such institutional forms of expression made by the body are, still today, gestures of humility (the church), respect (law courts), considerateness (hospitals) and attentiveness and commitment (school). If these ritualized gestures fail to be employed, then the representatives of institutions perceive this omission as a criticism of the social and societal legitimacy of their institutions. As a rule sanctions follow. As there are often people in these institutions who depend on them, the threat of sanctions is effective. Via the mimesis of institution-specific gestures, members of society submit to the normative requirements of its institutions.

Gender differences are also performed, repeated and affirmed by means of gestures. Thus, we can already see significant gender-specific differences in girls' and boys' games where use of gestural expression is practised via their different interests in games (cooperation and intimacy vs competition). Gender differences are also apparent in the way men and women sit, the space they take up when they are seated and how they arrange their legs. We find something similar expressed in the way they speak, eat and drink. Class differences are also evident in the way people use gestures. Bourdieu has studied these divergences in relation to taste and demonstrated that 'fine differences' lead to the establishment and consolidation of social hierarchies.[18] Divergences in body gestures and expressions play an important role in our perception of the way these differences are perceived. In his studies on the process of civilization, Elias has shown how gestures used at court were mimicked and gradually assumed and changed by the bourgeoisie.[19] In his study *Discipline and Punish*, Foucault showed how power becomes rooted in the body and also exerts a strong influence on the way the body expresses or portrays itself, that is, its gestures.[20] *The function of body gestures is first and foremost to produce, express and maintain social and cultural differences. Gestures are employed in a historical context which is structured by power, and it is only by examining this that we can determine their meaning.*

Gestures give us information about the values that are central to a society and provide insight into 'mentality structures'. If we look at the use of gestures in a medieval monastery, we can see what function of gestures can have in different areas of a society and how we can find out more about the relationship between body and symbol, present and history, religion and everyday life by studying how gestures are and have been used.[21] Gestures accompany spoken language but also have a 'life of their own' that has no direct relation to what is being said. Their meanings are often unclear. They often convey messages that add something to what is being said, whether by emphasizing certain aspects or by relativizing them or calling them into question. Frequently what is expressed in gestures is more closely linked to the speaker's feelings than to what he or she is saying. They are seen as a 'safer' way to express our inner lives than words, which are more consciously controlled.

Individuals, groups and institutions enact social life. They develop choreographies of human communal living. These performances of bodies, gestures and ritual expressions can be read or decoded as texts. Clifford Geertz rendered this view of social life as a text fruitful for cultural anthropology.[22] His attempt to capture social reality in what he has termed 'thick description' is in keeping with this view that social life can be read. Gestures hold an important position within the spectrum of social performances of the body as a whole. They are part of our sign, body and social language and can be read, like the more abstract signs of a text. This view of gestures needs to be further expanded by a perspective that takes into account their performative character and in which they are understood as aesthetic actions or cultural performances.

Gestures must first be grasped mimetically, before they can be read and decoded. *Someone who perceives a gesture understands it by imitating it, and in so doing is able to grasp the specific character of its bodily mode of expression and portrayal.* Although gestures are meaningful and can be analysed, it is only by reproducing them mimetically that we register their symbolic and sensory content. Important as it is to differentiate between various aspects of the meaning of gestures, it is only with the aid of mimesis that we can take in the mode of portrayal and expression incorporated in the gesture. The body then processes the gesture by mimetically absorbing the gestural enactment, and the medium is thus different from that of verbal communication. The specific nature of how another person expresses themselves through their body is captured through this mimetic perception of the gesture. *By performing gestures that are similar to those of other people, we experience their embodiedness and their world of feeling.* In imitating another person's gestures through mimesis, a person who behaves mimetically takes a step beyond their personal boundaries towards the world of the other person who is using their own body to express and portray themselves. In this way, it becomes possible to experience a world outside ourselves.

This 'stepping outside of personal boundaries' that occurs when a person behaves mimetically, stepping out of their own structures into someone else's world of gestural portrayal and expression, is experienced as being enriching and pleasurable. The inner world is expanded through the aisthetic-mimetic taking in of an outer world, and 'live' experiences become possible. These experiences are 'live' because the distinctive manner of being of the other person becomes apprehendable through the forces of mimesis. What happens in this process is not so much that the person behaving mimetically reduces the gestures of the other person to their own frame of reference as that they expand their perception of the gestures and points of reference of the other person. Although there is no clear dividing line between the two, the main thing is that the people who are perceiving expand mimetically in order to enter the worlds of portrayal and expression of other people. What happens is not so much that what is perceived is incorporated but that a person behaving mimetically expands in the direction of the body gestures of the other person. This outward expansion has associated images. The expansion outwards leads to a pleasurable enrichment of our lives.

12.4 Gestures as ways of meaning-making

In social situations, gestures are means of meaning-making. They express feelings and articulate moods. They express concepts and internal images of individuals and their understanding of the world. Conventionalized gestures also construct homologies between abstract and concrete collective images, thus influencing the thinking of individuals. They can be understood as bodily and symbolic portrayals of these images. Often neither the people making the gestures nor those who perceive them and react to them are aware of the feelings and moods they articulate. It is in this subconscious effect that much of their social significance is to be found. This is also true of institutional gestures, together with the values, norms and claims to power that they contain. These gestures, too, are perceived and processed mimetically by those who come into contact with the institutions without this process ever becoming conscious. Often institutions 'provide' types of gestures that have evolved in them over long periods of time and which their representatives use in order to express the social expectations of the institution. By using the gestures 'provided', the representatives of these institutions follow in the tradition of these institutions and their social expectations. Firstly, this process leads to an acquisition of ready-shaped social gestures. Secondly, since it is a mimetic process, the gestures that are part of the repertoire of the institution are not simply reproduced but can be shaped by the representatives of the institutions as they acquire them. The mimesis of gestures that have already been developed by the institution gives the representatives of the institution a high degree of creative freedom. This freedom leads to a gradual change in the way gestures are portrayed and expressed and the significance they have. The mimesis of the gestures belonging to an institution also includes a portrayal of existing traditions and changes that are made in them. This process is not simply imitating but also creatively embellishing the gestures in both form and meaning. Thus, the social meaning of gestures that have retained the same form despite new social developments can change. Studies on the history of gestures and how they evolve have produced impressive evidence of this.[23]

To the extent that institutions 'embody' their claims to power in the gestures of those who represent them, these claims to power are also perceived and sustained through the mimesis of these embodied gestures. Those at whom the claims to power are directed (its 'addressees') are included in the mimetic process of acquiring and creatively shaping the institutional values and norms. The way in which, in the mimesis of institutional gestures, the addressees of institutional acts play a part in shaping the effect that they exert in turn influences the form and content of the gestures of the institutions' representatives. This reciprocal relationship between the representatives and the addressees of institutional gestures is central to the understanding of the social function of gestures. The mimesis of institutional gestures results in both the representatives of institutions and the addressees identifying with the institution, whose claims to power are affirmed each time such a gesture is made. Gestures become emblems of institutions, by means of which they distinguish themselves from other institutions or social fields. People who share in the form and meaning of such emblematic gestures identify with the institution that created them. The mimetic use of gestures produces a social togetherness in the context of which social relations are regulated, partly through gestures. Feelings of belonging are generated and affirmed by the ritual use of gestures. This is true not only of institutions but also of professional, class and gender groupings and other special interest groups.

Gestures are movements of the body whose cultural meaning changes over the course of historical processes. Thus, in today's society sitting has a different function from the function it had in the Middle Ages or when human beings first became sedentary. The meaning of gestures changes even within limited historical periods, such as the Middle Ages. Social actions are gestural or accompanied by gestures which clarify their intentions. Mimetic processes are decisive in registering, reproducing and modifying the physicality and symbolism of gestures. Inasmuch as mimesis is the ability to express and portray a relationship to the world with the body, it also creates new gestures. In this production of new gestures, mimesis uses gestural elements which it disengages from their traditional context and introduces into the new context, altering them to fit it. Or it invents new forms of gesture from the range of possibilities of bodily expression. This is what happens, for example, in the gestures of making telephone calls, taking photographs, filming and making videos.

Gestures are only possible because humans are excentric and not instinct bound. They are movements of the body, but cannot be reduced to their corporeality. They have an underlying intentionality but cannot be reduced to this intentionality. Gestures are the expression and portrayal of feelings, and relate to objects and other people. In gestures, people experience themselves and the world simultaneously. As a rule we find a reduction in perspective in gestures which is characteristic of them. In gestures, human beings shape the world and are shaped by it at the same time. In other words, *gestures are two-way – that is, they are reflexive.*

Gestures are the expression and representation of practical knowledge grounded in the body. They cannot simply be acquired rationally from language and thought. Mimetic processes are necessary. By copying gestures and assimilating them, or making ourselves similar to them, we learn to make gestures appropriate to a specific scene, to use them and adapt or change them as circumstances demand. Historical studies of their anthropological function make clear how very important performative behaviour is, socially and culturally. Gestures help to create social continuity and announce social changes and then establish them in human behaviour. Through retaining gestures, often far-reaching changes in meaning are achieved which are initially almost imperceptible. The historical transformation of gestures affects their meanings, their sensory and physical make-up or both. The mimetic acquisition of gestural competence ensures that we can perform gestures by using movements of our body, deploy them in different social contexts and adapt them to the requirements of the situation. In the course of this mimetic acquisition, we incorporate the gestures. In other words, they become part of our body and movement fantasy and thus part of a practical knowledge that is grounded in the body. This gestural body knowledge develops largely unconsciously and thus independently of our ability to control it. For this very reason, however, it has lasting effects. *This focus on the mimetic, performative, corporeal, social, ludic and imaginative aspects of the gesture* opens up new perspectives in the field of international anthropological gesture research.[24]

IV

Mimesis and cultural learning

Cultural learning as mimetic learning

One of the most important forms of learning is mimetic learning, learning through imitation. Mimetic learning is not simply imitating or copying, but a process in which human beings expand their worldviews, action repertoires and behaviour by making reference to other people and worlds. Mimetic learning is productive. It is body based and connects the individual person to the world and other people. It creates practical knowledge and is therefore a constitutive element of social, artistic and practical actions. Mimetic learning is cultural learning and as such of central importance for child-raising and education.

13.1 Mimetic learning in early childhood

Mimetic processes are initially directed towards other people. It is in mimetic processes that infants and toddlers make reference to the people with whom they live, that is, their parents, older brothers and sisters and other relatives and acquaintances. They try to make themselves similar to these people, for instance by responding to a smile with a smile. However, they also elicit the corresponding responses from the adults by employing the abilities they have already learned. In these early interactive processes, toddlers also learn about feelings. They learn to produce them in themselves in relation to other people and to evoke them in other people. Their brains evolve in interactions with their environments, that is, certain of their potential capacities develop, while others decline. The cultural conditions of this early phase of life are inscribed in the children's brains and bodies. Anyone who has not learned to see, hear, feel or speak at an early age cannot learn these abilities at a later stage.

Recent studies in primate research have shown that although elementary forms of mimetic learning also take place in other primates, human beings have a special capacity to learn through mimesis. Cultural scientists do not find this surprising. In antiquity Aristotle believed that humans have a special aptitude for learning through mimesis and for taking pleasure in mimetic processes. In the last few years, drawing on research on the social behaviour of primates and using it for comparison, developmental psychologists and cognitive psychologists have been able to establish some characteristics of human learning at this early age and to define the special features of human mimetic learning in infants and toddlers. Michael Tomasello sums up these abilities of toddlers as follows:

> they identify with other persons; perceive other persons as intentional agents like the self; engage with other persons in joint attentional activities; understand many of the causal relations that hold among physical objects and events in the world; understand the communicative intentions that other persons express in gestures, linguistic symbols, and linguistic constructions; learn through role-reversal imitation to produce for others those same gestures, symbols, and constructions; and construct linguistically based object categories and event schemas.[1]

It is through these abilities that young children become able to participate in cultural processes. They can take part in enactments of the practices and skills of the social group in which they live and acquire the cultural knowledge of that group in this way. The abilities described are indicative of the central importance of models for mimetic learning processes in young children. Children's mimetic desire to emulate adults, to become similar to or like them, enables them to identify with other people, to see them as individuals who act intentionally and to direct their attention towards something together with them (joint attention). It is this desire to become similar to older people that motivates children to understand causal relationships between the objects of the world, to comprehend the intentions of other people as they communicate them in gestures, symbols and constructions and develop categories of objects and event schemata. Infants as young as nine months are already in possession of these abilities that are inherent in the human mimetic capacities and not available to other primates at any point in their lives.[2]

13.2 Mimetic learning: Education through imitation in antiquity

As far as we know today, it was in Sicily that the concept of mimesis first evolved. 'Mimesis' is a reference to the way in which wandering players performed a comic folk play. The word comes from the everyday culture of simple people and refers to the scenes staged as part of the festivities of rich people in order to entertain them. The stagings and performances developed were often ribald and disrespectful. Thus, the term 'mimesis' initially referred to cultural performative practices and had a pronounced body-related, sensory aspect. In the fifth century BC, the term 'mimesis' was widely used in Ionia and Attica. One could already distinguish between three different shades of meaning in the pre-Platonic era, and these remain useful for describing aspects of mimetic learning today. Mimetic behaviour means: firstly, *direct imitation of animals and human beings* through speech, song and dance; secondly, the *imitation of human actions*; and finally the *recreation of images* of persons or objects in a material form.[3] In the Platonic era, the term 'mimesis' was already commonly used to refer to processes of imitation, emulation, performance and expression.

We find the term 'mimesis' used in connection with child-raising and education for the first time in Book Three of Plato's *Republic*.[4] In this work, Plato expresses the view that mimesis is the main mechanism of child-raising and education and attributes exceptional power to mimetic processes. He sees this power as deriving from a pronounced human predisposition to mimesis. In his view it is this that makes motor, sensory and linguistic development and also mental, social and personal development possible, especially in childhood. Plato believed that children and adolescents experience and acquire social behaviours as they interact with other people and experience their behaviour, picking up and incorporating values and attitudes through all their senses. He attributed particular significance not only to visual perception but also to auditory perception. He thus emphasized the importance of music and its mimetic processing for the development of the capacity of the psyche or 'soul' for experience. He distinguished between different forms of music, to which he attributed a variety of different effects on the 'souls' of young people.[5]

According to the view developed by Plato in *The Republic*, the development and learning processes of youth are made possible by their mimetic desire, which 'forces' them to emulate a model. Plato proposed that human failings should be overcome and improvement achieved by choosing the right models. There has been some controversy about the radicality of this position, which defines the life and experiences of young people in terms of a normative anthropology and a normative theory of child-raising and education.

Aristotle was the first to critique Plato's view in his *Poetics*. Although he was just as convinced of the power of mimetic processes as Plato, he came to different conclusions about it. In his view, the solution is not to expunge from our experience what is unsatisfactory and incorrigible, but rather to confront it, get to grips with it and thus 'immunize' ourselves against its power to infect us. He proposed that the best way to protect ourselves against negative role models is not to avoid them, but to tackle them. Otherwise, he thought, young people would remain vulnerable to negative influences and unable to defend themselves, and they could only develop the resilience and personal strength if they reflected on the negative models. Similar ideas also play a role in civic education today. According to this rationale, people develop solid political attitudes through critical reflection, not by developing defences against opposing views. The same applies to attitudes and values in other fields of education. Today this position is supported by the psychoanalytic insights which have demonstrated the negative consequences of avoidance and defences for psychological development.

Due to the lasting effects of mimetic learning processes on the imagination, Plato demanded that its contents should be kept under strict control and Aristotle demanded that its effects should be subject to intensive processing. Not only ideas, attitudes and values, but also forms of social living and action are learned through mimetic processes. Since young people have differing backgrounds, what they assimilate is not a mere copy of the model. The mimetic process produces something different, and it is this that makes its results independent and creative. Thus the model that the young person adopts in the mimetic act is not simply a reproduction based on outward similarity, but the person who is behaving mimetically constructs something new in which there is room for difference, particularity and creativity.

13.3 Mimetic learning: Assimilating the world and constituting the subject

In his autobiography 'Berlin Childhood around 1900', Walter Benjamin gives a good example of how the world is assimilated in mimetic learning processes. He describes how he related to places, spaces, paths, houses, objects, events, etc. as a child, how he absorbed them into his internal image world, thus 'making them his own' in his own distinctive way. Benjamin's reminiscences show how a child experiences the world through mimesis. Like magicians, children dream up similarities between themselves and the outside world. They render streets, squares and spaces and the rooms of their parental homes accessible through mimesis. It is through processes of 'making themselves similar to' or 'like' the objects that children develop their magical interpretations of the world, in which the world of things takes on a life of its own and responds to them. They 'read' the world and in the process they 'create' likenesses.[6]

By stretching out their arms and rotating them, while producing the wind with their mouths, children play at becoming a 'windmill'. In so doing they expand their repertoire of experiences. They comprehend how the wind drives a mill and experience something of the power of the wind and the power of human exploitation of nature. They grasp the fascination of human productivity. In the mimetic act of transforming themselves into a 'windmill', they experience – at least in play – the extent to which they can exert power over nature. By turning their bodies into 'windmills', they familiarize themselves with a rudimentary form of machine and with the machine-like aspects of the human body. At the same time, they learn to use their bodies as instruments of performance and expression. They not only add to their concrete performative and expressive skills, but also experience what it is like to be able to use their bodies for certain purposes and thus to gain social recognition. Such mimetic processes are accompanied by symbolic interpretations and thus also contribute to the development of thought and speech capacities.

In this childhood world, not only images but also tones, noises and sounds, scents and smells, and experiences of touch play a large role. These non-visual impressions often reach beyond the images into the unknown and the unconscious. Thus, Benjamin writes of the intoxicating sound of the air, and thus the hum of the gas burner becomes the voice of the 'little hunchback' who whispers beseeching words over the threshold of the century.[7] Or, the world of what is visible and tangible is transformed into the echo of the telephone, the 'nocturnal noises', the invisible, the unrecognizable, the anonymous. It is through mimetic processes that some of the images and sounds of early childhood become established in the 'deeper ego', out of which they may be rendered conscious again by means of optical or acoustic stimuli. The act of recall forges a mimetic link to the content of the memory which represents it in a different, specific way each time. Memories differ in intensity and meaning every time they are recalled. The difference between different acts of recall of the same event can also be understood as the difference between the construction of recall and mimetic representation.

Benjamin thought that children's ability to establish a relationship with the world, to 'read' it, becomes incorporated in language and writing. He believed that 'this mimetic gift, which was earlier the basis for clairvoyance [. . .] found its way into language and writing [. . .] thus creating for itself in language and writing the most perfect archive of nonsensuous similarity'.[8] For Benjamin, being similar and becoming similar are central elements of child development through which the child's relationship to the world, language and itself gradually evolve.

These processes enable children to fit into the structural and power relations manifested in the symbolically encoded world. Only later do they develop the capacity to distance themselves from, criticize and modify them. Using their mimetic skills, children adopt the meanings of objects and of how other people act and represent things. They use mimetic movements to build bridges to the outside world. Their mimetic activity revolves around their attempts to relate to what is other, which they want not to incorporate but to become similar to. It is characteristic of the 'mimetic impulse' that in the act of receptive perception there comes a pause, a moment of passivity.

Mimetic encounters with the world take place through all the senses, which develop as these processes progress. The quality of sensory and emotional sensitivity in adult life is dependent on this capacity of children to render the world accessible to themselves. This applies especially to the development of aesthetic sensitivity and the ability to experience compassion, sympathy, liking and love. It is through our mimetic skills that we become able to comprehend other people's feelings and sensations, without reifying them or hardening ourselves to them.

13.4 Mimetic learning: Social actions and practical knowledge

As has been demonstrated by numerous research studies in recent years, the capacity for social action is acquired mimetically in cultural learning processes. In mimetic processes people develop the skills they need to play and participate in games and ritual actions, and to exchange gifts with each other. These skills differ from culture to culture. In order to be able to act 'correctly' in each of these situations, people need practical knowledge which they acquire through sensory, body-oriented mimetic learning processes in each of these fields of action. The cultural characteristics of these forms of social action can also only be acquired by re-enacting them, creating a close but not exact replica. Practical knowledge and social actions are strongly influenced by historical and cultural contexts. This is particularly evident in rituals and in the practical knowledge that is learned in them, in which repetition and the mimetic learning associated with it play a major role.[9]

Social actions are referred to as mimetic *if, as movements, they relate to other movements, if they can be understood as bodily enactments or performances and if they are actions in their own right which can be comprehended for themselves and make reference to other actions or worlds.*[10] Conversely, actions such as mental calculations, decisions, reflex-like or routine behaviour, and also one-off actions and violations of rules are not mimetic.

Wherever someone relates their behaviour to an already-existing social practice, thereby creating a social practice themselves, a mimetic relationship arises between the two, for example when someone performs a social practice, acts in accordance with a social model or expresses a social idea with their body. These are not – as we have seen – simply acts of imitation. Mimetic actions are not mere reproductions that copy a model exactly, but include the creation of something distinctively personal.

In contrast to mimicry, where the person simply adjusts to the given conditions, mimetic processes simultaneously produce both similarities to *and* differences from other situations or people to which they make reference. By 'making ourselves similar' to situations we have previously experienced and to culturally shaped worlds, we acquire the ability to orient ourselves in a social field. Through participating in the life practices of other people, we expand our own lifeworlds and create new ways of acting and experiencing for ourselves. In this process, receptivity and activity overlap and the given world becomes interwoven with our individuality as we relate to it mimetically. We recreate situations we have experienced previously or the world outside us and make them our own by duplicating them. Not until this process takes place does the excess drive of which we had been unaware become shaped into personal wishes and needs and into an imaginary.[11] The confrontation with the outside world and the development of the self take place in the same system. The outer and inner worlds gradually become increasingly similar and can only be experienced in this reciprocal relationship. Thus, similarities develop between inside and outside and they begin to correspond to each other. We make ourselves similar to the outside world and change in the process. In this transformation, our perceptions of the external world and of ourselves are altered.

In mimetic learning processes, previous social actions are repeated. They are staged and enacted and thus become performative.[12] The reference is not created through thinking theoretically, but aisthetically, through the senses.[13] The second social action differs from the first one in that it does not engage with it directly or alter it, but simply performs it once again. And yet the mimetic actions are demonstrative and performative; when they are performed, they generate their own aesthetic qualities. Mimetic processes refer to social worlds that people have already created, which can be either real or imaginary.

The dynamic nature of social actions has to do with the fact that the knowledge needed to perform them is practical knowledge. As such, it is less subject to rational control than analytical knowledge. This is also because practical ritual knowledge is not reflexive knowledge, where the person is self-aware. It is only reflexive where there is a conflict or crisis in which the actions that arise from it require justification. If the social practice is not called into question, the practical knowledge remains only semi-conscious, as it were. Like habitus knowledge, it embraces images, schemata and forms of actions that are used to enact social actions scenically, using the body, without reflecting on whether or to what extent they are appropriate. They are simply known and used in the performance of social practices.

Practical knowledge also includes the bodily movements used in scenic displays in social actions. Disciplined and controlled practical knowledge is developed through disciplining and controlling the movements of our bodies. This knowledge is stored in the body memory, thus enabling us to perform similar forms of symbolic and scenic action. This practical knowledge derives from the forms of social action and performance that have evolved in a culture. While it is therefore distinctive, it is also limited in terms of its historical and cultural potentials.

In mimetic processes, pre-existing worlds are modified and reshaped through imitation. This is the innovative element of mimetic acts. Social practices are mimetic when they relate to other actions and can themselves be grasped as social arrangements which are both independent social practices and linked to other actions. It is the development of practical knowledge in the course of mimetic processes that makes social actions possible. The practical knowledge that is relevant for social actions is bodily and ludic, while at the same time being historical and cultural. It is built up in *face-to-face situations*. Semantically, it is not unambiguous. It has imaginary components, is more than mere intentionality, has several shades of meaning and can be seen in social enactments and performances of religion, politics and everyday life.

13.5 Mimetic learning: Enculturation through simulation and differentiation

Finally, I would like to add some thoughts about the importance of mimetic learning processes for the development of communities, the generation of cultural knowledge and the upbringing and education of children as thinking and responsible individuals.

(1) In contrast to imitation and simulation, when we use the term 'mimesis', we are emphasizing that there is an external world that we can come closer to and to which we can make ourselves similar, but in which it is not possible for us to transcend ourselves and our preconceptions. Thus, there will always be a difference between our subjectivity and the outside world. This outside world towards which we move can be another person, part of the environment or a constructed imaginary world. In each of these cases, there is a movement towards an outside world. When this outside world is transformed by the senses and imagination into internal images, sound images and worlds of touch, smell and taste, in the course of mimetic learning processes, vivid experiences are produced that are inextricably connected with our corporeality.

(2) Mimetic learning processes are in fact inherent in our corporeality and therefore begin at a very early age. They take place before I and Thou become split and before the separation of subject and object. They play a decisive role in psychological and socio-development and the development of the persona and extend into the preconscious. Since they are inextricably linked to the earliest processes of the constitution of the body through birth, weaning and desire, their effects are very long-lasting.

(3) We experience the world, ourselves and other people through mimesis even before we develop thought processes and language. Mimetic processes are linked to the various senses. Mimetic abilities play an especially important role in the learning of motor skills, and language acquisition is also inconceivable without them. In early childhood, it is through mimetic practices that children experience the world.

(4) Sexual desire is awakened and developed in mimetic processes. Children experience the difference between the sexes and develop a gender identity. Desire behaves mimetically towards other desires – it is kindled and kindles itself. In the process, it develops a dynamic that frequently becomes opposed to the subject's intentions. Existing ideas are modified and new ones are tried out. Connections between constantly changing schemes and experiments are developed. Many of these processes take place unconsciously.

5) Mimetic processes support the polycentricity of the individual. They extend into layers of corporeality, sensuality and desire which are determined by forces that are different from those of the conscious mind. These include aggression, violence and destruction, which are likewise awoken and learned in mimetic processes. They can become especially powerful in group and

crowd situations, since in such situations the individual's centre of control and responsibility is replaced by the authority of the group or crowd and a kind of delirious contagion renders actions possible which the individual would not be capable of performing on their own.

6) It is in mimetic processes that children, young people and adults learn values, attitudes and standards that are embodied in the institutions of the family, school and business enterprises. As, for example, the discussion on the 'hidden curriculum'[14] has shown, the values that are actually operative in an institution may stand in contradiction to the institution's conscious image of itself. Awareness of these contradictions can be achieved by means of institutional analysis and the methods of ideology critique, consultancy and changes in the institution, providing a basis for corrective action.

7) The educational and socializing effects of individual people are also conveyed far more in mimetic processes than is generally assumed. Here again there is a discrepancy between the educator's perception of themselves and the effects of their actual actions. The unconscious and unintended effects on children and young people, which may, for example, be conveyed by the personalities of teachers and preschool teachers, are frequently long-lasting. The way in which individual teachers feel, think and make decisions, in particular, is experienced and learned in mimetic processes. Assimilation and rejection and the effects of these play a different role in each individual case, although this is difficult to assess. The difficulty of assessing the effects of educators' behaviour is also due to the fact that people evaluate the same behaviour of a teacher or preschool teacher differently at different stages of their life.

8) The process of making places, spaces and objects one's own through mimesis is of major importance for the development of the subject. Children relate to their environments through mimesis from early childhood onwards, and they experience them as 'peopled with animate beings'. They expand themselves into their environments by making themselves similar, absorb them into their internal imaginary worlds and broaden their skills and knowledge in this way. Since these worlds are always historically and culturally determined and the objects in them have meaning, that is, they are symbolically encoded, the children and young people become encultured in these mimetic processes.

9) Objects and institutions, imaginary figures and practical actions are embedded in societal power relations which are also conveyed, along with other information, through the processes of becoming similar. They are learned and experienced in mimetic processes, but they are not usually grasped to begin with. If experiences are to be fully fathomed, they need to be analysed and reflected

upon. It is frequently the case that they can only be appropriately assessed and judged once this work of analysis and reflection has been done. Mimetic processes are important for the development of lively experiences. Analysis and reflection are required for these experiences to develop.

10) Mimetic processes are ambivalent. The impulse to become similar is inherent in them and can be carried through independently of the value of the pre-existing world. Thus, people can make themselves similar to things that are stiff and lifeless which block their development or lead it in the wrong direction. Mimesis can degenerate into simulation and mimicry. However, it can also result in our 'expanding into' the world around us; it can bridge the gap to the outside world and thus lead to new learning experiences. Characteristically making ourselves similar to the outside world through mimesis is a non-violent process. The aim is not to shape or alter the world, but rather to develop and grow.

11) Mimetic processes can teach us to relate to other people in a non-instrumental way. Mimetic movements leave the other person as they are and do not attempt to change them. They are open to what is foreign in that they allow it to remain as it is and approach it, but do not try to dissolve the difference. The mimetic impulse to make ourselves similar to what is other accepts this difference; it forgoes clarity or non-ambiguity for the sake of the otherness of the other, who could only be rendered unambiguous by being reduced to the same, to something that is familiar. We ensure that our experience will be rich and the alien different by forgoing clarity.

12) In mimetic movements, we learn by interpreting a world that we have created from a world that went before, which has also been interpreted. We reinterpret a world that is already interpreted. This is true even when we repeat or simply reproduce. Thus, a gesture that is made over and over again creates meaning structures that are different from those it produced when it was made for the first time. It isolates an object or an event from its usual context and produces a perspective that differs from that in which the pre-existing world was perceived. Isolation and switching of perspectives are characteristics of aesthetic processes that are connected with the close affinity between mimesis and aesthetics. Mimetic reinterpretation is a novel perception, a seeing-as. In mimetic actions, there is an intention to recreate a symbolically constructed world in such a fashion that it is seen as a specific one.

14

The intangible cultural heritage

Intangible heritage is a central element of our cultural heritage and of the human imaginary. This is clearly expressed in the *masterpieces* and *second proclamation of the oral and intangible heritage*.[1] It is even more evident in the processes that since the passing of the 2003 UNESCO convention have led to intangible cultural practices being selected and rendered visible worldwide as cultural assets not only of a country or region, but of humanity as a whole. The convention, which was adopted by more than 180 states, distinguishes the following five domains of the intangible cultural heritage:

(a)   Oral traditions and expressions, including language as a vehicle of the intangible cultural heritage (e.g., traditional songs, sagas, fairy stories and idioms)

(b)   The performing arts (e.g. music, dance and forms of drama)

(c)   Social practices, rituals and festive events (e.g. parades and processions, carnivals and games)

(d)   knowledge and practices concerning nature and the universe (e.g. traditional healing procedures, agricultural knowledge)

(e)   Traditional craftsmanship

The cultural practices that exist in these domains in the individual countries and regions are diverse. There has also been a sharp increase in research on the cultural heritage. Widely differing perspectives have been selected as topics. For example, there is an initiative for a project promoted by the European Union which is concerned with the relationships between the intangible cultural heritage and sustainable regional development. Here the goal is to combine cultural traditions with economic and social regional development. In what follows, I show how bodily cultural practices, their performative aspect, the way in which they are passed down from one generation to the next through mimesis and the possibility of using them to enable people to experience alterity are all interconnected. The aim is to show what the specific characteristics of the intangible cultural heritage are and what role it plays in a globalized world that is determined by cultural diversity. We will be taking a closer look at four characteristics of the intangible cultural heritage that are important for understanding the cultural and societal significance of the intangible cultural heritage:

- The human body
- The performative character of social practices
- Mimesis and mimetic learning
- Otherness or alterity

14.1 The human body

Whereas architectural monuments are easy to identify and can usually be relatively well protected, the various forms of the intangible cultural heritage are much more difficult to recognize, transmit from each generation to the next, modify and sustain. The architectural works of the world cultural heritage are made of durable materials. The different forms of the intangible cultural heritage are less permanent and are subject to historical and cultural change. Whereas architectural works are tangible cultural objects, the forms and figurations of the intangible cultural heritage have the human body as a medium, and this is constantly changing. If we want to understand the special nature of the intangible cultural heritage, we must first grasp what a central role the body plays as its vehicle.[2]

Assuming that the human body is the most important medium of the intangible cultural heritage has several consequences. The body-based practices of the intangible cultural heritage are determined by the course of history and the temporality of the human body. They are dependent upon the dynamics of space and time. Unlike cultural monuments and objects, these practices are not fixed, but are subject to transformation processes that are tied to societal change and exchanges between human beings and cultural processes. Since they are linked to the dynamics of living, intangible cultural practices have the nature of processes and are much more sensitive to homogenizing and standardizing influences. They are therefore also more difficult to protect against the processes of globalization.

For the practices of the intangible cultural heritage to be staged and performed, each person needs to have a certain knowledge of their body. When practices such as dancing, playing games and rituals are staged and performed, it is frequently the case that a collective body arises out of the individual bodies. In order to understand this process, two viewpoints are important. Firstly, the intangible practices are historically and culturally dependent. They thus express and portray the respective society and help to create feelings of community and belonging. Secondly, there is an aesthetic aspect which is associated with the bodily aspects of the practices, and without which these practices and their effects cannot be fully understood.[3]

14.2 The performativity of social practices

The assumption that the human body is the medium for the practices of the intangible cultural heritage has implications for how these practices are perceived and understood. In my view, it is above all the performative nature of the rituals, games, dances and other practices that makes them socially and culturally sustainable. Since these practices are body based, we also need to take into account their physical aspect and investigate how these intangible cultural practices are executed by means of special 'arrangements' of the body. It is important, however, to consider from which body images and which images of social life the practices of the intangible cultural heritage are derived. At all events we need to investigate the historical and cultural dimensions of the way the body is viewed and used that are expressed in the social practices of the cultural heritage.

When we analyse the performative character of these practices, many intangible 'aspects' of culture and society which stage and perform differences and alterity become evident. As a result of their performative nature, these practices create communities and cultural identities and make it possible for a community to establish a cultural continuity of its members from one generation to the next. The practices of the intangible cultural heritage bring past, present and future into a dynamic relationship with each other. Not only do these practices pass on the traditional cultural values, they also help to adapt these values to people's current needs and requirements. Intangible cultural practices are windows on to a society that make it possible to grasp its cultural identity and dynamics. If they only embody traditional values and do not make reference to the concerns of contemporary society, they fail to fulfil their task, become stereotypical and lose their function of engendering community. If they adapt too fast to the challenges of globalization and relinquish their specific cultural character, they likewise fail to use their power to create social identity.

14.3 Mimesis and mimetic learning

Practices inherent to the intangible cultural heritage are learned by younger generations, for the most part in mimetic processes. Practical knowledge is acquired in mimetic processes as implicit 'tacit' knowledge, particularly when people participate in social stagings and performances. The social behaviour learned in mimetic processes is not simply copied, but rather reshaped in processes of creative imitation based on models and examples. In this process, those people who are behaving mimetically want to become similar to their models, but without actually becoming them, due to the differences between them and their models. These processes of 'becoming similar' differ from person to person and depend on how people behave towards the world, other people and themselves. In mimetic processes, people take an impression or imprint of the social world, so to speak, and make it into a part of themselves. In this process, the intangible cultural heritage is passed down to the next generation and altered in the process.[4]

It would be difficult to overestimate the significance of mimetic processes for the transmission of the practices of the intangible cultural heritage. These mimetic processes are sensory, tied to the human body, make reference to human behaviour and are often unconscious.[5] In these processes, people incorporate images and schemata of social practices which then become part of their internal image and imaginative worlds. Mimetic processes transfer the world of the intangible cultural heritage into the imaginary. They help to enrich and expand this imaginary world and thus also contribute to people's development and education. In mimetic processes, the intangible cultural heritage becomes part of the individual's practical knowledge. This knowledge develops in the context of bodily performances and plays an important role in generating modified forms of cultural performances. The practical knowledge results from mimetic processing of performative behaviour.[6]

Since mimesis and performativity are intertwined with each other in the development of practical knowledge, repetition plays a major role in the transmission of intangible cultural knowledge. If cultural competence is to develop, a behaviour that is socially shaped must be repeated. As it is repeated, some reference must be made to the current context, modifying the behaviour in the process. Without repetition, without the mimetic reference to something current or past, no cultural competence can develop. Repetition is therefore a central aspect of the transmission of intangible cultural heritage.[7]

14.4 Otherness

The practices of the intangible cultural heritage are important forms of expression of cultural diversity and otherness. In order to understand diversity, we need to be sensitized to the otherness of other people, which is enacted and expressed in the practices of the intangible cultural heritage. In order to avoid reducing difference to the same and homogenizing cultural diversity, we need to open up to cultural heterogeneity, that is, otherness or alterity. Only by developing a sense of the value of alterity can we prevent globalization processes from leading to a uniformity that reduces diversity.[8] Outstanding testimonies and everyday social practices of the intangible cultural heritage play an important role in promoting experiences of otherness.

Over the course of history, Western culture has developed the following three strategies to reduce alterity: *egocentrism, logocentrism* and *ethnocentrism.*[9]

Egocentrism. Elias, Foucault and Beck have described the processes that that play a role in the constitution of the modern subject and the development of egocentrism.[10] Technologies of the self are involved in the development of the subject. Many of these strategies are linked to the notion of a self-sufficient self that is supposed to lead its own life and has to develop its own life history. However, the self-sufficing self has multifarious unintended side effects. People are often overtaxed by the processes associated with self-determination. Other processes oppose self-determination and the hope of being able to act autonomously. While egocentrism is what constitutes the modern subject, giving it the strength to survive, to assert itself and adjust, egocentrism also results in an inability to accept differences and a tendency to reduce diversity. And although this subject is successful in its attempt to see others purely in terms of their functionality and usefulness, at the same time it frequently misses its mark. This insight opens up new perspectives for dealing with alterity as a new field of knowledge and research.

Logocentrism. Because of our logocentric bias, we view the Other through the eyes of European rationality. We only accept what follows the laws of rationality. Everything else is excluded. Those who uphold reason are right, even if this reason is reduced to a functional rationality. Thus, parents are usually considered to be right in conflicts with their children, and civilized people are considered to be more right than so-called primitive people, healthy people more so than sick people, and so on and so forth. A person who is rational is seen as being superior to those who have less developed forms of rational action at their disposal. The more a person's language and rationality deviate from the generally accepted norm, the more difficult it is to understand them. Nietzsche, Freud, Adorno and many others have criticized this attitude of self-sufficiency of rationality and pointed out that human life is only partly accessible to rationality.

Ethnocentrism. In the course of history, ethnocentrism has permanently destroyed many forms of otherness. Todorov, Greenblatt and other authors have analysed the processes that have led to the destruction of foreign cultures. The colonization of Central and South America in the name of Christ and the Christian kings is one of the most appalling examples.[11] The conquering of South America led to the subjugation of its indigenous cultures. The values, ideas and religions of the indigenous populations were replaced by the forms and contents of European culture. All that was foreign and different was destroyed. The indigenous peoples were unable to grasp the perfidiousness of the Spaniards. They learned from experience that their friendliness was not what it seemed to be. Promises were not made with the intention of keeping them, but with the intention of misleading and deceiving the natives. No action served the purpose it purported to serve. The colonializing behaviour was legitimized by the interests of the crown, the Christian mission and the assumed inferiority of the indigenous population. Together with the additional economic motives, this led to the destruction of differing kinds of worldview.

Egocentrism, logocentrism and ethnocentrism are interlinked. As strategies of creating a distorted image of the Other, they reinforce each other. Their common goal is to destroy otherness and replace it with what is familiar. The destruction of the diversity of cultures is the result. People were only able to survive if they adopted the culture of their conquerors. This was particularly tragic in cases where it led to the extinguishing of the local and regional cultures.

Heterological thinking. Practices of the intangible cultural heritage can sensitize people to alterity and help them gradually to learn to deal with foreignness and difference and to develop an interest in what is non-identical. If we are successful in perceiving the otherness in the practices of the intangible cultural heritage in our own culture, we can begin to develop an interest in what is foreign in other cultures and to value it. At the same time, we can learn to see ourselves through the eyes of others and thus to perceive ourselves from the standpoint of the Other, that is, heterologically.[12]

14.5 Future prospects

Exposure to practices of the intangible cultural heritage can lead to important experiences of intercultural diversity and alterity which are of major importance in our globalized world. For the countless people who today belong to *more* than one culture, the number of whom is rapidly increasing due to the large streams of migrants, this is an opportunity to learn to deal with the cultural differences within themselves, in their environments and in their encounters with other people. Since identity is not possible without alterity, intercultural education consists in forging a relational connection between an irreducible subject and numerous forms of alterity. In these processes hybrid forms of culture are also gaining in importance. At all events understanding other people helps our understanding of ourselves and vice versa. Grasping this interdependence leads us to the insight that our understanding of ourselves as subjects and others is limited. This insight also helps to counteract the risk that in response to the disenchantment of the world and the decreasing cultural diversity in the world people will encounter only themselves and what they themselves produce, and that as a result of this dearth of difference our experience of the world and ourselves will be diminished.

In contrast, encounters with practices of the intangible cultural heritage offer us countless opportunities to experience foreignness and alterity. This occurs through mimetic recreation of foreign configurations, arrangements and techniques. Mimetic imitation of foreign practices leads to the development of new hybrid practices in which it is not or no longer possible to clearly determine the origins of the individual structural elements. In view of the fact that more and more people are living in several cultures simultaneously, these hybrid forms of portrayal and expression that lead to new intangible cultural practices are gaining in importance.[13]

15

Family rituals

Rituals not only make a family into a community but also generate an imaginary of this community which forms a bond between the members of the family and is highly important for sustaining the family as a group. Feelings of mutual belonging, reliability and sharing common ground arise not only in the ritual practices of everyday life but also in the family's memories and aspirations for the future. These feelings are constantly (re-)produced and dynamically modified in rituals with the aid of mimetic processes.

Rituals establish a balance between stability and change in a family and provide the dynamics between the family members with a frame in which they can (re-)present or portray themselves and develop. Rituals structure the relationship between the generations and the sexes. They socialize, rear and educate the younger generation and form their imaginary.

Family rituals and how they are absorbed into the imaginary of the family members range from rituals performed at events that happen only once such as weddings, births, confirmations (first communions) and funerals, at one end of the spectrum, to the everyday rituals of shared mealtimes, outings, shopping trips and watching television together in the evening at the other, with the intensive, repetitive rituals of Christmas, birthday celebrations, family get-togethers and family holidays in the middle of the spectrum. If you ask people what they remember best from their childhoods, they often describe ritualized situations and arrangements in which the bonds within the family were strengthened.

Rituals are constantly taking place on the 'family stage'. They enact family traditions and patterns of family interactions and perform them. Rituals stage the symbolic knowledge shared by a family,[1] strengthen the family's portrayal of itself and support the reproduction of the family rules. Family rituals are social practices that are of central significance for the development of a family style and a family identity.

In view of the fact that there is an extensive body of research on families, it is surprising that researchers have paid relatively little attention to family rituals to date.[2] Some studies carried out in English-speaking countries have investigated the intergenerational nature of rituals.[3] Family rituals of transition have also been studied and typologies of rituals have been developed.[4] The uses of rituals in family therapy have also been investigated,[5] resulting in self-help guides for families. These guides give families tips on how they can structure rituals. For example, they point out how important it is for families to plan rituals, birthday celebrations, school-leaving celebrations and family trips together.

In Germany there have been very few comprehensive ethnographic studies providing insight into the processes of rituals and the constitution of the imaginaries of families, which might contribute as case studies to our understanding of the complex way in which family rituals function. There have been just a few studies that have investigated individual family rituals. These include, for example, the rituals of family mealtimes, of the transition from childhood to adolescence at confirmations and of family holidays.[6] Although today fewer and fewer people are living together in families or extended families, almost 66 per cent of young people still consider living together as a family to be pivotal for having a fulfilled life. Many family researchers, counsellors and therapists also see rituals as a means of enhancing feelings of family coherence, togetherness and solidarity and thus of promoting the keeping families together.

15.1 Central structural characteristics

With their rituals and stagings and performances, families present themselves to the outside world and themselves. Inward-looking rituals demonstrate to the family members what family it is that they are living in and with which they identify. Outward-looking family rituals present each family's unique style. In this way they provide the members of the family with a social identity. In this process, several characteristics, schemata and iconic representations of meaning are of special importance and are described in what follows.

Regulation of space and time. Family rituals alter how a family organizes space and time in its daily routines. Whereas on weekdays a family has breakfast and the conversations that accompany it within the space of twenty minutes in the kitchen, on Sundays the same family will have breakfast in the living room. They may light a candle and spend an hour chatting together. A time and space structure arises that differs markedly from that of breakfast in the kitchen and in which small 'family dramas' are staged and performed from time to time. For example, a small 'court scene' may be staged during a family breakfast, the wife reminding her husband to replace a salad server that he has broken. The son may immediately identify with his father and point out that he had too much to do and that that was the reason why he has not yet found time to buy a new salad server. Siding with her mother, his little sister points out that a person who has caused damage must rectify it. The daily conversations over meals contain numerous sequences in which gender behaviour is learned.

Rituals also create special space and time structures at large family celebrations. For example, on Christmas Eve the living room is altered by a number of objects that are only used on these days. One could say that they transform the everyday living room into the stage of the Christmas celebration, with the Christmas tree, the candles, the Christmas carols, foods eaten at Christmas and presents. They transform the everyday living room into a celebratory space for special actions. The way time is handled also changes: during the festivities, it slows down. The family members devote more time to each other than usual. For the present-giving, they get together in front of the Christmas tree. The present-giving ceremony is accompanied by intensive interactions and conversations between the family members which strengthen the feelings of intimacy and belonging. The space and time rules created by rituals make it possible to change interactive and communicative processes.

In rituals of transition where a family member or the whole family enters into a new social situation, changes in space and time play an important role.[7] For children, for example, these are transitions to a new type of school, which, because it is so important for the child's future life, is marked by a ritual and the temporal and spatial changes associated with it.

After the ceremony of the first day at school, a child no longer goes to nursery school, but to school, she/he becomes a schoolchild, a student. After starting school and making the transition into the space of school, far-reaching changes take place which are already prefigured in the ritual of the first day at school.[8]

Demonstrative and ludic character. Family rituals have a demonstrative component that is expressed both inwardly and outwardly in the ritual enactments. Rituals with an inward orientation are intended to show in what a 'unique' family its members live, while those directed towards the outside demonstrate each family's own specific style. The spectrum of ritual modes of presentation and action is broad. Each family therefore endeavours to develop its own distinctive style, from which its members derive their (family) identity.

In moments of social insecurity that arise in family crises, this component, in particular, can assume a greater importance. It then serves to demonstrate to the family members that they share a common ground and belong together, in spite of all their problems. The demonstrative character of rituals is expressed in their performativity, in *how* they are staged and performed. It results from the multidimensionality of rituals, in which several, sometimes even contradictory, layers of meaning are superimposed upon one another.[9]

Despite their conservative tendency family rituals are open to change. It is important that existing ritual schemes be constantly transformed. Without these dynamics of change, rituals become locked in stereotypes. Contrary to widespread misconceptions, they draw their strength from the fact that they do not contain any rigid repetitions, that is, they do not remain the same, but change in accordance with the time, space and context.[10] The dynamics of rituals result from the fact that in social life there are no simple copies. Every ritual action must be redesigned and carried out differently from before, and changes are therefore inevitable. Families construct variations on existing ritual schemes and are playful in how they implement the traditional performances and customs. Due to this freedom they enjoy them anew every time they stage and perform them. The present-giving in the family described earlier is a good example. Some of the presents were items of clothing that would have had to have been bought anyway. But wrapping them in Christmas paper and making presents out of them made them part of the Christmas ritual, and exchanging them allowed the family members to add playful comments to the flow of their feelings and to experience moments of intensive togetherness. If such playful or ludic variations are not present, young people, in particular, start to grumble and complain about the boredom of fixed rituals, which ultimately have to be replaced by new ones.

Performative character. The defining characteristic of family rituals is that the members of the family act together in them. Their actions are based on a mis en scène which leads to a ritual performance. In the case of the 'major' family rituals such as Christmas, birthday celebrations and holiday trips, this is clear. However, many everyday rituals also require a mis en scène. We see this with shared mealtimes, going-to-sleep rituals with small children and when families spend the evening together watching television. Sometimes these family rituals have a demonstrative character through which the family expresses aspects of its identity. Reading two versions of the nativity story can be understood as a family mis en scène or performance which expresses the fact that a religious affiliation is an important element of the family identity.

The performative character of family rituals has three aspects,[11] one of which consists in the fact that family rituals are cultural performances. They derive their meaning from the fact that they are part of a culture and can only be understood within the context of that culture. The Christmas festivities in Germany and the New Year's celebrations in Japan are examples of this. If we do not know anything about Japanese culture, we cannot understand the specific character of the New Year's celebrations. The family ritual needs to be contextualized in order to be able to grasp its historical and cultural character. Language and speech play an important role in the performance of family rituals. John Austin drew attention to the fact that utterances can be actions.[12] This is true, for example, of the blessing that is given to family members by a member of the clergy during a church service. Here the words of the blessing are a religious act. In the moment in which they are spoken, God's blessing is conveyed by the priest. And finally, the staging and performance, that is the performativity of family rituals, has an aesthetic quality which is of substantial importance for the effect of the ritual arrangement. Thus, for example, the aforementioned German family reported that they had spent the previous Christmas in Australia where there had not been a Christmas tree. It had not been Christmassy and wintry, but hot and summery. They had not been able to celebrate Christmas 'properly'. The Japanese family stressed how important it was on the morning of New Year's Day to eat the foods in very specific forms and arrangements. They explained that it was this that differentiated them from meals on other days; this was what made the New Year's meal special.

Repetition. Repetition is a constitutive element of family rituals.[13] However, there are differences in the frequency of the repetition. Everyday meals are repeated regularly, while the festive Christmas meal only takes place once a year. Rare rituals such as those conducted at weddings, births and funerals are of a high emotional intensity. Because they differ from the family's everyday life and emphasize significant events, they leave a lasting impression in the memories of the family members. When they are repeated, memories of previous rituals in which something special happened keep surfacing. Future celebrations are also imagined. Playing with ritual acts in the imagination in this way helps family members to feel assured of the special nature of the ritual proceedings in question. With everyday rituals in the family it is different – here it is less the individual stagings and performances that are remembered. Since they are intertwined, they are remembered more as repetitive arrangements. The socializing effects of these rituals arise mainly from the similarity and frequency of these ritual arrangements.

Memory and recall. Since the family is still one of the most important sites where learning takes place, many parents are aware of how important rituals and ritualizations are for the success of learning processes in the family. The repetitive character of ritual actions plays a central role in the development of the memory and the capacity to remember. The development of the *memory for routinized bodily skills* begins in early childhood aided by rituals and ritual arrangements, for example when children learn to walk or ride a bicycle, the same movements are repeated again and again. Ritualized everyday activities also leave traces in the *priming memory*, which contains unconscious perceptions that help children to orient themselves in their environments. Walter Benjamin's 'Berlin Childhood around 1900' gives many examples in which these processes are described.[14] The *perceptual memory* is developed in children's games that are repeated time and again and assure the consistency of their perception. When, for example, children twist their heads playfully and look at the world from an unusual perspective, they discover that their perception changes, but the world does not. This experience (re)assures them of the consistency of their perception of the world. Similarly, the acquisition of knowledge in *semantic memory* that can be recalled irrespective of context is dependent upon ritualized language games. To develop this memory, children repeat, for example, words or sentences together with their parents or older siblings for as long as they need to in order to be able to reproduce them in different contexts without help. Rituals are particularly important for the formation of the *autobiographical memory*, out of which memories can be transformed into intentional actions. These memories, which are available to the conscious mind, help subjects to assure themselves of their life histories and to develop their individuality.[15]

Rituals and ritual arrangements not only help to create the memories of individuals but are no less important for the creation of collective and family memories. In our family memories, we share memories of ritualized events with other members of our families. When we remember these events together, we feel that we belong to our family. The memories of such events are kept alive through the ritual repetition of family narratives. For the members of the family, their memory is the collective reference point that creates and sustains community between them. In crisis situations such as divorce, for example, the memories have to be reconstructed. Here rituals play an important role.

Mimetic learning. In ritual arrangements, numerous imitation processes take place in families, also between the generations. They make a central contribution to the formation of the identities of the individual family members and the collective identity of the family. The younger children, in particular, want to become like their parents and older siblings. This desire to 'become similar' has physical and sensual foundations. The child takes up, as it were, an 'imprint' of its parents and siblings into its inner world of images and imagination. This process, which takes place largely outside of consciousness, is not merely an act of copying but also an active and creative event. With the help of imitation, children 'create' themselves as social and cultural persons. They can only produce themselves as social and individual subjects with reference to their parents and siblings.

Due to the performative character of rituals, mimetic processes frequently take place in them. This also becomes clear in the small 'family tribunal' sketched out earlier. The son behaves mimetically towards the father and the daughter towards the mother. The behaviour of both has to do with the division of labour within the family and thus implicitly with questions of competence and power. Families organize work processes in ritualized action sequences. The ritualized nature of these sequences often conceal power relations by suggesting that everyone has always acted in this way, that it is thus 'natural' to continue to do so and that it is not therefore necessary to change them.[16]

A wide range of social skills are acquired in family rituals. This applies above all to the children who see *how* their parents act and acquire action skills of their own by imitating their parents' behaviour mimetically, the skills thus being based not in theoretical, but in practical knowledge. This knowledge that has been acquired mimetically through participation in rituals is an implicit practical knowledge that does not generally become conscious. Its central importance for the ability to lead a more or less successful life has long been underestimated; however, practical knowledge is of extraordinary importance for social action. This knowledge is acquired in the ritual processes of 'rendering oneself similar' to others through which it becomes increasingly possible to shape one's own world. In recent years, the mimetic character of the acquisition of this knowledge has been investigated and confirmed in several sciences working in different paradigms.[17]

Family rituals are normative stagings that make an important contribution to the shaping of the individual and collective imaginaries and thus to the formation of identity. They are physical performances and contribute to the development of individual skills and to the embodiment of relationships of authority and recognition. They are repetitive, are open to change and promote mimetic learning, in which homogeneity and collectivity, performativity and symbolism play a role. Especially today, when it is becoming more and more difficult for people to live together in families and there is often talk of the family being in crisis, rituals and their imaginary points of reference play an important role in supporting the way family members live together that has long escaped notice.

Whereas to date we have based our understanding mainly on families who live together, irrespective of whether the parents are married or not, the question of the meaning of rituals and imaginary schemata also arises in relation to the many families where the parents are divorced and the parents now need to maintain their relationships with their children, for the sake of the children. In family therapies there is widespread agreement that in the majority of cases modes of living together must be sought that ensure children unbroken stability in their relationships with their closest caregivers. Differences of opinion can usually be dealt with through rituals without having to be explicitly addressed every time they occur. Rituals help to apportion or assign responsibility for children. Also, in patchwork families, rituals offer new ways to create a sense of togetherness. Further research and work with rituals are needed to help us use their creative potential of rituals to shape different modes of family life.

Family happiness

One of the problems that is shamefully neglected today but is central to education and child-rearing is the question as to how children, young people and adults can be helped to lead a good and fulfilling life. It is not sufficient to equate education with the achievement of curricular learning objectives, however important this may be in the individual case. Such goals only account for the visible and measurable part of education. To use the iceberg simile, the goals of education, the achievement of which is generally what is measured, are only the (visible) tip of the iceberg, that is, the effects of the educational processes. However, the effects of education go much deeper than that, extending into layers of the personality which are not visible to others or the environment, and of which even the subjects themselves are often not aware. The ultimate goal of all educational efforts is to enable people to lead a fulfilled and happy life. In all phases of education, we must ask ourselves how our educational interventions help children, young people and adults learn how to lead a fulfilled life. When we speak of a happy life, this does not mean that transient periods of suffering are excluded. Without suffering, there can be no education for human beings. This was evident to the Greek philosopher Menander. He put it this way: *Ho me dareis anthropos ou paideuetai*: the human being who has not suffered ill-treatment has not been educated. It is of course nonetheless important to support young people to lead a fulfilled life through work, successful communication and interaction with other people and to take an interest in social and political tasks that currently face society.

Life history research is particularly important for educational science because it informs us about how people experience and process the events of their lives, including their upbringing and education. We learn how and why people attribute significance and meaning to the events of their lives and what significances and meanings these are. We need life history research in order to learn something about how educational interventions exert their effects at a deeper level. However, it is not only the narratives that are important. The images and the performativity of educational practices are no less important. In other words, in addition to life narratives there is also a need to reconstruct and conduct research on the images that live in the imaginaries of human beings and to reconstruct important performative practices. Educational ethnography has developed some important methods with which to obtain this information. These include narrative interviews, group discussions and methods of participatory and video-aided participant observation. With the first two methods, the task is to reconstruct and interpret the meanings constructed by subjects, groups and institutions with the aid of focusing metaphors. The observational methods aim to gain access to areas of life that are important to the subjects but of which they are not initially aware. The task here is to perceive, reconstruct and interpret the performative character of socializing and educational practices, that is, the staging and performance of the body. The transformation of performative actions into images and iconic signs plays an important role for memory. The domain of performative action and knowledge is particularly important for life history research, since it often has to do with practical, that is, implicit, knowledge that has an effect on our actions, but is beyond our awareness. If we are to understand the meaning of performative practices, we need to view them from the outside, even more so than with memories that can be expressed in language.

To illustrate this in more concrete terms, I would like to present some results from a German Japanese ethnographic study on the well-being and happiness of the family. In this study I wanted to show how important the quest for happiness and a fulfilled life is for people and how important the family is for achieving it, since it is often in our families that we have our first experiences of a successful life, but also of an unsuccessful one.

To lead a happy life, not only do we need to conduct our lives accordingly, but we must also have the associated images and schemata in our imaginaries. They provide an important basis for evaluating everyday family events.

16.1 Performing happiness in the family: A German Japanese study

Everybody wants to have a happy and fulfilled life. What do we understand by happiness? How are family and happiness linked? How do people lead a happy life and how does the family contribute to this? There are now countless self-help books, newspaper articles, television programmes and websites that seek to give answers to this question. In what follows, we look at the role played by the family in well-being and happiness.

We did not investigate what happiness is, but more cautiously posed the question as to how families stage their happiness, how they perform it and how they produce it. What a happy and fulfilled life looks like and how it is created is one of the central issues of religion and philosophy, sociology, psychology, education and anthropology. The answers vary. In fact, they may even contradict each other, and they are often so complex that they cannot be understood without considering the historical and cultural contexts in which they are given. The aim of this study was to describe and analyse how families create their well-being and happiness in six case studies in Germany and Japan. Following a long tradition in cultural anthropology, we investigated a family ritual that serves as a window on to our own and other cultures.

In three German Japanese research teams, we studied Christmas celebrations in three German families and the New Year's celebrations in three Japanese families. We wanted to find out how these families celebrate the annual festival that is most important for the family in such a way that their members are satisfied and happy. We were interested to see what commonalities and differences the culturally mixed research teams would identify in families from such different cultures. We used participant and video-supported observation, interviews and group discussions, photographs and films and also historical and cultural analyses to capture the different stagings and performances of family rituals and demonstrated how their performative character helped to create happiness in these families at these annual festivities. It was not easy to find six families who were willing to permit an international research team to be present at their family celebrations and to adhere to the criteria of *theoretical sampling* in their selection.[1] The families all belonged to the upper middle class, within which they covered a broad spectrum. In our mixed-culture teams, we found that there were different, overlapping cultural perspectives on the perception and interpretation of family rituals. This led to a new form of communicative validation which confronted us with numerous methodological problems due to the complexity of the study and the associated unanswered questions.[2]

Our ethnographic study on happiness in families from different cultural backgrounds also contributes to biographical research on emotions. With our research in these two very different cultures, we were able to investigate a broad spectrum of cultural differences within which the diversity of the ways in which happiness the families created happiness through ritual became very evident. Keeping these differences, which reached right into the depth structures of the families and their members, in mind, we were able to identify a number of elements that are transcultural and help to create happiness in families during the festive period. These will be described in what follows.

16.1.1 Happiness as the meaning and purpose of life: Some historical perspectives

How differently happiness can be understood is evidenced by the diversity of the terms used to denote it in the European cultures and Japan. To reconstruct them semantically and in a way that takes the context into account would require an analysis of its own, which would go beyond the scope of this chapter. However, a certain understanding of these terms helps us to appreciate the diversity of the aspects involved. In Middle High German, the word *gelücke* meant the positive outcome of an action or process. The word *fortuna* and other related expressions in the Romance languages still refer to that aspect of happiness that people experience simply by chance and for which they are not responsible. In contrast, *beatitudo* refers to being happy, a state to which people can in fact contribute. This aspect of happiness is also emphasized, for example, by the German saying 'everyone forges their own destiny'. We already find the corresponding distinction in Classical Greek, between *eutychia*, the happiness that is 'bestowed on' people, and, *eudaimonia*, the state of being happy, which people can help to create. This distinction is also found in other European languages. For instance, in English we speak of *luck* and *happiness*, while in French we find *chance* and *bonheur*. In the constitution of the United States, the *pursuit of happiness* is explicitly laid down as a human right.

For Socrates, a happy life, *eudaimonia*, consisted in leading one's life virtuously and in accordance with rational precepts, including the idea that it is better to suffer injustice than to inflict it on others. For Plato, a happy life became possible when a person was able to bring about goodness and beauty, that is, *kalokagathia*, in which the good, the beautiful and the just are united. A little later, Aristotle developed a stage model of happiness in which he considered it to be above the other human strivings such as honour, pleasure and rationality. For the Epicureans it is *ataraxia* and for the Stoics *apatheia*, dispassionateness, that are the decisive conditions of a happy life.

Seneca described the potentials of a happy life as follows: 'He that possesses prudence is also self-restrained, he that possesses self-restraint is also unwavering; he that is unwavering is unperturbed; he that is unperturbed is free from sadness; he that is free from sadness is happy. Therefore, the prudent man is happy, and prudence is sufficient to constitute the happy life.'[3]

16.1.2 Structural elements of happiness

Happiness is understood differently in Japan and Germany. The differences in understanding are also linked to corresponding differences in the social and cultural practices of generating happiness. These practices are an important part of a culture's intangible cultural heritage. They and the emotions and ideas associated with them play a substantial role in the development, sustaining and modification of cultural identity. These practices that families use to generate their happiness also help to create different cultural identities in Japan and Germany. By cultural identity we mean a cluster of characteristics which individuals and groups use to distinguish themselves from other individuals and groups. Within this group of characteristics, the broad spectrum of symbolizations and practices play an important role.

In view of the tendency towards homogenization and uniformization in and of the world that is associated with globalization, over the last two decades there has been an increasing emphasis on the importance of diversity, with a view to sustaining and promoting cultural identity. This development is clearly evident in the UNESCO Convention for the Safeguarding of the Intangible Cultural Heritage (2003) and the UNESCO Convention on the Protection and Promotion of the Diversity of Cultural Expressions (2005). In contrast to the uniformizing tendency, both conventions stress the necessity of upholding cultural difference and identity.[4] Rituals are among the most important forms of intangible cultural heritage. Everyday rituals in the family and those carried out on festive occasions play a central role. They help to create feelings of community and coherence and thus of family well-being and happiness. As a result, they have an important influence on the cultural identities of the family members. This became clear in the study on family rituals that we carried out at Christmas in Germany and at the New Year in Japan, which showed how family rituals help to engender a social and cultural identity in the family members. In the stagings of the German and Japanese family rituals, it became evident how similar, and yet how different the practices are that are used to produce well-being and happiness in the family. In what follows we give five examples of elements of structure that play a major role in organizing the rituals that make up the intangible cultural heritage, create the emotions of happiness and promote the development of cultural identity.

Language and imagination. Recent research on emotion has clearly shown how important it is from the perspective of the cultural sciences not to ontologize emotions of happiness. Emotions are not substances that can be isolated but are always in some way connected with a person's other characteristics. In many cases, language plays a part in creating the basis for emotions of happiness to arise and be felt. One example is the rhetoric of romantic love. Without it we would not have been able to develop our modern notions of love or expectations of happiness. If a culture does not have a word that is used to denote a certain aspect of happiness, it is likely to be difficult to identify the aspect of happiness to which this word refers in another language. The Japanese word *amae* is one example of this. If we were to try to describe this aspect of love and happiness, we might say something like 'being dependent on the love of another [person]' or 'surrendering oneself to the sweetness of the other'. In the Indo-European languages and the European imaginary, there is no word for this aspect of love and happiness. However, to be able to comprehend the Japanese mentality, it is important to have an understanding of this word that cannot be translated into English.[5] The question is to what extent the emotion of happiness and love that is expressed by this word can be understood by people in other cultures. There are several possible answers to this question. One of them proceeds from the assumption that people of other cultures can use linguistic descriptions to render this emotion understandable. Another is that this cannot suffice, since it is not only a knowledge of language that is required but also a knowledge of the ideas, emotional relationships and performative actions incorporated in the meaning of this word. While the first answer puts greater emphasis on the similarities in our human emotional faculties, the second directs the attention to cultural differences that are hard to overcome.

The flowing of emotions. Many emotions of happiness arise when we human beings interact with other people in ritual forms of communication, both between them and between them and us, and also when we use mimetic processes to better understand ourselves. These emotions can be described as flowing. This implies that emotions of happiness are altered by the practices of everyday life. They are superimposed on previous emotional experiences and create complexes of emotions. In this process emotional dispositions are selected and updated. One special characteristic of human emotionality is that it is influenced by moods that last for extended periods. These moods affect the 'tone' of emotions. 'The world of the happy man is a different one from that of the unhappy man.'[6] Emotions determine our relationships with other people and the world around us. They are evaluative, that is, they assess the events that we experience and prompt us to act in accordance with this assessment. Our emotional assessments of other people's actions are often made unconsciously or semi-consciously and are only partially accessible to our conscious minds. This evaluative aspect of emotions helps us to orient ourselves in the world and in our dealings with other people. It also helps us to make distinctions and to grasp the meanings of social situations, actions and connections. Its energy aspect enables individuals and communities to develop meaning and identity.[7]

Corporeality and performativity. Accentuating the performative nature of the production of happiness entails a shift in attention. We are then less interested in understanding ideas of happiness than in grasping how people articulate, (re-) present, modify and control the different feelings of happiness. In this case the goal is to explore the process in which happiness is staged and performed. This shifts the focus to the ways in which emotions are expressed by the body.[8] The corporeality and dramaturgy of emotions and the way in which they become habitual are important. In this connection rituals and gestures are of substantial importance.[9] This switch in perspectives is connected to developments that have led modern societies to be termed 'performative societies', where people's lifespaces become 'little theatres' in which they are constantly performing and marketing themselves and their roles in their communities.

Mimetic processes. Happy people often make other people happy too. This is partly attributable to the mimetic processes in which people 'make themselves similar' to or match each other. Just as when we laugh, when a person experiences a happy emotion, it is transmitted through the senses. Our bodies are infected by the joy and happiness of other people. Without our being conscious of it, we adapt to match the bodily movements and facial expressions of other people. We become 'sound boxes' for other people's happy emotions. We are infected by their happiness and our emotions enhance theirs. We can become happy ourselves through matching ourselves to their happy emotions in such a way that we are not happy in the same manner as they are, but in our own way. We reflect other people's happiness back to them and deepen their emotions. We perceive the concrete performative expression of happiness and learn the practices with which we stage and perform it and pass it down to future generations.[10]

Rituals. In all human societies, rituals help to deepen, channel and control emotions.[11] They lead their participants to make reference to each other. They are of central importance for the generation of happiness in the family. Their performativity creates social forms of happiness. In this process the movements of the body play an important role. Through shared actions, they create the social emotions of intimacy, affection and trust. Due to the dynamics of family rituals, no one ritual action is a mere copy of previous ones. While rituals are similar to each other, each time they are performed they also establish new practices and at the same time make reference to prior ones. If this does not happen, they lose their vitality and degenerate into stereotypes. Rituals are social practices in which people learn how they can create family stagings and performances that make other people happy and themselves as well. In ritual activities, all participants acquire the practical knowledge that they require.

Gestures. Gestures play an important role in rituals. Gestures are actions such as the offering of a sacrifice in a sacred ritual performed before a Buddhist family altar. Ringing a bell at the beginning of the present-giving on Christmas Eve can also be understood as a meaningful gesture in the Christmas ritual. In family rituals gestures are performative to a high degree – they are learned through mimesis. Gestures are movements of the body. They generate, represent and structure the flow of emotions. When they are staged and performed the meaning of a ritual frequently becomes condensed. Gestures help to create the social interactions and to guide the communications and interactions between the family members. They render something visible which we would not see without them. Gestures are spontaneous and ludic and organize transitions. They are inextricably linked to language, thought and the imagination. They are of great importance for the development of joint attention and human communication and co-operation. Gestures can contribute to the creation and presentation of emotions of well-being and happiness. [12]

16.1.3 The ethnography of happiness

Our German Japanese ethnographic study investigated the question as to the form of happiness, that is, how it is created through performance and rituals. A family's happiness is essentially produced, stabilized and renewed through ritual. We therefore also focused on the processes involved in creating happiness within the family. During the family celebrations, we looked at what kind of happiness the family expected to experience in their celebrations, how the family members staged family happiness, how they created situations of family happiness through their social interactions and how they finally experienced and understood their happiness. At the same time, we analysed what interactions the different members of the family performed and what happiness effects they had on both the social and the personal levels.

To investigate these questions, rather than limiting ourselves to the traditional quantitative or qualitative interview methods, we used an expanded range of methods. In the qualitative interviews, which used both narrative and episodic techniques, we focused on the contents, forms, preconditions and goals of family happiness. We therefore conducted most of them as group interviews. We also complemented them with ethnographic data obtained by means of participant observation (and observing participation), photographs and videos, and informal talks with the family members.[13] Our assumption was that the complexity of family happiness with its traditions, developments, current forms of performance, generative aspects and symbolic references can only be captured by combining visual, verbal and text data.

In order to be able to capture the complexity of family happiness, we restricted this ethnographic research design to the family ritual that was most important in each of the two cultures. It is not only in self-help guides for parents that the importance of rituals for the happiness of children and families is frequently stressed. Certain family rituals such as shared family meals, family holidays, birthdays, (leisure) activities and Christmas have also been considered to be of major significance for the happiness of families. We therefore believe that family rituals promote the performative generation of happiness within families, alongside a number of other functions: confirming the togetherness and shared identity of the family members, rendering visible the integration and solidarity of each individual, displaying and teaching values and traditions, creating a shared framework of action and also developing identities, roles and skills.

16.2 Christmas in a Berlin family, New Year in a Japanese family

In a project that was part of a Cluster of Excellence entitled 'Languages of Emotion' carried out at the Free University Berlin and a project attached to a Cluster of Excellence entitled 'Happiness' at the University of Kyoto, three German Japanese teams carried out research on the ritual of Christmas in three German families and the New Year ritual in three Japanese families. Although we cannot here go deeper into the methodological issues that are of interest when we do research in the cultural sciences in international teams, alongside all the differences between the ways in which these major family rituals are conducted, we can also identify some common features. In what follows I focus on two families, one in the Tegel district of Berlin and one in Higashimonobe, near Kyoto. The Berlin family consisted of the parents and four children and the Japanese family of the grandparents and the two families of their children.

Both the German and the Japanese family belonged to the middle class. They conducted the festivities in their own homes. Both families were religious. The families were selected by theoretical sampling and the questions and hypotheses on which theoretical sampling is based.

Christmas in a Berlin family. Arrival. As we (Shoko Suzuki and Christoph Wulf) approached the house of the Schultz family in Konradshöhe in a residential area of Berlin-Tegel on the afternoon of 24 December it had begun to rain slightly. Three of our small group were Japanese and one German. We drove through Tegel forest and then past numerous detached houses before arriving in the street where the Schultz family owned a semi-detached house. The family consisted of the two parents, that is, the mother, Frauke (an Evangelical protestant), the father, Ingo (a Catholic) and four children (all Evangelical protestants). The family were expecting us, and we were warmly greeted first by the mother and then by the father. The four children came out of their rooms in the two upper stories of the house, curious to see us. They were introduced to us. The family asked what we were expecting. We answered that they should take as little notice of us as possible and celebrate Christmas as they always do.

On this day of the year, the well-known Christmas carols transform the living room of this family into a sacred space. Opposite the table there was a seating area in an alcove with the Christmas tree and the presents lying beneath it. The fir tree was decorated with red Christmas baubles, wooden decorations, red ribbons and a string of electric Christmas tree lights. This was the sacred centre of the living room and the family's staging of happiness on Christmas Eve.

Church service. In the early evening, we walked with the mother, Frauke, and Kevin to an Evangelical church a few minutes away, where the other members of the family had kept seats for us. The bells started ringing and the pastor walked up to the altar. After a brief organ piece, he greeted the congregation, remembered those who were not present and the sick and asked God to bless the Christmas congregation. The congregation then sang the carol 'Es ist ein Ros entsprungen' (*Engl.* Lo, How a Rose E'er Blooming). This was followed, as every year, by a reading of the nativity story from the Gospel of St. Luke. The congregation then sang 'Vom Himmel hoch, da komm ich her' (*Eng.* From Heaven above to Earth I come). The pastor then gave a sermon about the star that can only be seen with the heart and shines like God, warming us with His love. This was followed by an interpretation of the three gifts presented to Jesus by the Three Kings from the East, in which gold was equated with dignity, honour and recognition, frankincense with the soul that rises up to God and myrrh with encouragement and healing. The service ended with another piece of organ music and more Christmas carols sung by the whole congregation.

When we arrived back at the Schultz's house, they began their present-giving ceremony. It was introduced by Frauke reading the Christmas story of 'How Jesus came into the World', once more in the Berlin vernacular, while the family sat close together in front of the Christmas tree. Everyone clapped enthusiastically when this story was announced. It was evidently part of the family tradition to listen to this 'modern version' of the story of the nativity. It was the same story as in the Gospel of Luke, but read in the Berlin dialect it sounded so different that everybody had to listen very closely to be able to recognize and understand it.

The present-giving ceremony took more than two hours. As each of the six members of the family received a present from the other members, and the children several from their parents, a large number of gifts were exchanged. The present-giving was experienced as very intense and pleasurable by all family members. Elias, the eldest child, received the first present. It was a DVD of the film *The Dead Poets Society*. He unpacked it with everyone looking on. Everybody was waiting, curious to see what the present was. There were several comments. 'That's the one you wanted', 'Cool', 'I want to see that film too'. The three other children also picked up the DVD and looked at it. It was clear from the giving of this present and the accompanying comments that this DVD was a present not only for Elias but for the whole family. The attention of all the family members meant that the gift became part of the family community. Although it belonged to the eldest son, all the others were involved in the process of giving and receiving. All members of the family identified with him as the person receiving the gift. Each of them imagined themselves in his shoes for a moment and shared in his pleasure. With this present it was less its material value than the attention paid to Elias and how he was honoured that were important.

A present for the mother that the children had to go and fetch from another room and which looked as if it could be a picture, occasioned special attention. There was great astonishment when the gift turned out to be a doormat for the front door with the inscription 'Hotel Mama'. The mother was particularly pleased with this present. She understood it as a validation and a token of recognition for herself and her commitment to the family. The comments of all the other members of the family were correspondingly lengthy. In particular they demonstrated in front of the whole family how much they appreciated her for always being there and caring for them. The father, Ingo, captured what everyone was feeling when he said, 'Mummy is happy now'.

During the present-giving the family were sitting huddled close together in the seats in front of the Christmas tree. Their bodies touched each other. There were drawn-up legs next to stretched-out arms, hips against bent knees and heads on the shoulders of siblings. Everyone was pressed up against everyone else in front of the Christmas tree. Some were sitting on the sofa, others on the floor, leaning against their siblings' knees, while others were balanced on the arms of the sofa. The alcove in front of the Christmas tree was filled with the family's intertwined bodies. A collective body was formed, the dynamics of which arose out of their movements as they gave each other their presents. The present-giving ceremony was essentially a physical process. The giving and receiving of the presents was accompanied by many gestures and comments. The physical proximity played an important role. Parents and children touched each other, expressing their pleasure and gratitude in this way. Oscillating gestures expressing emotion were exchanged especially between the mother and her children. The bodies of those handing over presents leaned towards the bodies of the other, creating sensual closeness, festive enjoyment, intimacy and feelings of belonging together. Touching each other allowed them to directly feel the presents and the other members of the family. The mother touched and stroked her presents several times, as if she could sense and incorporate them through her sense of touch. In these gestures of reciprocal physical present-giving, the Schultz family created a special form of collective family body.[14]

Family happiness. We visited the family again on Christmas Day. We wanted to have a conversation with them about how they view the happiness of their family, to complement the impressions we had gained on Christmas Eve. We wanted not only to observe how the family stages and performs its happiness on that day, but also to hear what the family thought their happiness consisted in. We wanted to find out what aspects were important to them, what weights they attached to these aspects and how they talked about their happiness.

  The parents of the Schultz family told us that they tried to make it possible for their children to have everything that is important in life and make them happy, not only at Christmas, but also in their day-to-day family life. The material circumstances that enabled them to fulfil their own wishes and those of their children were also important. After this it was especially the day-to-day care of the children by the mother that both parents considered important. Frauke had given up her job as a physiotherapist in order to be able to dedicate herself to the care of her children – to begin with even against her own convictions. As father, Ingo had given his continuing support to this decision, without which the time-consuming care of the children would not have been possible. His job allowed him frequently to work from home. Quite spontaneously, he stressed that in their daily lives the children received all-inclusive care. 'There's all-inclusive and XXL all-inclusive care.'[15]

Both parents considered it especially important that their children should have a hot meal at lunchtime every day and that one of them should look after them. For example, the mother accompanied each of the children to the door as they left and said goodbye to them personally. She also opened the door to each child on their return from school, even if they had already long had their own keys. Recently Frauke had got up at 4.30 am every morning to make breakfast for one of her sons who was doing a period of practical training, thus ensuring that he had a good meal to start his day. Both parents said that the children needed different things at different times and that what these things were differed from one child to another and could not always be predicted in advance. Frauke said she thought her children should consider themselves fortunate that she went along with most things. In the last twenty years, the parents of the Schultz family had seen their task in life as being to devote themselves completely to their children. I shall now interrupt my ethnographic description and come to the New Year celebrations in the Japanese family and their staging of family happiness, in which I participated together with Shoko Suzuki, my colleague from Kyoto University.

New Year celebrations in a Japanese family living in a village. The village of Higashimonobe is located north of Lake Biwa, the largest lake in Japan. It is a typical rice-growing area (low-lying and flat with an ample supply of water). The village has a long history and old traditions that are closely linked to the cultivation of rice. For instance, the irrigation channels play an important role. They ensure the order and maintenance of the fields. The village is oriented towards the water system. Originally almost all the families in the village were employed in the cultivation of rice, which is reflected in the fact that the houses were built close together. However, today only a few families still cultivate rice. All the families bear the name of the head of the family who first moved to live in this village with his family as a special family name.

The Japanese call 31 December Omisoka. In the past at Omisoka all the shops would receive new decorative hangings for the entrances to their houses. Each house has a small house shrine where candles are lit at Omisoka, and the family gives thanks for the fact that they have had a good year and also ask for a good year to come. On the evening of 31 December, people eat *soba* (long noodles like spaghetti that are made of buckwheat). Soba is a symbol of longevity. In the night from 31 December to 1 January, the bells are rung 108 times in all temples at midnight (*joya*). This Buddhist ritual is intended to remove negative desires. As a rule people are not supposed to sleep on this night. Tradition has it that anyone who does sleep will later have more white hair and face wrinkles. In the past, people also used to spend the night in the shrine (without going to sleep). A big fire is therefore lit at the shrine.

Joya is a very holy fire. It is lit to receive the year god of the coming year. All the villagers wait for the arrival of the god (which is why they must not sleep). There are twelve year gods: mouse, cow, tiger, rabbit, dragon, snake, horse, sheep, monkey, bird (hen), dog and wild boar. When the year god comes, the human beings – or at least the Japanese – are reborn.

On 1 January, two representatives of the village council have to go to the Nogita shrine and prepare to receive the other villagers. Shortly after sunrise, the other villagers come to the shrine to welcome the New Year. In the past, everybody used to wear a kimono on this occasion. Today nobody wears a kimono anymore, but they do put on official clothes. Each person brings with them three units of rice wrapped in white paper (one each for the two shrines and one for a temple in the village). They begin with the shrines and then go to the temple. They then briefly visit their relatives (particularly the fathers of the families and the oldest son) to wish them a happy New Year. Then they can finally eat a light breakfast. Just before 7.00 am, a drum is beaten in the temple as a signal that the temple service to which the villagers are going (a Buddhist mass in the main hall of the temple) is about to begin. The fathers of the families bring a coin wrapped in white paper with them, while the women bring an *isho*, a sack of rice. Later New Year's greeting cards are written to friends, colleagues and so on, usually a lot of them.

The house of the Oda family where we (Shoko Suzuki and Christoph Wulf) saw the old year out and welcomed the New Year in consisted of two rooms joined together to make one large one, next to which there were another two rooms that were separated from each other. A large kitchen adjoined one of these rooms. There were six more rooms on the first (upper) floor. At the front end of the large living room opposite the front door, there was a fine Buddhist family altar and, to the left of it, the tokonoma, a scrolled picture with some holy characters on it. In front of this was a bunch of flowers arranged in the Ikebana style. On the left of the flowers was the front of a Shinto shrine that hung on the wall above head level. Below this some sacred vessels were arranged. On the other long wall opposite the Shinto shrine, there were some photographs of the great-grandparents and great-great-grandparents, next to the Buddhist temple. The Buddhist temple and the Shinto shrine were next to each other and formed the sacred centre of the house. In this case the separation of Buddhist and Shinto shrines that was striven for in the Meiji era evidently either did not happen or was later reversed. The Buddhist temple had special significance for the Oda family. The family belonged to the *Jōdo Shinshū school of Japanese Buddhism*, in which the great-grandfather had been a lay preacher and with which the family still felt close ties. The temple contains some holy scriptures that were passed down to the family by the great-grandfather. A text in Old Japanese from one of them was read out in the course of the New Year's ceremony. Today the temple had been decorated. A special triangular cloth that is used only at the turn of the year, freshly cut flowers, new candles and, later, two rice cakes placed one on top of the other with a mandarin symbolized the turn of the year and the wishes and hopes for a healthy and happy life that Japanese people associate with it. Over the door of the large living room looking towards the entrance hall of the house, there was an *ootsue*, an image of the devil that is widespread in the Shiga District around Lake Biwa. It shows a devil carrying hiking equipment, including a rolled-up sleeping mat on his back and a rice bowl on his belly. One of his horns is mutilated, and the other looks funny rather than threatening. This devil only has limited access to the powers of evil. Over the opening between this room and the one next door, which is mainly used by the children as a playroom, there is a picture of Mount Fuji as a reminder of the most important sacred places in Japan, where the love of nature, religious feeling and aesthetic sensations come together.

Visit to the cemetery. A visit to the cemetery is an integral component of the New Year's celebrations. We set off for the cemetery in late afternoon. The graves of the deceased were on the outskirts of the village, next to a modern motorway. For the Japanese, graves are the entrance to the world of their ancestors. All the families in the village have a stone grave here in which the remains of their deceased relatives are laid to rest following cremation. As we approached the grave of the Oda family, it began to snow lightly.

Grandfather Makato conducted the ritual. First, he replaced flowers on the grave with new ones. He then lit two candles and placed them in containers that were protected from the wind. He also lit some incense sticks and placed them in the beakers provided. He then poured some water over the top of the grave. Finally, he took out two small books, out of which he, his son and his grandson read some prayers. It was gradually becoming dark and the snow was falling more heavily. We drove home.

The New Year's dinner. The women are responsible for preparing the New Year's dinner. Usually the daughter-in-law has to learn the customs and traditions of the family into which she has married, for example how the family chops vegetables, how they cook, how they season the dishes and how they decorate the table and plates. The young woman is expected to follow what her mother-in-law does. Grandmother Oda learned these things in the same way when she was a young daughter-in-law. After her mother-in-law died, she slowly began to prepare the dishes as she herself liked to do. As time passed, she also began to take the wishes of the younger generation and her grandchildren into account in her preparations for the New Year's dinner, also some elements of Western cuisine. Today her own daughter-in-law was helping her to prepare the dinner. As she had done herself, today her daughter-in-law was learning how to prepare the family dinner in accordance with the traditions and customs of the Oda family. In an interview with us, grandmother Kayoko explained the meaning of the preparations for the traditional family meal.

Family happiness. A little later we asked the eldest son, Yasuo, and his wife Nanako to give us an interview about happiness in the family. We asked them about their ideas of happiness and how they experienced happiness. Yasuo began to talk as if it were quite natural. Nanako joined in later on. Both of them talked about their ideas of happiness and how the happiness of the family was threatened by the fact that their son Kijoichi had a heart defect. The family was important for Yasuo and Nanako. Yasuo said that he tried to spend time with his children and to play with them as much as possible. He added that he wanted to enable them to have memories of their childhoods that were as pleasant as his own. His own memories reflected the love of his father Makato, and he tried to create similar memories for his children. The transmission of parental love to the next generation takes place in a mimetic process, which lays the foundations for experiencing happiness later on in life.[16]

The morning of New Year's Day. We visited the Oda family again in the early morning of New Year's Day. When we arrived at their house, before six o'clock in the morning, everyone was already awake and dressed in festive clothes, ready to celebrate the first day of the New Year. We set off in the dark with the grandfather and his son to visit a shrine and a temple to ask for happiness and luck in the New Year. It had begun to snow again. On the way we met many villagers, most of whom were men, who, like us, were on their way to the sacred places to ask for a blessing for the New Year. The women had stayed at home to prepare the first and particularly important meal of the New Year. When we arrived at the shrine, two priests in blue robes were sitting there. The gifts of money that had been prepared the day before were handed over, the bell was rung, and its sounds rang out. People clapped their hands twice and drank a bowl of rice wine. Then we continued to the Buddhist temple. We wished a Happy New Year to everyone we met on the way, and they wished us one, too: *Akemaskite omedeto gozaimasu . . .*

16.3 The conditions for family happiness

Although we cannot make a conclusive statement as to what the necessary conditions for family happiness are, we can name three central characteristics on the basis of our ethnographic data:

- The happiness that is experienced during the New Year's celebrations is a shared happiness that is created through stagings and performance within the family.
- The happiness that families experience arises during the New Year's celebrations in and with the support of performative practices.
- Families differ from other communities in the practices that they use to increase their happiness.

In our study on the staging and performance of happiness in the Oda family at the New Year, two practices of the family were particularly important: (1) the sacred practices rooted in Shintoism and Buddhism that generate the happiness of the family studied; (2) the practices and symbolic modes of eating and drinking that are closely linked to these sacred practices. The sacred practices establish a connection with the cosmic order and assign the lives of the individuals their place in the succession of ancestors and generations. The eating and drinking practices are experienced as pleasurable and promoting togetherness. They help to support the family's sense of identity, enhance the communication between the generations and the sexes and thus ensure the continued existence of the family.

16.4 Transcultural elements of family happiness

In the family rituals we studied in Germany and Japan, we found that the five elements of eating meals, praying, giving gifts, remembering and being together have special importance for the creation of happiness in families. Depending on the focus of the descriptions and interpretations, we were able to distinguish some shared and some differing aspects in each of these elements. Each element can be understood as a *unitas multiplex*, a unit with multiple aspects. The goal of the descriptions and interpretations is to relate the shared and differing aspects to each other, while at the same time avoiding focusing on only one of the two perspectives while neglecting the other. Only an approach that oscillates between the two perspectives can avoid making unacceptable conceptual and methodological reductions. The difficulty of elucidating the *unitas multiplex* of these elements of family rituals was described by Wittgenstein in his thoughts on the 'family resemblances' between games.[17] The spectrum of family happiness investigated in our study includes many different forms, resemblances and differences, and thus we were faced with a complexity that is basically boundless, but within which resemblances arise that enabled us to perceive and structure it. One fundamental question that arises is whether cultural phenomena are at all comparable, and where the potentials and limits of the comparison lie, and another is the question as to what commonalities can be found in respect to the happiness of families.[18]

The two ritual family celebrations have several characteristic elements, which, however, took very different forms in the two families. To conclude, we give a brief outline in six points of the commonalities and differences between the ways the two families conducted this major family ritual.[19]

(1) In both families the sacred foundation of the family ritual played an important role. The German family, which transformed its living room into a sacred space with the Christmas tree, numerous candles and the familiar Christmas carols, went to a Christmas service at a nearby Evangelical protestant church. There they met other members of the parish. They gave each other their gifts and read the nativity story again in two different versions. It was read in the Berlin vernacular, which transformed it into a new story, but without changing its substance. In the second version the story was 'translated' into a modern newspaper report that shows how strong the resistance to the events of Christmas would be in the world of today too.

In the Japanese family, a visit was made to the family grave on the last day of the year. Very early in the morning of New Year's Day, the family went to two temples. On the way there, the villagers greeted each other and wished each other a healthy and happy New Year. The New Year's ritual was carried out at both temples. Then the families returned home to participate in another ritual conducted by the grandfather in the presence of the whole family before the Buddhist altar in the living room, following which they had their New Year's meal, which the women had prepared during the night.

(2) The meal was the focal point of the celebration. The Japanese family sat around a table on the floor in front of the Buddhist house temple. On New Year's Day, special dishes were cooked. The family discussed their symbolic meaning for the New Year as they ate. The family members sat close together and spoke little. The German family sat at their dining table and did not talk much about the dishes they were consuming. The mother stressed that she was 'not a great cook' and that she refused to make a special effort on this day. It was mainly the discussions that took place at the dining table that created the sense of togetherness in the family. Its intensity is typical of the style of this family.

(3) The exchanging of gifts played a role in both family rituals. While this role was more or less peripheral in the Japanese family, in the German family it was central. It was less its material value than its social significance that made it the focus of the family ritual. The two-hour present-giving ceremony took place in the armchairs and sofa grouped together in front of the Christmas tree. All members of the family sat there, close together. Each member of the family made comments on the usefulness of the present to its recipient and on its social and aesthetic qualities.

(4) Families create their feelings of togetherness by means of narratives in which the members of the family remember events that they experienced together. In the narratives they relate the present as they are experiencing it to the family's overall frame of reference and articulate shared plans for the future. Family narratives create, confirm and sustain feelings of togetherness.

(5) The family members make time for each other and time to be together during the festive rituals. They enjoy being together and being with each other. In the German family this was expressed in the lengthy and affectionate conversations. In the Japanese family it was the games the adults played with the children in which the children received special attention. In the conversations in the German family that we recorded, the children commented again and again that they would later have a family and children of their own and that they wanted their families to follow the same model as that of their own family. In the Japanese family the value that this family ritual with the three generations had for all participants was expressed in the preparation of the meals by the grandmother, her daughter and her daughter-in-law together and the family's deep appreciation of the meal.

(6) One marked difference between the German and the Japanese family resulted from the significance of the parents and previous generations for the family members. The German family visited the parents of the father, who lived close by and whom the family saw from time to time, on the afternoon of

Christmas Day. They sent parcels containing presents to the mother's parents, who lived quite a long way away. They phoned them during the Christmas celebrations. In the Japanese family, the ritual in which three generations participated was performed in the grandparents' home. Until recently it had been four generations. The family also visited the family grave on the last day of the old year, in order to remember their ancestors, to thank them and to ask them for a blessing for the New Year. The grandfather carried out the ritual with water, fire and flowers and organized the reading of sacred quotes, in which he also included his small grandson.

In our conversations with the members of both families, it became clear how important the Christmas and New Year's rituals were for the coherence of the family and the happiness of its members. By talking about past and future Christmases and New Year's celebrations, both families integrated their current experience of the family festivities into their family histories and their expectations for the future. This led to an emotional intensity and a feeling of togetherness which the family members experienced as family happiness. Durkheim was right to draw attention to how important the sacred character of such rituals is for the family,[20] allowing it to assume its societal and social function. As they perform such rituals families represent their values, norms and rules in their performative practices and the narratives that accompany them and generate their meaning. These family values, norms and rules are (re-) created in these processes and incorporated in the behaviour of the family members. They are then confirmed again and again by repetition. The members of the family are not conscious of these values, norms and rules and the feelings that are associated with them as abstract values. Rather they are embedded in scenic actions, conversations and behaviours that only become conscious when there is conflict or when questions are asked that require justifications. The values, norms and rules are part of a know-how that enables the family members to act correctly in accordance with the situation.

Conclusion

The power of images

Human beings live with images. Perceptual images enable us to access the world and other people. Memory images give us access to the past. Images projected into the future help us to develop new plans for action. Images render visible what would otherwise remain invisible. They have power over human beings who can lose their way in them. Images are a substitute for things that are absent and make them present. At the same time, they are the expression of a deficit, which is particularly evident in images of drives and desire and is common to all human beings. They also possess a visible energy which forms us into social and cultural beings. This is evident in our perception of the world and in the wide array of images that exist. The word 'image' denotes a broad spectrum of all sorts of images. Depending on the criteria used to differentiate between them, the numerous 'image types' have both common and divergent elements. Wittgenstein's concept of 'family resemblance' is an excellent way of describing the relationship between the 'image types'. It is the differing aspects of each 'family resemblance' that make it possible nevertheless to refer to all the different 'image types' as *images*.

Images are generated by the process of imagination. Although neuroscientific research has demonstrated that the energy currents of the imagination can be visualized, these energy currents nonetheless remain invisible if they do not become manifest in images. As in the terminology of neuroscience, in this context the word 'image' is used to denote not only the results of the process of seeing but also those of perception by the other senses. The effects of this multifaceted imagination can be traced over the entire evolution of *Homo sapiens*. We see these effects, for instance, in the early hand axes and bone markings, in the remains found in graves that reveal how humans pictured the world beyond, and in cave paintings. Without the image-generating power of the imagination, there would have been no evolution of humankind. Over the course of history, we find an increasing number and variety of images. We can find evidence of the effects of the imagination in both diachronic studies of history and synchronic studies of different cultures.

The imagination manifests itself in various iconic forms. Of particular importance are perceptual and memory images and also images projected into the future. However, pathologies of imagination, visions and dreams also all have their own different iconic forms. We therefore took as the starting point for our analysis the theories of concepts of imagination and their relationship to fantasy and the faculty of imagination. There are three different points of departure: the fact that different images show a family resemblance, the role that imagination has played in the evolution of humanity beings and the different iconic forms in which imagination expresses itself. It became clear that mental images play a major role in the different ways in which emotions are experienced. We also saw how ludic elements are involved in the imagination.

Without the imagination, it is not possible to play games. The imagination generates the required framework and the make-believe that is necessary for the actions in the game to take place. The imagination helps to create the 'as if' nature of the games which suspends the 'reality' of the situation and transforms it into the world of the game. The imagination develops images and schemata which, because they are performative, shape the game, and in turn generate images which take root in the collective and individual imaginaries. They can be combined differently in new contexts.

It is similar with dance. Here imaginary worlds are created where people portray and express themselves, worlds which we find it pleasurable to create and participate in. Here too the imagination becomes performative. The imagination is evident in performances of dance and also in the movements of the body. As the 'imagination of movement', it is an essential component of dance.

Similarly, the staging and performance of rituals, and the practical knowledge out of which they are created, is not possible without drawing on the images and schemata of the imaginary. As with games and dances, rituals also contain an imageless body knowledge, which is put on display and can be understood to have resulted from the body's learning processes. The imagination and the imaginary play a part in shaping these social practices. They would not be possible if there were no memory images to enable us to fall back on our knowledge of earlier stagings and performances when we are in new situations. At the same time, ritual arrangements also create action sequences that can be absorbed into the social and cultural imaginary with the aid of the imagination. The body and the imagination become performative, thus facilitating the dynamic of rituals, a dynamic that is open to change.

Because they are iconic, gestures can condense the essence of rituals into a single scene, or rather into an image that is performative and expresses the meaning of the whole ritual. Because they are iconic, gestures are easily memorable. They simplify and intensify rituals and generate an image to which people can also attach their emotions. As actions without words, gestures are stagings and performances of the body. They have a 'family resemblance' and are grasped in mimetic processes. Gestures are early forms of communication which express an implicit body knowledge and do not need to be conscious.

Cultural learning is to a large extent mimetic learning that takes place with the aid of the imagination. The processes upon which this learning is based are largely unconscious. People behaving mimetically take an 'impression' of social and cultural events and integrate it into their imaginaries, where it becomes mixed up with images, schemata and models that are already there. This results in their 'becoming similar' to social and cultural practices that have already been created. A dynamic process of re-creation takes place, during which variations and innovations are made. Much of our implicit practical knowledge is acquired mimetically, especially in childhood. This includes, for example, feelings, the ability to walk upright and language. Since the imagination and the imaginary are performative, this helps us to stage and perform body-based practices and permits actions to emerge. Participating in the practices of our intangible cultural heritage and the mimetic processing of the respective practices promotes the forming of a collective and individual identity.

Family rituals, and the contribution they make to the development of the imaginary of the individual, play an important role in the forming of personal identity. We would not develop an individual identity without family practices and their repetition and modification in rituals. If we are to lead a fulfilled life, we need family well-being and happiness. The individual imaginary, for which we need the practical knowledge that enables us to stage happiness, is acquired in mimetic processes. As we saw in our German/Japanese ethnographic study, despite all the cultural differences between Germany and Japan there are also transcultural aspects of family happiness that appear to be common to people of different cultures.

The results of these studies prompt us to ask how we should understand the relationship between universal, culture-specific imaginaries and personal imaginaries in the globalized world of the Anthropocene. In our globalized world, images and our image worlds are very important for human co-existence. The spectrum of images contains global icons that can be seen all over the world as well as regional, local and individual images that are not so well known. There are also commonalities and differences between the images of the globalized world. We all share an overall human imaginary. This has also been called a *unitas multiplex*, a unity with diverse parts, which people share in varying degrees. It is clear that great changes are taking place in 'human images' and in the human imaginary. With digitalization and globalization the iconic is acquiring a universality and power that we have never known before. During the Covid-19 pandemic, where social distancing is required, images are acquiring an additional importance. They become substitutes for the presence of other people and facilitate new forms of presence brought to us via media. In these processes, whereby many areas of life are undergoing a digital transformation, electronic images are becoming increasingly important. On the one hand, they are becoming a substitute for engaging with the materiality of things. On the other hand, in so doing, they permit us to have new forms of connections and communication via icons. As media of the imagination, images generate new possibilities of creative action in our everyday lives, science and the arts. Here, for example, it is the development of contemporary art into global art that leads to new image worlds.

The globalization of contemporary art shows that large changes are taking place in human beings, in their images and in the human imaginary. Whereas modern art and its images used to be centred on Europe and the United States and was largely Euro-American, the situation today is changing and moving in the direction of global contemporary art. Dynamic art scenes and art markets with numerous museums and exhibitions have now emerged in China, India, Brazil and the Arab world. Global art is no longer Euro-American but polycentric.[1] This development mirrors the changes in the human imaginary, in whose changing structures, schemata and images the dynamics of globalization are manifested. With the aid of the electronic media, locally and regionally produced images are broadcast worldwide. These processes are having lasting effects on the expansion and restructuring of the human imaginary in all parts of the world. This development epitomizes what is happening in other areas of the globalized world, where new image worlds are arising that are taking hold of imaginaries throughout the world in mimetic processes. We can distinguish between two contradictory tendencies in this process. The first is oriented towards disseminating the same images the world over and homogenizing our collective and personal imaginaries. The second emphasizes cultural diversity and the importance of the diversity of the imaginary in a broad range of cultural and social variations. Both tendencies influence the way we see the world and us human beings in it. In the Anthropocene, an age in which human beings have become a telluric power determining the destiny of the planet, it is the global images of the violence of war, the threatened destruction of the climate and biodiversity and the pollution of our seas, land and air that go round the world and open our eyes to the destructive effects of the modern age and industrialization.[2] These images interconnect with the very different images that form part of our individual experience, which constitute the uniqueness of the individual.[3]

Political, economic, social and cultural power constellations play a major role in both of these tendencies. It is through the variety of different images that imaginaries are formed. This often happens implicitly rather than explicitly. The power structures inherent in the images which find expression in them are transmitted tacitly and exert an influence on the structures and schemata of our imaginaries. These power structures that are also rooted in our imaginaries are performative and affect the shaping of the world and people's relationships with each other. The images that we have in our imaginaries influence how we handle the challenges of the Anthropocene and of sustainable development, one of the greatest challenges of our time.[4]

With modernization, industrialization and the developments of the twentieth century, we have seen a growth in the importance of the media and medialization in the way images are created and the imaginary expanded. It is possible to distinguish four media groups which are determined according to the means and conditions of how they are produced and received in:[5] (1) primary media as means of direct human contact without a device; (2) secondary media which require devices in order to be produced but not perceived; (3) tertiary media, which require devices on the part of the producer and the consumer; (4) quaternary media, which require the use of devices, but neither spatial nor temporal correspondence is necessary. These also include the electronic media where the consumer can actively decide when, where and how they want to use them. There has been a sharp increase in the importance of these in the globalized world of the Anthropocene.

At a time when many processes of life had to take place on a virtual level during the Covid-19 pandemic, people became fully aware of the potential of the electronic media and the growth in their importance.[6] There was a large increase in people communicating via electronic media in order to be able to maintain the requirement for social distancing. Whereas people's bodies presented the danger of infection, the images of people were 'hygienic' and offered protection from infection. This led to an acceleration in the digital transformation of society together with the processes of abstraction that are part and parcel of this. An exploratory study on the role of the internet in the lives of young people in several countries and continents examined the extent to which digitalization has become an essential component in the everyday life of the young.[7] The distinction between an offline and online world no longer means anything to this generation. The online world is an integral part of their everyday world. The links between online and offline are part of the lifeworld of the young and permit fast, uncomplicated communication. They make it possible, for example, to meet up on the spur of the moment, to communicate through the exchange of feelings and thoughts and discussion of issues and problems and to develop new forms of social interaction. For many young people the idea of going back to a world without this type of communication is unimaginable. They are, as some young people put it, always ready to communicate (*pready*). Most young people want to be instantly contactable, just as they want to be able to instantly contact others. They aspire to being always available, knowing that others are also available and want the flexibility this requires. The importance of images and written and spoken language is diminishing in favour of new connections which had never seemed possible before. These have repercussions on the use of images and written and spoken in youth culture. Images become means of communication for the young. The spectrum ranges from selfies to screenshots. Increasingly young people communicate their situation, their concerns, their emotions with the help of images. This turns them into producers, that is, persons who are productive through the creation or conscious selection of images. Digital media are an essential component of young people's lives; they have a great potential for education. By producing texts, images and videos, digital media offer young people the opportunity to learn in an autonomous and creative way. The young also deploy their bodies and their emotions in their handling of digital media; digital methods allow them to create forms of expression and social experiences that were previously unknown. They create new forms of recognition and appreciation, as well, of course, as contempt and hate. Digital media permit the use of new tools and promote the development of new skills. They support processes of decentralizing education and making it more individual. They contribute towards digital literacy and multiliteracy. Much of the fascination of digital media also lies in their connection with alternative forms of education and the media that can be used in education.

The upsurge in electronic media is accompanied by an acceleration in our living and communication processes. In these forms of communication, spatial distance becomes meaningless. The new media are intensifying globalization. The interconnectedness that they bring has led to a decentralization of power and the development of polycentrism in global society. Here, the iconic character of the electronic media plays an important role in producing the communication and interaction structures. The transformation of the world into a world where icons dominate is becoming increasingly important. There are ever fewer encounters with the material substance of the world. In education, for example, images and films serve as a substitute for the encounter with things. Children and young people experience the actuality of the world in images of the world. In their virtual world, they have less experience of the resistance and contrariness of things. It is a pared-down image of the world that comes into being, one that factors out the limitations of human possibilities and suggests that 'anything is possible'.[8]

However, much doubt has been expressed over this dictum of modern times. People are becoming increasingly aware that they have become a force that is determining the fate of our planet and that this development is by no means positive but has resulted in numerous negative side effects. It has created new iconic worlds, such as climate change, the destruction of biodiversity, a disruption to biogeochemical cycles, the acidification of the oceans and the pollution of the planet, with the risk of destroying the foundations of human, animal and plant life. In addition, we have images of traffic and travel, prosthetics and robotics, all stemming from the global spread of machines. In genetics and biotechnology as well, we find new image worlds – unseen until now – such as the double-helix structure of DNA, cloned animals, endless genome sequences from the human genome project and depictions of gene manipulation by CRISPR–Cas9. These newly created image worlds are gradually becoming part of, and also a basis for, a new understanding of ourselves as human beings and of our world.[9]

These image worlds and the many others that have come into being as a consequence of globalization and modernization distinguish the Anthropocene from other historical periods such as the Renaissance, the Middle Ages and Classical Antiquity. The imaginary of the Anthropocene contains performative images that challenge us to shape the world. These images are disseminated and adopted worldwide in mimetic processes and become woven into a collective imaginary that connects people with each other. It consists of performative images of events and actions, which initiate individual and collective feelings, actions and attitudes and result in many people having a sense of a collective responsibility and a feeling of solidarity for the future and the planet.

Over the last decades, new image worlds have arisen out of the situation of the Anthropocene that we find ourselves in, and this shows clearly the dichotomy inherent in our positions as humans on our planet. It has long been the case that the traditional distinction between nature and culture no longer applies – there are hardly any areas of nature that are not impacted by human beings. Whereas in Antiquity and Christendom, human beings were seen as part of nature; in the modern age their position changed and instead they came to be understood as subjects confronting nature as an object. And in the Anthropocene, the human being is seen as being entwined with nature in an existential way.

Human actions have an impact on nature which, having changed by them, then has a reverse impact on humans in response. Thus, quite rightly, the relationship between nature and culture is described as a dialectical one or as a network relationship in which all actions are contingent and generate unforeseeable effects. Gradually human beings are beginning to see themselves as part of nature again and to develop a less violent, sustainable relationship with it.

Such changes in the way we view the world and ourselves are only possible if they go hand in hand with a similar change in human imaginaries and image worlds. Certain images help us to understand what the Anthropocene means – examples are the atomic explosion in Hiroshima, the 'blue planet' in the infinity of the cosmos, the melting of the glaciers, the seas filled with plastic detritus, the burning rainforests, the endless rubbish mountains and also the images of people fighting for their lives against Covid. These images take possession of our collective and individual imaginaries and shape the way we feel about life.

If the world community is to achieve the goals for sustainable development set in 2015 in New York, then it also needs new image worlds from the strategies for sustainability to make these goals concrete and give people the chance to transform them in their individual imaginaries through mimetic processes. If this is successful and people's imaginaries are transformed by a change in values and role models, feelings and attitudes, rituals and gestures, there is perhaps hope that the changes that the Anthropocene demands will follow. This is, however, by no means certain. Important as the power of the imagination is in realizing our hopes for the future, it also remains an open question as to whether cognition of the problems and commitment to action will be enough to present a solution.

Notes

Introduction

1 Wallenhorst, N., and Wulf, C., eds (2021), *Dictionnaire d'anthropologie Prospective*, Paris: Vrin; Wallenhorst, N., and Wulf, C., eds (2022), *Handbook of the Anthropocene*, Basingstoke: Springer Nature.

2 Gil, Capeloa I., and Wulf, C., eds (2015), *Hazardous Future. Disaster, Representation and the Assessment of Risk*, Berlin: de Gruyter.

3 Wulf, C. (2022), *Education as Human Knowledge in the Anthropocene. An Anthropological Perspective*, London: Routledge.

4 Kontopodis, M., Varvantakis, C., and Wulf, C., eds (2017), *Global Youth in Digital Trajectories*, London: Routledge.

5 Jonas, H. (1994), '*Homo pictor. Von der Freiheit des Menschen*'. In: Boehm, G. (ed.), *Was ist ein Bild?*, Munich: Wilhelm Fink, 105–124; Blacking, J., ed. (1977), *The Anthropology of the Body*, London: Academic Press; Belting, H. (2011), *An Anthropology of Images*, Princeton: Princeton University Press; Huppauf, B., and Wulf, C., eds (2009), *Dynamics and Performativity of Imagination. The Image between the Visible and the Invisible*, London: Routledge; Wulf, C. (2013), *Anthropology. A Continental Perspective*, Chicago: The University of Chicago Press; Wulf, C. (2009). *Anthropologie. Geschichte – Kultur – Philosophie*, Cologne: Anaconda (2nd edn, first edn, Reinbek 2004: Rowohlt).

6 Huppauf, and Wulf, *Dynamics and Performativity of Imagination*.

7 Kamper, D. (1986), *Zur Soziologie der Imagination*, Munich: Hanser, 32ff.

8 Gebauer, G., and Wulf, C. (1995), *Mimesis. Culture - Art – Society*, Berkeley: University of California Press.

9 Brandstetter, G., and Wulf, C., eds (2007), *Tanz als Anthropologie*, Munich: Wilhelm Fink.

10 Cf. Wulf, C. (2005), *Zur Genese des Sozialen. Mimesis, Performativität, Ritual*, Bielefeld: transcript; Wulf, C. (2013), *Das Rätsel des Humanen. Eine Einführung in die historische Anthropologie*, Munich: Wilhelm Fink; Wulf, C., and Zirfas, J., eds (2004), *Die Kultur des Rituals. Inszenierungen. Praktiken. Symbole*, Munich: Wilhelm Fink; Wulf, C., and Zirfas, J. (2004), 'Performative Welten. Eine Einführung in die systematischen, historischen und methodischen Dimensionen

des Rituals'. In: Wulf, C., and Zirfas, J. (eds), *Die Kultur des Rituals. Inszenierungen. Praktiken. Symbole*, Munich: Fink, 7–46.

11 Wulf, C., Althans, B., Audehm, K., Bausch, C., Göhlich, M., Sting, S., Tervooren, A., Wagner-Willi, M., and Zirfas, J. (2010), *Ritual and Identity. The Staging and Performing of Rituals in the Lives of Young People*, London: Tufnell.

12 Cf. Kendon, A. (2004), *Gesture: Visible Action as Utterance*, Cambridge: Cambridge University Press; McNeill, D. (1992), *Hand and Mind. What Gestures Reveal About Thought*, Chicago, London: Chicago University Press; McNeill, D. (2005), *Gesture and Thought*, Chicago, London: Chicago University Press; Wulf, C., and Fischer-Lichte, E., eds (2010), *Gesten – Inszenierung, Aufführung, Praxis*, Paderborn: Wilhelm Fink.

13 Wulf, C., Althans, B., Audehm, K., Blaschke, G., Ferrin, N., Kellermann, I., Mattig, R., and Schinkel, S. (2011), *Die Geste in Erziehung, Bildung und Sozialisation. Ethnographische Feldstudien*, Wiesbaden: Springer VS.

14 Wulf, C., and Zirfas, J., eds (2005), *Ikonologie des Performativen*, Munich: Wilhelm Fink; Wulf, C., and Zirfas, J., eds (2007), *Pädagogik des Performativen. Theorien, Methoden, Perspektiven*, Weinheim, Basel: Beltz.

15 Kress, G., Selander, S., Säljö, R., and Wulf, C., eds (2021), *Learning as Social Practice. Beyond Education as an Individual Enterprise*, London: Routledge.

16 Wulf, *Anthropology*.

17 Wulf, C., Suzuki, S., Zirfas, J., Kellermann, I., Inoue, Y., Ono, F., and Takenaka, N. (2011), *Das Glück der Familie: Ethnographische Studien in Deutschland und Japan*, Wiesbaden: Springer VS.

Chapter 1

1 Heidegger, M. (2002), 'The Age of the World Picture'. In: Martin Heidegger (ed.), *Off the Beaten Track*, Cambridge: Cambridge University Press.

2 Ibid., 69.

3 Ibid., 70.

4 Denis, M. (1991), *Image and Cognition*, Harvester: Wheatsheaf, IX.

5 Michaels, A., and Wulf, C., eds (2014), *Exploring the Senses*, London: Routledge.

6 Schulze, H., and Wulf, C., eds (2007), 'Klanganthropologie', *Paragrana Internationale Zeitschrift für Historische Anthropolog*ie, 16: 2.

7 Wulf, C. ed. (2010), 'Kontaktzonen', *Paragrana Internationale Zeitschrift für Historische Anthropologie*, 19: 2.

8 Changeux, J.-P. (2002), *L'Homme de vérité*, Paris: Odile Jacob.

9 Mitchell, W. J. T. (1986), *Iconology: Image, Text, Ideology*, Chicago: University of Chicago Press, 10.

10 Großklaus, G. (2004), *Medien-Bilder. Inszenierung der Sichtbarkeit*, Frankfurt/M.: Suhrkamp, 9.

11 Wunenburger, J.-J. (1995), *L'imagination*, Paris: Presses Universitaires de France.

12 Straus, E. (1956), *Vom Sinn der Sinne. Ein Beitrag zur Grundlegung der Psychologie*, Berlin, Göttingen, Heidelberg: Springer.

13 Ibid., 212.

14 Howes, D., ed. (1991), *The Varieties of Sensory Experience*, Toronto, Buffalo: University of Toronto Press, 260.

15 Michaels and Wulf, *Exploring the Senses*.

16 Cf. Obert, M. (2006), 'Imagination'. In: Huppauf, B., and Wulf, C., (eds), *Dynamics, and Performativity of Imagination. The Image between the Visible and the Invisible*, London: Routledge, 116–134; Jullien, F. (2009), *The Great Image Has No Form. On the Nonobject through Painting*, Chicago: University of Chicago Press; Escande, Y. (2003), *Traités chinois de peinture et de calligraphie*, Paris: Klincksieck.

17 quoted by Jullien, *The Great Image Has No Form*, 8.

18 Ibid., 13.

19 Wulf, *Anthropology*; Gebauer, and Wulf, *Mimesis*.

20 Jullien, *The Great Image Has No Form*, 229.

21 Appadurai, A. (1996), *Modernity at Large: Cultural Dimensions of Globalization*, Minneapolis: University of Minnesota Press.

22 Jullien, *The Great Image Has No Form*, 252.

23 Obert, 'Imagination', 145.

24 Ibid., 149.

25 Ibid., 152.

Chapter 2

1 See the following seminal works on the theory of the image: Bourdieu, P. (1984), *Distinction: A Social Critique of the Judgement of Taste*, Cambridge, MA: Harvard University Press; Bourdieu, P. (2013), *Outline of a Theory of Practice*, Cambridge; Cambridge University Press; Boehm, G. (1994), 'Die Bilderfrage'. In: Boehm, G. (ed.), *Was ist ein Bild?*, Munich: Wilhelm Fink, 325–43; Kämpf, H., and Schott, R., eds (1995), *Der Mensch als homo pictor? Die Kunst traditioneller Kulturen aus der Sicht von Philosophie und Ethnologie*, Bonn: Bouvier; Schäfer, G., and Wulf, C., eds (1999), *Bild – Bilder – Bildung*, Weinheim: Deutscher Studienverlag; Böhme, G. (2001), *Aisthetik. Vorlesungen über Ästhetik als allgemeine Wahrnehmungslehre*, Munich: Wilhelm Fink; Maar, C., and Burda, H., eds (2004), *Iconic Turn. Die neue Macht der Bilder*, Cologne: Dumont; Großklaus, *Medien-Bilder*. Wiesing, L. (2005), *Artifizielle Präsenz. Studien zur Philosophie des Bildes*, Frankfurt/M.:

Suhrkamp; Wulf, and Zirfas, *Ikonologie des Performativen*; Huppauf, and Wulf, *Dynamics and Performativity of Imagination*; Imai, Y., and Wulf, C. eds (2007), *Concepts of Aesthetic Education. Japanese and European Perspectives*, Münster, New York: Waxmann; Debray, R. (1992), *Vie et mort de l'image. Une histoire du regard en Occident*, Paris: Gallimard; Seel, M. (2000), *Ästhetik des Erscheinens*, Frankfurt/M.: Suhrkamp; Sachs-Hombach, K., and Schirra, R. J., eds (2013), *Origins of Pictures*, Cologne: von Halem; Didi-Huberman, G. (1990), *Devant l'image*, Paris: Minuit; Marin, L. (1993), *Des pouvoirs de l'image*, Paris: Seuil; Mondzain, M.-J. (1996), *Image, icône, économie. Les sources byzantines de l'imaginaire contemporain*, Paris: Seuil; Bredekamp, H. (2010), *Theorie des Bildakts*, Berlin: Suhrkamp; Mersch, D. (2010), *Posthermeneutik,* Berlin: Akademie Verlag; Seitz, S., Graneß, A., and Stenger, G. eds (2018), *Facetten gegenwärtiger Bildtheorie*, Wiesbaden: Springer; Uhlig, B., Lieber, G., and Pieper, I. eds (2019). *Erzählen zwischen Bild und Text*, Munich: Kopaed; Hermann, B., ed. (2019), *Anthropologie und Ästhetik: Interdisziplinäre Perspektiven*, Paderborn: Wilhelm Fink.

2   The term 'fantasy' is related to the Greek *phainestai*, where the emphasis is on something appearing, or rather being made to appear; The Latin word *imaginatio* is different in that it places the emphasis on the process of imagining (lit. taking in the image), or the embodiment of images, which is also emphasized in the German concept of 'Einbildungskraft'.

3   Iser, W. (1993), *The Fictive and the Imaginary: Charting Literary Anthropology*, Baltimore: John Hopkins Press; Sartre, J.-P. (2001), *The Psychology of the Imagination*, London: Routledge.

4   Leroi-Gourhan, A. (1993), *Gesture and Speech*, Cambridge, MA: MIT Press, 192.

5   Wulf, *Anthropology*. Wulf, C., ed. (2010), *Der Mensch und seine Kultur. Hundert Beiträge zur Geschichte, Gegenwart und Zukunft des menschlichen Lebens*, Cologne: Anaconda.

6   Belting, H. (2001), *Bild-Anthropologie*, Munich: Fink, p. 144.

7   Kant, I. (1998), *Critique of Pure Reason*, Cambridge: Cambridge University Press, 256.

8   Boehm, 'Die Bilderfrage'.

9   Ibid., 343.

10 Belting, *Bild-Anthropologie*, 89.

11 McLuhan, M. (1964), *Understanding Media. The Extension of Man*, New York: Mentor.

12 Baudrillard, Jean (1994), *Simulacra and Simulation*, Ann Arbor: The University of Michigan Press.

13 Belting, *Bild-Anthropologie*, 121.

14 Ibid., 123.

Chapter 3

1 Sartre, *Imagination*, 141.

2 Hume, D. (1739/1896), *A Treatise of Human Nature*, L. A. Selby-Bigge (ed.), Oxford: Clarendon Press, 50.

3 Bergson, H. (1912/2004), *Matter and Memory*, Mineola: Dover Publications.

4 Proust, M. (2002), *Finding Time Again in Search of Lost Time*, Vol VI, London: Allen Lane/Penguin, 179.

5 'La seule imagination me rend compte de ce qui peut être' (André Breton, Manifeste du surréalisme, 1924).

6 Bachelard, G. (1969), *The Poetics of Space*, Boston: Beacon Press, xxxiv.

7 Wunenburger, *L'imagination*, 38; Wunenburger, J.-J. (2012), *Gaston Bachelard, poétique des images*, Paris: Mimesis.

8 Rousseau, J.-J. (1979), *Emile or On Education*, New York: Basic Books, 38.

9 Halbwachs, M. (1992), *On Collective Memory*, Chicago: The University of Chicago Press.

10 Goldstein, E. B. (2005), *Cognitive Psychology*, Belmont: Wadsworth Publishing.

11 Rizzolatti, G., and Craighero, L. (2004), 'The Mirror-Neuron System', *Annual Review Neuroscience*, 27: 169–92.

12 Simon, G. (1988), *Le regard, l'être et l'apparence dans l'optique de l'Antiquité,* Paris: Seuil.

13 Kepler, J. (1997), 'Der Vorgang des Sehens'. In: Konersmann, R., (ed.), *Kritik des Sehens*, Leipzig: Reclam, 105.

14 Macho, T. (2000), 'Ist mir bekannt, dass ich sehe?'. In: Belting, H., and Kamper, D. (eds), *Der zweite Blick. Bildgeschichte und Bildreflexion*, Munich: Wilhelm Fink, 215.

15 There is no doubt that this position is a continuation of that of Kant, according to which the 'I think' 'must be able to accompany all my representations'. Kant (Kant, *Critique of Pure Reason*, 246) and Roth (Roth, Gerhard (2000), *Brain Evolution and Cognition*, New York: Wiley) hold a similar view, stating that there is a difference between an attentive consciousness, which is actualized in perception, and a consciousness of one's own self and personal identity.

16 Sartre, *L'imagination*, 171.

17 Ibid., 172.

18 Sartre, ibid., p.184.

19 Benz, E. (1969), *Die Vision. Erfahrungsformen und Bilderwelt*, Stuttgart: Klett.

20 Bloch, E. (1995), *The Principle of Hope*, Cambridge, MA: MIT Press. Blacking, *The Anthropology of the Body*.

21 Descartes, René (1641), *Meditations on First Philosophy in Which the Existence of God and the Distinction Between Mind and Body Are Demonstrated.*

22 Sartre, *Imagination*, 195.

23 Ibid., 206.

Chapter 4

1 Diderot, D. (1875), *Œuvres complètes de Diderot*, Paris: Garnier Frères, 364.

2 Hobbes, T. (2012), *Leviathan*, Dover: Dover Philosophical Classics, 9.

3 Malebranche, N. (1997), *The Search after Truth*, Cambridge: Cambridge University Press, 134.

4 Descartes, *Meditations*, 1.20.

5 Descartes, R. (1988), 'The Passion of the Soul'. In: Cottingham, John, Stoothoff, Robert, Murdoch, Dugald and Kenny, Anthony (eds), *Selected Philosophical Writings*, Cambridge: Cambridge University Press, Article 21.

6 Descartes, *Meditations* I, Article 20,111.

7 Ibid., Article 20, 226.

8 Bodmer, J. J. (1966), *Critische Abhandlung von dem Wunderbaren in der Poesie* (Reprint of the 1740 edition), Stuttgart: Metzler.

9 Kant, *Critique of Pure Reason*, 211; Breitinger, J. J. (1966), *Critische Dichtkunst*. 2 volumes (Reprint of 1849 edition), Stuttgart: Metzler.

10 Mattenklott, G. (2009), 'On Imagination'. In: Huppauf, B., and Wulf, C. (eds), *Dynamics and Performativity of Imagination. The Image between the Visible and the Invisible*, London: Routledge, 54.

11 Bedecke deinen Himmel, Zeus,/ Mit Wolkendunst! / Und übe, dem Knaben gleich,/ Der Disteln köpft,/ An Eichen dich und Bergeshöh'n!/ Mußt mir meine Erde/ Doch lassen steh'n:'

12 Novalis (1997), *Philosophical Writings*, New York: State University of New York, 118.

13 Aristotle (1987), *De Anima (On the Soul)*, London: Penguin Classics, 433b, 29.

14 Merleau-Ponty, M. (1968), *The Visible and the Invisible*, Evanston: Northwestern University Press.

15 Bachelard, G. (1983), *Water and Dreams: An Essay on the Imagination of Matter*, Florida: Pegasus Foundation; Bachelard, G. (1988), *Air and Dreams: An Essay on the Imagination of Matter*, Florida: Pegasus Foundation.

16 Durand, G. (1999), *The Anthropological Structures of The Imaginary*, Brisbane: Boom Bana Publications.

17 Wunenburger, *Imagination*, 31.

18 Wulf, *Das Rätsel des Humanen*.

19 Kretschmar, T. (2016), *The Power of Inner Images*, London: Routledge.

20 Bachelard, *The Poetics of Space*; Bachelard, G. (1980), *La terre et les rêveries de la volonté*, Paris: Corti; Bachelard, G. (1999), *Water and Dreams*; Bachelard, G., (2011), *Air and Dreams*; Bachelard, G., (1985), *La psychoanalyse du feu*, Paris: Gallimard.

21 Durand, *The Anthropological Structures of The Imaginary*.

22 Blumenberg, H. (1985), *The Legitimacy of the Modern Age*, Cambridge, MA: MIT Press;

   Blumenberg, H. (1987), *The Genesis of the Copernican World*, Cambridge, MA: MIT Press.

23 Ricoeur, P. (1974), *The Conflict of Interpretations. Essays in Hermeneutics*, Ihde, D. (ed.), London: Continuum, 3–56;

   Ricoeur, P. (1975), *Le metaphore vive*, Paris: Seuil.

24 Bergson, *Matter and Memory*, pl. vi f.

25 Leroi-Gourhan, *Gesture and Speech*, 96ff.

26 Durand, *The Anthropological Structures of the Imaginary*.

27 Ibid., 52.

28 Jousse, M. (1974/1978), *L'anthropologie du geste*, 3 vols, Paris: Gallimard.

29 Morin, E. (2005), *The Cinema, or The Imaginary Man*, Minneapolis: University of Minnesota Press.

30 Gide, A. (1973), *The Counterfeiters*, New York: Vintage Books, 71.

31 Rousseau, J.-J. (1996), *The Confessions*, Ware: Classics of World Literature, 38.

32 Aristotle, *De Anima*, 43.

33 Jung, C. G. (2005), *Aspects of the Masculine*, London: Routledge, 130.

34 Lacan, J. (2001), 'Les complexes familiaux dans la formation de l'individu. Essai d'analyse d'une fonction en psychologie'. In: *Autres écrits*, Paris: Editions du Seuil, 23–84.

35 Bachelard, *Water and Dreams*, 17.

36 Wunenburger, *L'imagination*, 60.

37 Ibid., 64, author's translation.

38 Ibid., 65.

39 Bhabha, H. K. (1994), *The Location of Culture*, London: Routledge; Wulf, C., ed. (2016), *Exploring Alterity in a Globalized World*, London: Routledge.

40 Mitchell, *Iconology*.

41 Imdahl, M. (1994), 'Ikonik. Bilder und ihre Anschauung'. In: Boehm, G. (ed.), *Was ist ein Bild?*, Munich: Wilhelm Fink, 318.

42 Ibid., 319.

43 Morin, *The Cinema*, 208.

44 Caillois, R. (2001), *Man, Play, and Games*, Champaign: University of Illinois Press.

45 de Montaigne, M. (1976), *Complete Essays*, Palo Alto: Stanford University Press, 773.

Chapter 5

1 Bachelard, *Poetics of Space*; Bachelard, *Water and Dream*.

2 Bachelard, *Air and Dreams*, 109.

3 Ibid., 111–112.

4 Ibid., 28.

5 Ibid., 261.

6 Ibid., 94, italics in original.

7 Durand, *The Anthropological Structures of the Imaginary*, 42.

8 Ibid., 61.

9 Ibid.

10 In his writings on archetypes, Durand cites C. G. Jung. However, he uses only one of the definitions that are to be found in Jung's works. Recently, several Jungian analysts have drawn attention to the fact that Jung defined archetype in several different ways at different times, some of which contradict each other. Today a clearer distinction is made between archetypes and archetypal images. See https://www.thesap.org.uk/resources/articles-on-jungian-psychology-2/about-analysis-and-therapy/complexes-and-archetypes/.

11 Ibid., 62.

12 Ibid., 63, italics mine.

13 Ibid., 55.

14 Resina, J. R., and Wulf, C., eds (2019), *Repetition, Recurrence, Returns. How Cultural Renewal Works*, Lanham: Lexington Books/Roman & Littlefield.

15 Wittgenstein, L. (1993), *Letzte Schriften über die Philosophie der Psychologie: Das Innere und das Äußere*, Frankfurt/M.: Suhrkamp.

16 Ricoeur, *The Conflict of Interpretations*, 12. Ricoeur, *Le metaphore vive*.

17 Durand, *The Anthropological Structures of The Imaginary*.

18 Wunenburger, *L'imagination*, 69.

Chapter 6

1 Translator's note: All quotes from works by Dietmar Kamper have been translated into English by the translators of the present book.

2 Kamper, *Zur Soziologie der Imagination*, 134.

3 Ibid., 135.

4 Ibid., 127f.

5 Ibid., 138.

6 Ibid., 142.

7 Ibid., 144.

8 Ibid., 85.

9 Kamper, D. (1995), *Unmögliche Gegenwart. Zur Theorie der Phantasie*, Munich: Wilhelm Fink, 23.

10 Wulf, C., and Kamper, D., eds (2002), *Logik und Leidenschaft. Erträge Historischer Anthropologie*, Berlin: Reimer.

11 Rilke, R. M. (1977), *Possibility of Being: A Selection of Poems*, New York: New Directions, 108–9.

12 Kamper, *Zur Soziologie der Imagination*, 32f.

13 Ibid., 25.

14 Ibid.

15 Ibid., 45.

16 Ibid., 46.

17 Ibid., 57.

18 Ibid., 58.

19 Barthes, R. (1981), *Camera Lucida: Reflections on Photography*, New York: Hill and Wang.

20 Ibid., 65.

21 Ibid.

22 Ibid., 67.

23 Baudrillard, cited in Carlsson, M. (2013), 'Red Bull Stratos – At the Edge of the Obscene', *International Journal of Baudrillard Studies*, 10 (2), retrieved; and Ibid., 39.

24 Ibid., 80.

25 Ibid.

26 Ibid., 91.

27 Ibid., 136.

28 Ibid.

Chapter 7

1 For more on the connection between embodiment or incorporation and practical knowledge, see also Bourdieu, 1990, 54.

2 Leroi-Gourhan, *Gesture and Speech*.

3 Augé, M. (1999), *An Anthropology for Contemporaneous Worlds*, Palo Alto: Stanford University Press.

4 Gruzinski, S. (2001), *Images at War: Mexico from Columbus to Blade Runner, 1492–2019*, trans. H. MacLean, Durham: Duke University Press.

5 Kontopodis, Varvantakis, and Wulf, *Global Youth in Digital Trajectories*; Wulf, *Education as Human Knowledge in the Anthropocene. An Anthropological Perspective*.

6 Belting, *Anthropology of Images*.

7 Alliez, cited in Belting, *Bild-Anthropologie*, 25.

8 Flusser, V. (1990), *Writings*, Minneapolis: University of Minnesota Press, 116.

9 Merleau-Ponty, *The Visible and the Invisible*, 133.

10 Cf. Virilio, P. (1989), *War and Cinema, The Logistics of Perception*, London: Verso; Virilio, P. (1990), *L'inertie polaire. Essai sur le contrôle d'environnement,* Paris: Christian Bourgois; Virilio, P. (2010), *The University of Disaster*, Cambridge: Polity.

11 Gehlen, A. (1988), *Man*, New York: Columbia University Press, 316.

12 Flügge, J. (1963), *Die Entfaltung der Anschauungskraft*, Heidelberg: Quelle & Meyer, 93.

13 Gehlen, *Man*, 309.

14 Iser, *The Fictive and the Imaginary*.

15 Adorno, T., Albert, H., Dahrendorf, R., Habermas, J., Pilot, H., and Popper, K. R., eds (1969), *The Positivist Dispute in German Sociology,* London: Heinemann, 51.

16 Hume, *A Treatise of Human Nature*, 19.

17 Coleridge, S. (1907), *Biographia Literaria*, Oxford: Clarendon Press, 202.

18 Sartre, Jean-Paul, (2001), *The Imagination*, London: Routledge.

19 Lacan, J. (1949), 'Le Stade du miroir comme formateur de la fonction du Je: telle qu'elle nous est révélée dans l'expérience psychanalytique'. In: *Revue française de psychanalyse*, 449–55.

20 Castoriadis, C. (1987), *The Imaginary Institution of Society*, Cambridge: Polity Press, 127.

Chapter 8

1 Brandstetter, G., Buchholz, M., Hamburger, A., and Wulf, C. eds (2018), 'Balance, – Rhythmus – Resonanz', *Paragrana. Internationale Zeitschrift für Historische Anthropologie*, 27: 1.

2 Bourdieu, P. (1990), *The Logic of Practice*, Palo Alto: Stanford University Press, 53.

3 Krais, and Gebauer (2002), *Habitus*, Bielefeld: transcript, 37.

4 Bourdieu, *Distinction*, 175–6.

5 Ibid.

6 Ibid., 194–5.

7 Ibid., 196.

8 Butler, J. (1990), *Gender Trouble. Feminism and the Subversion of Identity*, London and New York: Routledge.

9 Fischer-Lichte, E., and Wulf, C., eds (2004), 'Praktiken des Performativen'. *Paragrana. Internationale Zeitschrift für Historische Anthropologie*, 13: 251–309.

10 Bourdieu, P. (1997), 'Eine sanfte Gewalt. Pierre Bourdieu im Gespräch mit Irene Dölling und Margareta Steinrücke'. In: Dölling, I., and Krais, B. (eds), *Ein alltägliches Spiel,* Frankfurt/M.: Suhrkamp, 222.

11 Krais, and Gebauer, *Habitus*, 51.
12 Ibid., 56.

Chapter 9

1   de Cervantes Saavedra, Miguel (1615), *Don Quixote*. Available online: http://www
    .spanisharts.com/books/quijote/chapter8.htm, chapter 8.
2   Schürmann, E. (2008), *Sehen als Praxis. Ethisch-ästhetische Studien zum Verhältnis
    von Sicht und Einsicht*, Frankfurt/M.: Suhrkamp.
3   Cf. Buytendijk, F. J. J. (1933), *Wesen und Sinn des Spiels. Das Spielen des Menschen
    und der Tiere als Erscheinungsform der Lebenstriebe*, Berlin: Wolff; Huizinga, J.
    (1971), *Homo ludens*, Boston: Beacon Press; Fink, E. (1960), *Spiel als Weltsymbol*,
    Stuttgart: Kohlhammer.
4   Wittgenstein, *Letzte Schriften über die Philosophie der Psychologie*; Gebauer,
    G. (1997), 'Spiel'. In: Wulf, C., (ed.), *Vom Menschen. Handbuch Historische
    Anthropologie* Weinheim, Basel: Beltz, 1038–48.
5   Gebauer, G., and Wulf, C. (1998), *Spiel, Ritual, Geste. Mimetisches Handeln in der
    sozialen Welt*, Reinbek: Rowohlt, 192.
6   Caillois, *Man, Play, and Games*.
7   Geertz, C. (1973), 'Thick Description: Toward an Interpretative Theory of Culture'.
    In: *The Interpretation of Cultures*, New York: Basic Books, 3–30.
8   Resina, and Wulf, *Repetition*.
9   Bateson, G. (1955), 'A Theory of Play and Fantasy', *In Psychiatric Research Reports*,
    1955: 177–8.
10 Elias, N., and E. Dunning, E. (1986), *Quest for Excitement. Sport and Leisure in the
    Civilizing Process*, Oxford: Blackwell.
11 Gebauer, and Wulf, *Spiel, Ritual, Geste*, 205.
12 Ibid., 207.
13 Cf. Gebauer, and Wulf, *Spiel, Ritual, Geste*, 210; Thorne, B. (1993), *Gender Play.
    Girls and Boys in School*, Buckingham: Open University Press; Tervooren, A. (2001),
    'Pausenspiele als performative Kinderkultur'. In: Wulf, Christoph et al. *Das Soziale
    als Ritual. Zur performativen Bildung von Gemeinschaften*, Opladen: Leske &
    Budrich, 205–48.

Chapter 10

1   Jung, V. (1977), *Handbuch des Tanzes*, Hildesheim, New York: Olms; Brandstetter,
    and Wulf, *Tanz als Anthropologie*; Klein, G., and Malte, F. (2011), *Die Kultur des
    HipHop*, Frankfurt/M.: Suhrkamp.

2 Wulf, and Kamper, *Logik und Leidenschaft*.

3 Dinkla, S., and Leeker, M., eds (2002), *Tanz und Technologie. Auf dem Weg zu medialen Inszenierungen*, Berlin: Alexander.

4 Brandstetter, and Wulf, *Tanz als Anthropologie*.

5 Boetsch, G., and Wulf, C., eds (2005), 'Rituels', Vol 43, Paris: CNRS Éditions; Wulf, *Anthropologie. Geschichte – Kultur – Philosophie*; Wulf, *Anthropology*, 199 ff.

6 Featherstone, M. (1995), *Undoing Culture. Globalization, Postmodernism and Identity*, London, Thousand Oaks: Sage; Wulf, *Der Mensch und seine Kultur*; Wulf, *Exploring Alterity in a Globalized World*.

7 Wulf, *Anthropology*; Wulff, Helena, ed. (2007), *The Emotion. A Cultural Reader*, New York, Oxford: Berg.

Chapter 11

1 Resina, and Wulf, *Repetition*.

2 Wulf, C. (2006), 'Praxis'. In: Kreinath, J., Snoek, J. A. M, and Stausberg, M. (eds), *Theorizing Rituals: Issues, Topics, Approaches, Concepts*, Leiden: Brill, 395–411.

3 Wulf, *Zur Genese des Sozialen*.

4 Kraus, A., Budde, J, Hietzge, M., and Wulf, C., eds (2021), *Handbuch Schweigendes Wissen. Erziehung, Bildung, Sozialisation und Lernen*, 2nd edn, Weinheim and Basel: Beltz Juventa; Kraus, A., and Wulf, C., eds (2022), *Handbook of Embodiment and Learning*, London: Palgrave, Macmillan.

5 Wulf, C., and Zirfas, J., eds (2003), 'Rituelle Welten', *Paragrana. Internationale Zeitschrift für Historische Anthropologie*, 12 (1).

6 Wulf, *Education as Human Knowledge in the Anthropocene. An Anthropological Perspective*.

7 Cf. the following ethnographic publications of the Berlin Ritual and Gesture Study: Wulf, C., Althans, B., Audehm, K., Bausch, C., Jörissen, B., Göhlich, M., Sting, S., Tervooren, A. Wagner-Willi, M., and Zirfas, J. (2001), *Das Soziale als Ritual. Zur performativen Bedeutung von Gemeinschaft*, Opladen: Leske & Budrich; Wulf, C., Althans, B., Audehm, K., Bausch, C., Jörissen, B., Göhlich, M., Mattig, R., Tervooren, A., Wagner-Willi, M., and Zirfas, J. (2004), *Bildung im Ritual. Schule, Familie, Jugend, Medien*, Wiesbaden: Springer VS; Wulf, C., Althans, B., Audehm, K., Blaschke, G., Ferrin, N., Jörissen, B., Göhlich, M., Mattig, R., Schinkel, S., Tervooren, A., Wagner-Willi, M., and Zirfas, J. (2007), *Lernkulturen im Umbruch. Rituelle Praktiken in Schule, Medien, Familie und Jugend*, Wiesbaden: Springer; Wulf et al., *Ritual and Identity*; Wulf et al., *Die Geste in Erziehung, Bildung und Sozialisation*.

8 Bausch, C. (2006), *Verkörperte Medien. Bilder der Gemeinschaft, Aufführung der Körper*, Bielefeld: transcript.

9 Frazer, J. G. (2009), *The Golden Bough. A Study in Magic and Religion*, Oxford: Oxford University Press; Otto, R. (1958), *The Idea of the Holy*, Oxford: Oxford University Press; Eliade, M. (1961), *The Sacred and the Profane: The Nature of Religion*, New York: Harper Torchbooks.

10 Durkheim, E. (1912), *The Elementary Forms of the Religious Life*, London: George Allen and Unwin Ltd; van Gennep, A. (1960), *The Rites of Passage*, London: Routledge & Paul; Sahlins, M. (1976), *Culture and Practical Reason*, University of Chicago Press.

11 Geertz, *Thick Description: Toward an Interpretative Theory of Culture*.

12 Bell, C. (1992), *Ritual Theory, Ritual Practice*, New York: Oxford University Press; Grimes, R. (1995), *Beginnings in Ritual Studies*, Columbia: University of South Carolina Press; Turner, V. (1982), *From Ritual to Theatre. The Human Seriousness of Play*, New York: PAJ Publications.

13 Bourdieu, *Outline of a Theory of Practice*. Schechner, R. (1977), *Essays on Performance Theory 1970-1976*, New York: Drama Book Specialists; Wulf, *Anthropology*; Tambiah, S. (1979), 'A Performative Approach to Ritual', *Proceedings of the British Academy*, 65: 113–63.

14 Wulf, 'Praxis'.

15 Grimes, *Beginnings in Ritual Studies*.

16 Girard, R. (1977), *Violence and the Sacred*, Baltimore: John Hopkins University Press.
Girard, R. (1996), *The Scapegoat*, Baltimore: The Johns Hopkins University Press.

17 Wulf, *Der Mensch und seine Kultur*.

18 Wulf et al., *Bildung im Ritual*.

19 Wulf et al., *Lernkulturen im Umbruch*.

20 Wulf et al., *Die Geste in Erziehung, Bildung und Sozialisation*.

21 Glaser, B. G., and Strauss, A. (1969), *The Discovery of Grounded Theory*, Chicago: Chicago University Press; Strauss, A., and Corbin, J. (1994), 'Grounded Theory. An Overview'. In: Denzin, N. K., and Lincoln, Y. S. (eds), *Handbook of Qualitative Research*, Thousand Oaks: Sage, 273–85.

22 Cf. Flick, U., ed. (2013), *The Sage Handbook of Qualitative Data Analysis*, Thousand Oaks: Sage Publications; Flick, U. (2018), *Doing Triangulation and Mixed Methods*, Thousand Oaks: Sage Publications; Bohnsack, R. (2003), *Rekonstruktive Sozialforschung. Einführung in qualitative Methoden*, Opladen: Leske und Budrich; Tervooren, 'Pausenspiele als performative Kinderkultur'. Tervooren, A., Engel, N., Göhlich, M., Miethe, I., and Reh, S. eds (2014), *Ethnographie und Differenz in pädagogischen Feldern. Internationale Entwicklungen erziehungswissenschaftlicher Forschung*, Bielefeld : transcript.

23 Wulf, C., Göhlich, M., and Zirfas, J., eds (2001), *Grundlagen des Performativen. Eine Einführung in die Zusammenhänge von Sprache, Macht und Handeln*, Weinheim, Munich: Juventa; Wulf, and Zirfas, *Pädagogik des Performativen.*

24 Wulf, C., Suzuki, S., Zirfas, J., Kellermann, I., Inoue, Y., Ono, F., and Takenaka, N. (2011), *Das Glück der Familie: Ethnographische Studien in Deutschland und Japan*, Wiesbaden: Springer VS.

25 Goffman, E. (1974), *Frame-Analysis. An Essay on the Organization of Experience*, New York: Harper and Row.

26 Austin, J. L. (1962), *How to Do Things with Words*, Cambridge, MA: Harvard University Press.

27 Butler, *Gender Trouble*; Butler, J. (1993), *Bodies That Matter. On the Discursive Limits of 'Sex'*, London and New York: Routledge Classics.

28 UNESCO (1996), *Learning, the Treasure within: Report to UNESCO of the International Commission on Education for the 21st Century*, Paris: UNESCO.

29 Wulf, *Education as Human Knowledge in the Anthropocene.*

30 Wulf, *Anthropology*; Wulf, *Das Rätsel des Humanen.*

31 Mollenhauer, K., and Wulf, C., eds (1996), *Aisthesis/Asthetik. Zwischen Wahrnehmung und Bewusstsein*, Weinheim: Deutscher Studienverlag; Schäfer, G., and Wulf, *Bild – Bilder – Bildung*; Wulf, *Education as Human Knowledge in the Anthropocene.*

32 Frazer, J. G. (2009), *The Golden Bough. A Study in Magic and Religion*, Oxford: Oxford University Press.

33 Gebauer, and Wulf, *Mimesis.*

34 Wulf, and Zirfas, *Die Kultur des Rituals.*

35 van Gennep, *The Rites of Passage.*

36 Resina, and Wulf, *Repetition.*

37 Wulf et al., *Das Soziale als Ritual*; Wulf et al., *Bildung im Ritual*; Wulf et al., *Lernkulturen im Umbruch*; Wulf et al., *Die Geste in Erziehung, Bildung und Sozialisation.*

38 Wulf, 'Praxis'; Boetsch, and Wulf, 'Rituels'; Kraus, Budde, Hietzge, and Wulf, *Handbuch Schweigendes Wissen*, 1917, second edn, 2021.

Chapter 12

1 Cf. Wulf et al., *Das Soziale als Ritual*; Wulf et al., *Bildung im Ritual*; Wulf et al., *Lernkulturen im Umbruch*; Wulf et al., *Ritual and Identity*; Wulf et al., *Die Geste in Erziehung, Bildung und Sozialisation.*

2 Cf. Flusser, V. (1990), *Writings*, Andreas Ströhl (ed.), Minneapolis: University of Minnesota Press; Flusser, V. (1993), 'Eine neue Einbildungskraft'. In: Flusser, V.

(ed.), *Lob der Oberflächlichkeit. Für eine Phänomenologie der Medien*, Bensheim: Bollmann, 251–331; Egidi, M., Schneider, O., Schöning, M., Schütze, I., and Torra-Mattenklott, C., eds (2000), *Gestik. Figuren des Körpers in Text und Bild*, Tübingen: Narr; Müller, C., and Posner, R., eds (2004), *The Semantics and Pragmatics of Everyday Gestures*, Berlin: Weidler; Prange, K. (2005), *Die Zeigestruktur der Erziehung. Grundriss der operativen Pädagogik*, Paderborn: Schöningh; Kraus, Budde, Hietzge, and Wulf, *Handbuch Schweigendes Wissen*.

3 Wulf et al., *Die Geste in Erziehung, Bildung und Sozialisation*.

4 Agamben, G. (2000), 'Notes on Gesture'. In: *Means Without End: Notes on Politics*, Minneapolis: University of Minnesota Press.

5 Mead, G. H. (2015), *Mind, Self, and Society*, London: University of Chicago Press.

6 Kendon, *Gesture: Visible Action as Utterance*. McNeill, *Gesture and Thought*.

7 Gal, M., Friedlander, E., Wulf, C., and Zuckermann, M., eds (2014), 'Art and Gesture', *Paragrana. Internationale Zeitschrift für Historische Anthropologie*, 23: 1.

8 Goldin-Meadow, S. (2005), *Hearing Gesture. How Our Hands Help Us Think*, Cambridge, MA, London: Harvard University Press.

9 Bremmer, J., and Roodenburg, H., eds (1992), *A Cultural History of Gesture*, Ithaca, London: Cornell University Press.

10 Birdwhistell, R. L. (1952), *Introduction to Kinesics. An Annotation System for the Analysis of Body Motion and Gesture*, Louisville: University Louisville Press; Birdwhistell, R. L. (1970), *Kinesics and Context. Essays on Body Motion Communication*, Philadelphia: University of Pennsylvania Press.

11 Darwin, C. (1979), *The Expression of the Emotions in Man and Animals*, London: Murray.

12 Morris, D., Collett, P., Marsh, P., and O'Shaughnessy, M. (1979), *Gestures Their Origins and Distribution*, London: Jonathan Cape.

13 Calbris, G. (1990), *The Semiotics of French Gestures*, Bloomington, Indianapolis: Indiana University Press.

14 Benthien, C., and Wulf, C., eds (2001), *Körperteile. Eine kulturelle Anatomie*, Reinbek: Rowohlt.

15 Plessner, H. (1983), 'Conditio Humana'. In: Plessner, H. (ed.), *Gesammelte Schriften*, vol. 8, Frankfurt/M.: Suhrkamp.

16 McNeill, *Hand and Mind*; McNeill, *Gesture and Thought*.

17 Darwin, *The Expression of the Emotions in Man and Animals*.

18 Bourdieu, *Distinction*.

19 Elias, N. (1994), *The Civilizing Process: Sociogenetic and Psychogenetic Investigations*, Hoboken: Blackwell.

20 Foucault, M. (1977), *Discipline and Punish: The Birth of the Prison*, New York: Vintage Books.

21 Schmitt, J.-C. (1990), *La raison des gestes dans l'Occident médiéval*, Paris: Galimard.

22 Geertz, 'Thick Description: Toward an Interpretative Theory of Culture'.

23 Starobinski, J. (1994), *Gute Gaben, schlimme Gaben. Die Ambivalenz sozialer Gesten*, Frankfurt/M.: Fischer.

24 Wulf, and Fischer-Lichte, *Gesten – Inszenierung, Aufführung, Praxis*; Wulf et al., *Die Geste in Erziehung, Bildung und Sozialisation*.

Chapter 13

1 Tomasello, M. (1999), *The Cultural Origins of Human Cognition*, Cambridge , MA: Harvard University Press, 161.

2 Tomasello, M. (2008), *Origins of Human Communication*, Cambridge, MA: MIT Press.

3 Else, G. F. (1958), 'Imitation in the 5th Century', *Classical Philology*, 53 (2): 79.

4 Plato, 1979, *The Republic*, trans. D. Lee, 2nd edn, Harmondsworth: Penguin, 149 ff.

5 Gebauer, and Wulf, *Mimesis*, chapters 2–5.

6 Benjamin, W. (2006), *Berlin Childhood Around 1900*, Cambridge: Belknap.

7 Ibid., 122.

8 Eiland, H., and Jennings, M. W. (2014), *Walter Benjamin: A Critical Life*, Cambridge, MA: Harvard University/Belknap Press, 697.

9 Resina, and Wulf, *Repetition*.

10 Gebauer, and Wulf, *Spiel, Ritual, Geste*.

11 Gehlen, *Man*.

12 Wulf, Göhlich, and Zirfas, *Grundlagen des Performativen*; Wulf, and Zirfas, *Pädagogik des Performativen*.

13 Cf. Rizzolatti, and Craighero, *The Mirror-Neuron-System*.

14 Giroux, H., and D. Purpel, D., eds. (1983), *The Hidden Curriculum and Moral Education*, Berkeley, California: McCutchan Publishing Corporation.

Chapter 14

1 Cf. UNESCO, *Learning, the Treasure within*; UNESCO (2001), *First Proclamation of Masterpieces of the Oral and Intangible Heritage of Humanity*, Paris: UNESCO; UNESCO (2002), *Medium Term Strategy 2002–2007*, Paris: UNESCO; UNESCO (2003a), *Convention for the Safeguarding of Intangible Cultural Heritage*, Paris: UNESCO; UNESCO (2003b), *Second Proclamation of Masterpieces of the Oral and Intangible Heritage of Humanity*, Paris: UNESCO; UNESCO (2004), *Museums International: Views and Visions of the Intangible*,

Paris. UNESCO; UNESCO (2005), *Übereinkommen über den Schutz und die Förderung der Vielfalt kultureller Ausdrucksformen*, DUK, Bonn: Deutsche UNESCO-Kommission.

2 Kraus, and Wulf, *Handbook of Embodiment and Learning*.

3 Cf. Wulf, Göhlich, and Zirfas, *Grundlagen des Performativen*; Wulf, and Zirfas, *Pädagogik des Performativen*; Fischer-Lichte, and Wulf, 'Praktiken des Performativen'.

4 Gebauer, and Wulf, *Mimesis*; Resina, and Wulf, *Repetition*.

5 Lakoff, G., and Johnson, M. (1999), *Philosophy in the Flesh. The Embodied Mind and Its Challenge to Western Thought*, New York: Basic Books.

6 Alkemeyer, T., Brümmer, K., Kodalle, R., and Pille, T., eds (2009), *Ordnung als Bewegung. Choreografien des Sozialen*, Bielefeld: transcript.

7 Resina, and Wulf, *Repetition*.

8 Cf. Todorov, T. (1996), *The Conquest of America. The Question of the Other*, New York: Harper; Greenblatt, S. (1992), *Marvellous Possessions: The Wonder of the New World*, Chicago: University of Chicago Press; Gruzinski, S. (2001), *Images at War: Mexico from Columbus to Blade Runner, 1492-2019*, Durham: Duke University Press; Gruzinski, S. (1999), *La pensée métisse*, Paris: Fayard; Waldenfels, B. (1990), *Der Stachel des Fremden*, Frankfurt/M.: Suhrkamp; Waldenfels, B. (2010), *Sinne und Künste im Wechselspiel. Modi ästhetischer Erfahrung*, Berlin: Suhrkamp; Wulf, *Exploring Alterity in a Globalized World*.

9 Waldenfels, *Sinne und Künste im Wechselspiel*.

10 Elias, *The Civilizing Process*; Foucault, *Discipline and Punish*; Beck, U., Vossenkuhl, W., and Ziegler, U. E. (1995), *Eigenes Leben. Ausflüge in die unbekannte Gesellschaft, in der wir leben*, Munich: Beck.

11 Todorov, *The Conquest of America*; Greenblatt, *Marvellous Possessions*.

12 Wulf, *Exploring Alterity in a Globalized World*.

13 Wulf, *Education as Human Knowledge in the Anthropocene*.

Chapter 15

1 Douglas, M. (1986), *How Institutions Think*, New York: Syracuse University Press.

2 Morgenthaler, C., and Hauri, R., eds (2010), *Rituale im Familienleben: Inhalte, Formen und Funktionen im Verhältnis der Generationen*, Weinheim, Munich: Juventa.

3 Keppler, A. (1994), *Tischgespräche. Über Formen kommunikativer Vergemeinschaftung am Beispiel der Konversation in Familien*, Frankfurt/M.: Fischer.

4 Quinn, W. H., Newfield, Neal, Protinsky, A., and Howard, O. (1985), 'Rites of Passage in Families with Adolescents', *Family Process*, 24: 101–11; Wolin, S. J., and Bennett, L. A. (1984), 'Family Rituals', *Family Process* 23: 401–20.

5 Imber-Black, E., Roberts, J., and Whiting, R. A., eds (1988), *Rituals in Families and Family Therapy*, New York: Norton; Bowen, M. (1978), *Family Therapy in Clinical Practice*, New York: Jason Aronson.

6 Morgenthaler, and Hauri, *Rituale im Familienleben.*

7 van Gennep, *The Rites of Passage.*

8 Kellermann, I. (2008), *Vom Kind zum Schulkind. Die rituelle Gestaltung der Schulanfangsphase,* Opladen: Budrich UniPress.

9 Turner, V. (1969), *The Ritual Process: Structure and Anti-Structure*, Chicago: Aldine.

10 Michaels, A., and Wulf, C., eds (2012), *Emotions in Rituals and Performances*, London: Routledge.

11 Wulf, and Zirfas, *Pädagogik des Performativen*; Wulf, C., and Zirfas, J., eds (2014), *Handbuch Pädagogische Anthropologie*, Wiesbaden: Springer VS.

12 Austin, *How to Do Things with Words.*

13 Resina and Wulf, *Repetition.*

14 Benjami, *Berlin Childhood around 1900.*

15 Tulving, E. (2005), 'Episodic Memory and Autonoesis: Uniquely Human?', In: Terrace, H. S., and Metcalfe, J. (eds), *The Missing Link in Cognition: Self-knowing Consciousness in Man and Animals*, New York: Oxford University Press, 3–56.

16 Bourdieu, *Outline of a Theory of Practice.*

17 Tomasello, *Origins of Human Communication*; Tomasello, *The Cultural Origins of Human Cognition*; Iacoboni, M. (2008), *Mirroring People. The New Science of How We Connect with Others*, New York: Farrar, Straus and Giroux.

Chapter 16

1 Glaser, and Strauss, *The Discovery of Grounded Theory.*

2 Cf. Bohnsack, R. (2003), *Rekonstruktive Sozialforschung*; Bohnsack, R. (2009), *Qualitative Bild- und Videointerpretation: Die dokumentarische Methode*, Opladen, Farmington Hills: Barbara Budrich; Flick, *The Sage Handbook of Qualitative Data Analysis*; Flick, *Doing Triangulation and Mixed Methods.*

3 Seneca (65/1917), Ad Lucillium Epistulae Morales. Engl. Trans. *Moral letters to Lucilius* by R. M. Gummere, London: Heinemann, letter 85, p. 1. Available online: https://en.wikisource.org/wiki/Moral_letters_to_Lucilius on.

4 Wulf, *Exploring Alterity in a Globalized World.*

5 Wulf and Suzuki, *Das Glück in der Familie.*

6 Wittgenstein, L. (2003), Tractatus Logico-philosophicus. Tr by DF Pears and BF McGuiness, London and New York: Routledge. p. 87. 6.43.

7   Cf. Wulf, and Kamper, eds (2002), *Logik und Leidenschaft*; Greco, M., and Stenner, P., eds (2008), *Emotions. A Social Science Reader*, London, New York: Routledge; Harding, J., and Pribram, E. D., eds (2009), *Emotions: A Cultural Studies Reader*, London, New York: Routledge; Wulf, C., Poulain, J., and Triki, F. eds, (2011), 'Emotionen in einer transkulturellen Welt', *Paragrana Internationale Zeitschrift für Historische Anthropologie*, 20: 2; Klien, Susanne, and Wulf, Christoph (2013), 'Well-being', *Paragrana: Internationale Zeitschrift für Historische Anthropologie*, 22: 1.

8   Ekman, P. E., Sorenson, R., and Ellsworth, P. (1982), *Emotions in the Human Face*, New York: Pergamon.

9   Wulf, and Fischer-Lichte, *Gesten*; Kraus, and Wulf, *Handbook of Embodiment and Learning*.

10 Gebauer, and Wulf, *Mimesis*; Suzuki, S., and C. Wulf, (2007), *Mimesis, Poiesis and Performativity in Education*, Münster, New York: Waxmann.

11 Cf. Wulf, and Zirfas, *Die Kultur des Rituals*; Michaels, A., and Wulf, C., eds (2011), *Images of the Body in India*, London: Routledge; Michaels, and Wulf, *Emotions in Rituals and Performances*; Michaels, and Wulf, *Exploring the Senses*; Michaels, A., and Wulf, C, eds (2020), *Science and Scientification in South Asia and Europe*, London: Routledge.

12 Wulf, and Fischer-Licht, *Gesten*; Wulf et al., *Die Geste in Erziehung, Bildung und Sozialisation*.

13 Bohnsack, *Qualitative Bild- und Videointerpretation*.

14 Butler, *Bodies That Matter*.

15 20:58-21:05 of the CD 25.12.

16 Klien, and Wulf, 'Well-being'.

17 Wittgenstein, L. (1960), 'Philosophische Untersuchungen'. In: Wittgenstein, L. (ed.), *Schriften. Vol. I*, Frankfurt/M.: Suhrkamp, 73.

18 Antweiler, C. (2016), *Our Common Denominator. Human Universals Revisited*, New York & Oxford: Berghahn Books.

19 Wulf et al., *Das Glück der Familie*.

20 Durkheim, *The Elementary Forms of the Religious Life*.

Conclusion

1   Weibel, P., and Buddensieg, A., eds (2007), *Contemporary Art and the Museum: A Global Perspective*, Ostfildern: Hatje Cantz.

2   Belting, H., and Buddensieg, A., eds (2009), *The Global Art World. Audiences, Markets, and Museums*, Ostfildern: Hatje Cantz.

3   Reckwitz, A. (2019), *Die Gesellschaft der Singularitäten. Zum Strukturwandel der Moderne*, Berlin: Suhrkamp.

4   Wallenhorst, and Wulf, *Dictionnaire d'anthropologie Prospective*; Wallenhorst, and Wulf, *Handbook of the Anthropocene.*

5   Pross, H. (1970), *Publizistik: Thesen zu einem Grundcolloquium*, Neuwied: Luchterhand, 129.

6   *Paragrana*, Internationale Zeitschrift für Historische Anthropologie (2021), Den Menschen neu denken, 30 (1).

7   Kontopodis, Varvantakis, and Wulf, *Global Youth in Digital Trajectories.*

8   Wulf, *Education as Human Knowledge in the Anthropocene.*

9   Wallenhorst, and Wulf, *Dictionnaire d'anthropologie Prospective*; Wallenhorst, and Wulf, *Handbook of the Anthropocene.*`

References

Adorno, T., H. Albert, R. Dahrendorf, J., Habermas, H. Pilot, and K. R. Popper, eds (1969), *The Positivist Dispute in German Sociology*, trans. G. Adey and D. Frisby, London: Heinemann.

Agamben, G. (2000), 'Notes on Gesture', in *Means Without End: Notes on Politics*, trans. C. Cesarino, and V. Binetti. Minneapolis: University of Minnesota Press.

Alkemeyer, T., K. Brümmer, R. Kodalle, and T. Pille, eds (2009), *Ordnung als Bewegung. Choreografien des Sozialen*, Bielefeld: transcript.

Antweiler, C. (2016), *Our Common Denominator. Human Universals Revisited*, New York & Oxford: Berghahn Books.

Appadurai, A. (1996), *Modernity At Large: Cultural Dimensions of Globalization*, Minneapolis: University of Minnesota Press.

Aristotle (1987), *De Anima (On the Soul)*, trans. H. Lawson-Tancred, London: Penguin Classics.

Aristotle (1996), *Poetics*, trans. Malcolm Heath, London: Penguin Classics.

Aristotle (2007), *Aristotle on Memory and Recollection. Text, Translation, Interpretation and Reception in Western Scholasticism* by D. Bloch, Leiden: Brill.

Augé, M. (1999), *An Anthropology for Contemporaneous Worlds*, Palo Alto: Stanford University Press.

Austin, J. L. (1962), *How to Do Things with Words*, Cambridge, MA: Harvard University Press.

Bachelard, G. (1969), *The Poetics of Space*, trans. M. Jolas, Boston: Beacon Press.

Bachelard, G. (1980), *La terre et les rêveries de la volonté*, Paris: Corti.

Bachelard, G. (1983), *Water and Dreams: An Essay on the Imagination of Matter*, Florida: Pegasus Foundation.

Bachelard, G. (1988), *Air and Dreams. An Essay on the Imagination of Movement*, trans. E. R. Farrell and C. F. Farrell, Dallas: Dallas Institute Publications.

Bachelard, G. (1997), *La psychoanalyse du feu*, Paris: Gallimard.

Barthes, R. (1981), *Camera Lucida: Reflections on Photography*, New York: Hill and Wang.

Bateson, G. (1955), 'A Theory of Play and Fantasy', *Psychiatric Research Reports*, 2(39): 177–8.

Baudrillard, Jean (1994), *Simulacra and Simulation*, Ann Arbor: The University of Michigan Press.

Bausch, C. (2006), *Verkörperte Medien. Bilder der Gemeinschaft, Aufführung der Körper*, Bielefeld: transcript.

Beck, U., W. Vossenkuhl, and U. E. Ziegler (1995), *Eigenes Leben. Ausflüge in die unbekannte Gesellschaft, in der wir leben*, Munich: Beck.

Bell, C. (1992), *Ritual Theory, Ritual Practice*, New York: Oxford University Press.

Belting, H. (1990), *Bild und Kult. Eine Geschichte des Bildes vor dem Zeitalter der Kunst*, Munich: Beck.

Belting, H. (2001), *Bild-Anthropologie*, Munich: Wilhelm Fink.

Belting, H. (2011), *An Anthropology of Images*, Princeton: Princeton University Press.

Belting, H., and A. Buddensieg, eds (2009), *The Global Art World. Audiences, Markets, and Museums*, Ostfildern: Hatje Cantz.

Benjamin, W. (2006), *Berlin Childhood Around 1900*, Cambridge: Belknap.

Benthien, C., and C. Wulf, eds (2001), *Körperteile. Eine kulturelle Anatomie*, Reinbek: Rowohlt.

Benz, E. (1969), *Die Vision. Erfahrungsformen und Bilderwelt*, Stuttgart: Klett.

Bergson, H. (1912/2004), *Matter and Memory*, Mineola: Dover Publications.

Bhabha, H. K. (1994), *The Location of Culture*, London: Routledge

Birdwhistell, R. L. (1952), *Introduction to Kinesics. An Annotation System for the Analysis of Body Motion and Gesture*, Louisville: University Louisville Press.

Birdwhistell, R. L. (1970), *Kinesics and Context. Essays on Body Motion Communication*, Philadelphia: University of Pennsylvania Press.

Bloch, E. (1995), *The Principle of Hope*, Cambridge, MA: MIT Press.

Blacking, J., ed. (1977), *The Anthropology of the Body*, London: Academic Press.

Blumenberg, H. (1985), *The Legitimacy of the Modern Age*, trans. R. M. Wallace, Cambridge, MA: MIT Press.

Blumenberg, H. (1987), *The Genesis of the Copernican World*, trans. R. M. Wallace, Cambridge, MA: MIT Press.

Bodmer, J. J. (1966), *Critische Abhandlung von dem Wunderbaren in der Poesie* (Reprint of the 1740 edition), Stuttgart: Metzler.

Boehm, G., ed. (1994a), *Was ist ein Bild?*, Munich: Wilhelm Fink.

Boehm, G. (1994b), 'Die Bilderfrage', in G. Boehm (ed.), *Was ist ein Bild?*, 325–43, Munich: Wilhelm Fink.

Boehm, G. (2001), *Homo Pictor*, Munich, Leipzig: Saur.

Böhme, G. (2001), *Aisthetik. Vorlesungen über Ästhetik als allgemeine Wahrnehmungslehre*, Munich: Wilhelm Fink.

Boetsch, G., and C. Wulf, eds (2005), 'Rituels', *Hermès*, 43, Paris: CNRS Éditions.

Bohnsack, R. (2003), *Rekonstruktive Sozialforschung. Einführung in Qualitative Methoden*, Opladen: Leske und Budrich.

Bohnsack, R. (2009), *Qualitative Bild- und Videointerpretation: Die dokumentarische Methode*, Opladen, Farmington Hills: Barbara Budrich.

Bossard, J. H. S., and E. S. Boll (1950), *Ritual in Family Living. A Contemporary Study*, Philadelphia: University of Pennsylvania Press.

Bourdieu, P. (1982a), 'Les rites comme actes d'institution', *Actes de la recherche en sciences sociales*, 32: 58–63.

Bourdieu, P. (1984), *Distinction: A Social Critique of the Judgement of Taste*, trans. Richard Nice, Cambridge, MA: Harvard University Press.

Bourdieu, P. (1990), *The Logic of Practice*, trans. Richard Nice, Palo Alto: Stanford University Press.

Bourdieu, P. (1997), 'Eine sanfte Gewalt. Pierre Bourdieu im Gespräch mit Irene Dölling und Margareta Steinrücke', in Irene Dölling, and Beate Krais (eds), *Ein alltägliches Spiel*, 218–29, Frankfurt/M.: Suhrkamp.

Bourdieu, P. (2013), Outline of a Theory of Practice, trans. R. Nice, Cambridge: Cambridge University Press.

Bowen, M. (1978), *Family Therapy in Clinical Practice*, New York: Jason Aronson.

Brandstetter, G. (1995), *Tanz-Lektüren. Körperbilder und Raumfiguren der Avantgarde*, Frankfurt/M.: Fischer.

Brandstetter, G., and C. Wulf, eds (2007), *Tanz als Anthropologie*, Munich: Wilhelm Fink.

Brandstetter, Gabriele, M. Buchholz, A. Hamburger, and C. Wulf, eds (2018), 'Balance, – Rhythmus – Resonanz', *Paragrana. Internationale Zeitschrift für Historische Anthropologie*, 27: (1).

Bredekamp, H. (2010), *Theorie des Bildakts*, Berlin: Suhrkamp.

Breitinger, J. J. (1966), *Critische Dichtkunst*, 2 volumes, (Reprint of 1849 edition), Stuttgart: Metzler.

Bremmer, J., and H. Roodenburg, eds (1992), *A Cultural History of Gesture*, Ithaca: Cornell University Press.

Bush, S. (1971), *The Chinese Literati on Painting. Sushih (1037) to Tung Ch'ich'ang (1555–1636)*, Cambridge: Cambridge University Press.

Butler, J. (1990), *Gender Trouble. Feminism and the Subversion of Identity*, London and New York: Routledge.

Butler, J. (1993), *Bodies That Matter. On the Discursive Limits of '"Sex"'*, London and New York: Routledge Classics.

Buytendijk, F. J. J. (1933), *Wesen und Sinn des Spiels. Das Spielen des Menschen und der Tiere als Erscheinungsform der Lebenstriebe*, Berlin: Wolff.

Caillois, R. (2001), *Man, Play, and Games*, trans. Meyer Barash, Champaign: University of Illinois Press.

Calbris, G. (1990), *The Semiotics of French Gestures*, Bloomington, Indianapolis: Indiana University Press.

Carlsson, M. (2013), 'Red Bull Stratos – At the Edge of the Obscene', *International Journal of Baudrillard Studies*, 10 (2): Available online: http://www2.ubishops.ca/b audrillardstudies/vol10_2/v10-2-carlsson.html (accessed 5 September 2017).

Castoriadis, C. (1987), *The Imaginary Institution of Society*, trans. K. Blamey, Cambridge: Polity Press.

de Cervantes Saavedra, Miguel (1615), *Don Quixote*. Available online: http://www.span isharts.com/books/quijote/chapter8.htm

Changeux, J.-P. (2002), *L'Homme de vérité*, Paris: Odile Jacob.

Coleridge, S. (1907), *Biographia literaria*, Oxford: Clarendon Press.

Darwin, C. (1979), *The Expression of the Emotions in Man and Animals*, London: Murray.

Debray, R. (1992), *Vie et mort de l'image. Une histoire du regard en Occident*, Paris: Gallimard.

Denis, M. (1991), *Image and Cognition*, trans. C. Greenbaum, Harvester: Wheatsheaf.

Descartes, R. (1988), 'The Passion of the Soul', in trans. J. Cottingham, R. Stoothaoff, and D. Murdoch, *Selected Philosophical Writings*, Cambridge: Cambridge University Press.

Descartes, René (1641), *Meditations on First Philosophy in Which the Existence of God and the Distinction Between Mind and Body are Demonstrated*. Available online: http://www.public.iastate.edu/~jwcwolf/Papers/DESI-III.HTM

Diderot, D. (1875), *Œuvres complètes de Diderot*, Paris: Garnier Frères.

Didi-Huberman, G. (1990), *Devant l'image*, Paris: Minuit.

Dieckmann, B., C. Wulf, and M. Wimmer, eds (1997), *Violence. Nationalism, Racism, Xenophobia*, Münster, New York: Waxmann.

Dinkla, S., and M. Leeker, eds (2002), *Tanz und Technologie. Auf dem Weg zu medialen Inszenierungen*, Berlin: Alexander-Verlag.

Douglas, M. (1986), *How Institutions Think*, New York: Syracuse University Press.

Durand, G. (1999), *The Anthropological Structures of The Imaginary*, Brisbane: Boom Bana Publications.

Durkheim, E. (1912), *The Elementary Forms of the Religious Life*, trans. Joseph Ward Swain, London: George Allen and Unwin Ltd.

Egidi, M., O. Schneider, M. Schöning, I. Schütze, and C. Torra-Mattenklott, eds (2000), *Gestik. Figuren des Körpers in Text und Bild*, Tübingen: Narr.

Eiland, H., and M. W. Jennings (2014), *Walter Benjamin: A Critical Life*, Cambridge, MA: Harvard University/Belknap Press.

Ekman, P. E., R. Sorenson, and P. Ellsworth (1982), *Emotions in the Human Face*, New York: Pergamon.

Eliade, M. (1961), *The Sacred and the Profane: The Nature of Religion*, New York: Harper Torchbooks.

Elias, N. (1994), *The Civilizing Process: Sociogenetic and Psychogenetic Investigations*, Hoboken: Blackwell.

Elias, N. and E. Dunning (1986), *Quest for Excitement. Sport and Leisure in the Civilizing Process*, Oxford: Blackwell.

Else, G. F. (1958), 'Imitation in the 5th Century', *Classical Philology*, 53 (2): 73–90.

Escande, Y. (2003), *Traités chinois de peinture et de calligraphie*, Paris: Klincksieck.

Featherstone, M. (1995), *Undoing Culture. Globalization, Postmodernism and Identity*, London, Thousand Oaks: Sage.

Fink, E. (1960), *Spiel als Weltsymbol*, Stuttgart: Kohlhammer.

Fischer-Lichte, E., and C. Wulf, eds (2001), 'Theorien des Performativen', *Paragrana. Internationale Zeitschrift für Historische Anthropologie*, 10 (1).

Fischer-Lichte, E., and C. Wulf, eds (2004), 'Praktiken des Performativen', *Paragrana. Internationale Zeitschrift für Historische Anthropologie*, 13 (1).

Flick, U., ed. (2013), *The Sage Handbook of Qualitative Data Analysis*, Thousand Oaks: Sage Publications.

Flick, U. (2018), *Doing Triangulation and Mixed Methods*, Thousand Oaks: Sage Publications.

Flügge, J. (1963), *Die Entfaltung der Anschauungskraft*, Heidelberg: Quelle & Meyer.

Flusser, V. (1990), *Writings*, Andreas Ströhl (ed.), trans. Erik Eisel, Minneapolis: University of Minnesota Press.

Flusser, V. (1993), 'Eine neue Einbildungskraft', in V. Flusser (ed.), *Lob der Oberflächlichkeit. Für eine Phänomenologie der Medien*, 251–331, Bensheim: Bollmann.

Foucault, M. (1977), *Discipline and Punish: The Birth of the Prison*, New York: Vintage Books.

Frazer, J. G. (2009), *The Golden Bough. A Study in Magic and Religion*, Oxford: Oxford University Press.

Freud, S. (1900/1953), *The Interpretation of Dreams*, Standard Edition, 4–5, London: Hogarth Press.

Gal, M., E. Friedlander, C. Wulf, and M. Zuckermann, eds (2014), 'Art and Gesture', Paragrana. Internationale Zeitschrift für Historische Anthropologie, 23 (1).

Gebauer, G. (1997), 'Spiel', in C. Wulf (ed.), *Vom Menschen. Handbuch Historische Anthropologie*, 1038–48, Weinheim, Basel: Beltz.

Gebauer, G., and C. Wulf, eds (1993), *Praxis und Ästhetik. Neue Perspektiven im Denken Pierre Bourdieus*, Frankfurt/M.: Suhrkamp.

Gebauer, G., and C. Wulf (1995), *Mimesis. Culture – Art – Society*, trans. Don Reneau, Berkeley: University of California Press.

Gebauer, G., and C. Wulf (1998), *Spiel, Ritual, Geste. Mimetisches Handeln in der sozialen Welt*, Reinbek: Rowohlt.

Gebauer, G., and C. Wulf (2003), *Mimetische Weltzugänge. Soziales Handeln – Rituale und Spiele – ästhetische Produktionen*, Stuttgart: Kohlhammer.

Geertz, C. (1973), 'Thick Description: Toward an Interpretative Theory of Culture', in *The Interpretation of Cultures*, New York: Basic Books, 3–30.

Gehlen, A. (1988), *Man, His Nature and Place in the World*, trans. C. McMillan and Karl A. Pillemer, New York: Columbia University Press.

van Gennep, A. (1960), *The Rites of Passage*, London: Routledge & Paul.

Gide, A. (1973), *The Counterfeiters. A novel*, trans. D. Busy, New York: Vintage Books.

Gil, Capeloa I., and C. Wulf, eds (2015), *Hazardous Future. Disaster, Representation and the Assessment of Risk*, Berlin: de Gruyter.

Girard, R. (1977), *Violence and the Sacred*, Baltimore: John Hopkins University Press.

Girard, R. (1996), *The Scapegoat*, Baltimore: The Johns Hopkins University Press.

Giroux, H., and D. Purpel, eds (1983), *The Hidden Curriculum and Moral Education*, Berkeley: McCutchan Publishing Corporation.

Glaser, B. G. and A. Strauss (1969), *The Discovery of Grounded Theory*, Chicago: Chicago University Press.

Goethe J. W. (1988), *Gedichte*, Berlin and Tübingen: Aufbau.

Goffman, E. (1974), *Frame-Analysis. An Essay on the Organization of Experience*, New York: Harper and Row.

Goldin-Meadow, S. (2005), *Hearing Gesture. How Our Hands Help Us Think*, Cambridge, MA, London: Harvard University Press.

Goldstein, E. B. (2005), *Cognitive Psychology*, Belmont: Wadsworth Publishing.

Greco, M., and P. Stenner, eds (2008), *Emotions. A Social Science Reader*, London and New York: Routledge.

Greenblatt, S. (1992), *Marvellous Possessions: The Wonder of the New World*, Chicago: University of Chicago Press.

Grimes, R. (1995), *Beginnings in Ritual Studies*, Columbia: University of South Carolina Press.

Großklaus, G. (2004), *Medien-Bilder. Inszenierung der Sichtbarkeit*, Frankfurt/M.: Suhrkamp.

Gruzinski, S. (2001), *Images at War: Mexico from Columbus to Blade Runner, 1492–2019*, trans. H. MacLean, Durham: Duke University Press.

Gruzinski, S. (1999), *La pensée métisse*, Paris: Fayard.

Halbwachs, M. (1992), *On Collective Memory*, Chicago: The University of Chicago Press.

Hamburger, M. (1984), *Goethe: Poems and Epigrams*, London: Anvil Press Poetry.

Harding, J., and E. D. Pribram, eds (2009), *Emotions: A Cultural Studies Reader*, London, New York: Routledge.

Heidegger, M. (2002), 'The Age of the World Picture', in J. Young and K. Haynes (eds) and trans., Martin Heidegger: Off *the Beaten Track*, Cambridge: Cambridge University Press, 57–84.

Hermann, B., eds (2019), *Anthropologie und Ästhetik: Interdisziplinäre Perspektiven*, Paderborn: Wilhelm Fink.

Hobbes, T. (2012), *Leviathan*. Dover: Dover Philosophical Classics.

Howes, D., ed. (1991), *The Varieties of Sensory Experience*, Toronto, Buffalo: University of Toronto Press.

Huppauf, B., and C. Wulf, eds (2009), *Dynamics and Performativity of Imagination. The Image between the Visible and the Invisible*, New York, London: Routledge.

Huizinga, J. (1971), *Homo Ludens*, Boston: Beacon Press.

Hume, D. (1739/1896), *A Treatise of Human Nature*, L. A. Selby-Bigge (ed.), Oxford: Clarendon Press. Available online: https://people.rit.edu/wlrgsh/HumeTreatise.pdf (accessed 29 September 1919).

Imai, Y., and C. Wulf, eds (2007), *Concepts of Aesthetic Education. Japanese and European Perspectives*, Münster, New York: Waxmann.

Imber-Black, E., J. Roberts, and R. A. Whiting, eds (1988), *Rituals in Families and Family Therapy*, New York: Norton.

Imdahl, M. (1994), 'Ikonik. Bilder und ihre Anschauung', in G. Boehm (ed.), *Was ist ein Bild?*, 300–24, Munich: Wilhelm Fink.

Iser, W. (1993), *The Fictive and the Imaginary: Charting Literary Anthropology*, Baltimore: John Hopkins Press.

Iacoboni, M. (2008), *Mirroring People. The New Science of How We Connect with Others*, New York: Farrar, Straus and Giroux.

Jonas, H. (1994), 'Homo pictor. Von der Freiheit des Menschen', in G. Boehm (ed.), *Was ist ein Bild?*, 105–24, Munich: Wilhelm Fink.

Jousse, M. (1974/1978), *L'anthropologie du geste*, 3 vols, Paris: Gallimard.

Jullien, F. (2009), *The Great Image Has No Form*. On the Nonobject through Painting, trans. J. M. Todd, Chicago: University of Chicago Press.

Jung, C. G. (2005), *Aspects of the Masculine*, London: Routledge.

Jung, V. (1977), *Handbuch des Tanzes*, Hildesheim, New York: Olms (Reprint of the Edition Stuttgart 1930).

Kämpf, H., and R. Schott, eds (1995), *Der Mensch als homo pictor? Die Kunst traditioneller Kulturen aus der Sicht von Philosophie und Ethnologie*, Bonn: Bouvier.

Kamper, D. (1981), *Zur Geschichte der Einbildungskraft*, Munich: Hanser.

Kamper, D. (1986), *Zur Soziologie der Imagination*, Munich: Hanser.

Kamper, D. (1995), *Unmögliche Gegenwart. Zur Theorie der Phantasie*, Munich: Wilhelm Fink.

Kant, I. (1998), *Critique of Pure Reason*, trans. P. Guyer and A. W. Wood, Cambridge: Cambridge University Press.

Kellermann, I. (2008), *Vom Kind zum Schulkind. Die rituelle Gestaltung der Schulanfangsphase*, Opladen: Budrich UniPress.

Kendon, A. (2004), *Gesture: Visible Action as Utterance*, Cambridge: Cambridge University Press.

Kepler, J. (1997), 'Der Vorgang des Sehens', in R. Konersmann (ed.), *Kritik des Sehens*, 105–15, Leipzig: Reclam.

Keppler, A. (1994), *Tischgespräche. Über Formen kommunikativer Vergemeinschaftung am Beispiel der Konversation in Familien*, Frankfurt/M.: Fischer.

Klein, G., and F. Malte (2011), *Die Kultur des HipHop*, Frankfurt/M.: Suhrkamp.

Klien, Susanne, and Christoph Wulf (2013), 'Well-Being', *Paragrana: Internationale Zeitschrift für Historische Anthropologie*, 22 (1).

Kontopodis, M. C. Varvantakis, and C. Wulf, eds (2017), *Global Youth in Digital Trajectories*, London: Routledge.

Krais, Beate, and Gebauer Gunter (2002), *Habitus*, Bielefeld: transcript.

Kraus, A., J. Budde, M. Hietzge, and C. Wulf, eds (2021), *Handbuch Schweigendes Wissen. Erziehung, Bildung, Sozialisation und Lernen*, 2nd edn, Weinheim and Basel: Beltz Juventa.

Kraus, A., and C. Wulf, eds (2022), *Handbook of Embodiment and Learning*, London: Palgrave, Macmillan.

Kreinath, J., J. Snoek, and M. Stausberg, eds (2006), *Theorizing Rituals. Issues, Topics, Approaches, Concepts*, Leiden, Boston: Brill.

Kress, G., S. Selander, R. Säljö, and C. Wulf, eds (2021), *Learning as Social Practice. Beyond Education as an Individual Enterprise*, London: Routledge.

Kretschmar, T. (2016), *The Power of Inner Images*, London: Routledge.

Lacan, J. (1949), 'Le Stade du miroir comme formateur de la fonction du Je: telle qu'elle nous est révélée dans l'expérience psychanalytique', in *Revue française de psychanalyse*, 449–55

Lacan, J. (2001), 'Les complexes familiaux dans la formation de l'individu. Essai d'analyse d'une fonction en psychologie', in *Autres écrits*, 23–84, Paris: Editions du Seuil.

Lakoff, G., and M. Johnson (1999), *Philosophy in the Flesh. The Embodied Mind and Its Challenge to Western Thought*, New York: Basic Books.

Laotse (1990), *Tao Te Ching. The Classic Book of Integrity and the Way*, New York: Bantam Books.

Le Breton, D. (1998), *Les passions ordinaires. Anthropologie des émotions*, Paris: Armand Colin.

Leroi-Gourhan, A. (1993), *Gesture and Speech*, trans. A. Bostock Berger, Cambridge, MA: MIT Press.

Maar, C., and H. Burda, eds (2004), *Iconic Turn. Die neue Macht der Bilder*, Cologne: Dumont.

Macho, T. (2000), 'Ist mir bekannt, dass ich sehe?' in H. Belting, and D. Kamper (eds), *Der zweite Blick. Bildgeschichte und Bildreflexion*, 211–28, Munich: Wilhelm Fink.

Malebranche, N., (1997), *The Search After Truth*, Cambridge: Cambridge University Press.

Marin, L. (1993), *Des pouvoirs de l'image*, Paris: Seuil.

Mattenklott, G. (2009), 'On Imagination', in Huppauf, B., and Wulf, C. (eds), *Dynamics and Performativity of Imagination. The Image between the Visible and the Invisible*, 25–41, New York and London: Routledge.

McLuhan, M. (1964), *Understanding Media. The Extension of Man*, New York: Mentor.

McNeill, D. (1992), *Hand and Mind. What Gestures Reveal About Thought*, Chicago, London: Chicago University Press.

McNeill, D. (2005), *Gesture and Thought*, Chicago, London: Chicago University Press.

Mead, G. H. (2015), *Mind, Self, and Society*, London: University of Chicago Press.

Merleau-Ponty, M. (1968), *The Visible and the Invisible*, Evanston: Northwestern University Press.

Mersch, D. (2002), *Ereignis und Aura. Untersuchungen zu einer Ästhetik des Performativen*, Frankfurt/M.: Suhrkamp.

Mersch, D. (2010), *Posthermeneutik*, Berlin: Akademie Verlag.

Michaels, A., and C. Wulf, eds (2011), *Images of the Body in India*, London: Routledge.

Michaels, A., and C. Wulf, eds (2012), *Emotions in Rituals and Performances*, London: Routledge.

Michaels, A., and C. Wulf, eds (2014), *Exploring the Senses*, London: Routledge.

Michaels, A., and C. Wulf, eds (2020), *Science and Scientification in South Asia and Europe*, London: Routledge.

Mitchell, W. J. T. (1986), *Iconology: Image, Text, Ideology*, Chicago: University of Chicago Press.

Mollenhauer, K., and C. Wulf, eds (1996), *Aisthesis/Asthetik. Zwischen Wahrnehmung und Bewusstsein*, Weinheim: Deutscher Studienverlag.

Mondzain, M.-J. (1996), *Image, icône, économie. Les sources byzantines de l'imaginaire contemporain*, Paris: Seuil.

de Montaigne, M. (1976), *Complete essays*, Palo Alto: Stanford University Press.

Morgenthaler, C., and Hauri, R., eds (2010), *Rituale im Familienleben: Inhalte, Formen und Funktionen im Verhältnis der Generationen*, Weinheim, Munich: Juventa.

Morin, E. (2005), *The Cinema, or The Imaginary Man*, Minneapolis: University of Minnesota Press.

Morris, D., P. Collett, P. Marsh, and M. O'Shaughnessy (1979), *Gestures Their Origins and Distribution*, London: Jonathan Cape.

Müller, C., and R. Posner, eds (2004), *The Semantics and Pragmatics of Everyday Gestures*, Berlin: Weidler.

Novalis (1997), *Philosophical Writings*, trans. M. Mahony Stoljar, New York: State University of New York.

Obert, M. (2006), 'Imagination', in B. Huppauf, and C. Wulf (eds), *Dynamics, and Performativity of Imagination. The Image between the Visible and the Invisible*, 116–34, New York and London: Routledge.

Otto, R. (1958), *The Idea of the Holy*, trans. J. W. Harvey, Oxford: Oxford University Press.

Plato (1979), *The Republic*, trans. D. Lee, 2nd edn, Harmondsworth: Penguin

Plessner, H. (1983), 'Conditio Humana', in H. Plessner, Otto Dux, O. Marquard, and El Ströker (eds), *Gesammelte Schriften*, vol. 8, Frankfurt/M.: Suhrkamp.

Prange, K. (2005), *Die Zeigestruktur der Erziehung. Grundriss der operativen Pädagogik*, Paderborn: Schöningh.

Pross, Harry (1970), *Publizistik: Thesen zu einem Grundcolloquium*, Neuwied: Luchterhand.

Proust, M. (2002), 'Finding Time Again [Le temps retrouvé, 1927]', in *In Search of Lost Time*, vol VI, trans. I. Patterson, London: Allen Lane/Penguin

Quinn, W. H., Neal Newfield, A. Protinsky, and O. Howard (1985), 'Rites of Passage in Families with Adolescents', *Family Process*, 24: 101–11.

Reckwitz, A. (2019), *Die Gesellschaft der Singularitäten. Zum Strukturwandel der Moderne*, Berlin: Suhrkamp.

Resina, J. R., and C. Wulf, eds (2019), *Repetition, Recurrence, Returns. How Cultural Renewal Works*, Lanham: Lexington Books/Roman & Littlefield.

Ricoeur, P. (1974), *The Conflict of Interpretations. Essays in Hermeneutics*, D. Ihde (ed.), London: Continuum.

Ricoeur, P. (1975), *Le metaphore vive*, Paris: Seuil.

Rilke, R. M. (1977), *Possibility of Being: A Selection of Poems*, trans. J. Blaire Leishman, New York: New Directions.

Rizzolatti, G., and L. Craighero (2004), 'The Mirror-Neuron System', *Annual Review Neuroscience*, 27: 169–92.

Roth, G. (2000), *Brain Evolution and Cognition*, New York: Wiley.

Rousseau, J.-J. (1996), *The Confessions*, Ware: Classics of World Literature.

Rousseau, J.-J. (1979), *Emile or On Education*, trans. Allan Bloom, New York: Basic Books.

Sachs-Hombach, K. (2003), *Das Bild als kommunikatives Medium. Elemente einer allgemeinen Bildwissenschaft*, Cologne: von Halem.

Sachs-Hombach, K., ed. (2005), *Bildwissenschaft. Disziplinen, Themen, Methoden*, Frankfurt/M.: Suhrkamp.

Sachs-Hombach, K., and R. J. Schirra, eds (2013), *Origins of Pictures*, Cologne: von Halem.

Sahlins, M. (1976), *Culture and Practical Reason*, Chicago: University of Chicago Press.

Sartre, J.-P. (2001), *The Psychology of the Imagination*, London: Routledge.

Schäfer, G. and C. Wulf, eds (1999), *Bild – Bilder – Bildung*, Weinheim: Deutscher Studienverlag.

Schechner, R. (1977), *Essays on Performance Theory 1970–1976*, New York: Drama Book Specialists.

Scheunpflug, A., and C. Wulf, eds (2006), *Biowissenschaft und Erziehungswissenschaft*, Zeitschrift für Erziehungswissenschaft, Beiheft 5, Wiesbaden: Verlag für Sozialwissenschaften.

Schmitt, J.-C. (1990), *La raison des gestes dans l'Occident médiéval*, Paris: Galimard.

Schulze, H., and C. Wulf, eds (2007), 'Klanganthropologie', *Paragrana* Internationale Zeitschrift für Historische Anthropologie, 16 (2).

Schürmann, E. (2008), *Sehen als Praxis. Ethisch-ästhetische Studien zum Verhältnis von Sicht und Einsicht*, Frankfurt/M.: Suhrkamp.

Seel, M. (2000), *Ästhetik des Erscheinens*, Frankfurt/M.: Suhrkamp.

Seitz, S., A. Graneß, and G. Stenger, eds (2018), *Facetten gegenwärtiger Bildtheorie*, Wiesbaden: Springer.

Seneca (65/1917), *Ad Lucillium Epistulae Morales*. Engl. trans. Moral letters to Lucilius by R. M. Gummere, London: Heinemann. Available online: https://en.wikisource .org/wiki/Moral_letters_to_Lucilius (accessed 5 October 2019).

Simon, G. (1988), *Le regard, l'être et l'apparence dans l'optique de l'Antiquité*, Paris: Seuil.

Starobinski, J. (1994), *Gute Gaben, schlimme Gaben. Die Ambivalenz sozialer Gesten*, Frankfurt/M.: Fischer.

Straus, E. (1956), *Vom Sinn der Sinne. Ein Beitrag zur Grundlegung der Psychologie*, Berlin, Göttingen, Heidelberg: Springer.

Strauss, A., and J. Corbin (1994), 'Grounded Theory. An Overview', in N. K. Denzin and Y. S. Lincoln (eds), *Handbook of Qualitative Research*, 273–85, Thousand Oaks: Sage.

Suzuki, S., and C. Wulf, eds (2007), *Mimesis, Poiesis and Performativity in Education*, Münster, New York: Waxmann.

Tambiah, S. (1979), 'A Performative Approach to Ritual', *Proceedings of the British Academy*, 65: 113–63.

Tervooren, A. (2001), 'Pausenspiele als performative Kinderkultur', in Christoph Wulf et al., *Das Soziale als Ritual. Zur performativen Bildung von Gemeinschaften*, 205–48, Opladen: Leske & Budrich.

Tervooren, A., N. Engel, M. Göhlich, I. Miethe, and S. Reh, eds (2014), *Ethnographie und Differenz in pädagogischen Feldern. Internationale Entwicklungen erziehungswissenschaftlicher Forschung*, Bielefeld: transcript.

Thomas, J. (1998), *Virgile, Bucoliques, Géorgiques*, Paris: Ellipses.

Thorne, B. (1993), *Gender Play. Girls and Boys in School*, Buckingham: Open University Press.

Todorov, T. (1996), *The Conquest of America. The Question of the Other*, New York: Harper.

Tomasello, M. (1999), *The Cultural Origins of Human Cognition*, Cambridge, MA: Harvard University Press.

Tomasello, M. (2008), *Origins of Human Communication*, Cambridge, MA: MIT Press.

Tulving, E. (2005), 'Episodic Memory and Autonoesis: Uniquely human?' in H. S. Terrace, and J. Metcalfe (eds), *The Missing Link in Cognition: Self-knowing Consciousness in Man and Animals*, 3–56, New York: Oxford University Press.

Turner, V. (1969), *The Ritual Process: Structure and Anti-Structure*, Chicago: Aldine.

Turner, V. (1982), *From Ritual to Theatre. The Human Seriousness of Play*, New York: PAJ Publications.

Uhlig, B., G. Lieber, and I. Pieper, eds (2019), *Erzählen zwischen Bild und Text*, Munich: Kopaed.

UNESCO (1996), *Learning, the Treasure within: Report to UNESCO of the International Commission on Education for the 21st Century*, Paris: UNESCO.

UNESCO (2001), *First Proclamation of Masterpieces of the Oral and Intangible Heritage of Humanity*, Paris: UNESCO

UNESCO (2002), *Medium Term Strategy 2002–2007*, Paris: UNESCO.

UNESCO (2003a), *Convention for the Safeguarding of Intangible Cultural Heritage*, Paris: UNESCO.

UNESCO (2003b), *Second Proclamation of Masterpieces of the Oral and Intangible Heritage of Humanity*, Paris: UNESCO.

UNESCO (2004), *Museums International: Views and Visions of the Intangible*, Paris: UNESCO.

UNESCO (2005), *Übereinkommen über den Schutz und die Förderung der Vielfalt kultureller Ausdrucksformen*, by DUK, Bonn: Deutsche UNESCO-Kommission.

Virilio, P. (1989), *War and Cinema, The Logistics of Perception*, London: Verso.

Virilio, P. (1990), *L'inertie polaire. Essai sur le contrôle d'environnement*, Paris: Christian Bourgois.

Virilio, P. (2010), *The University of Disaster*, Cambridge: Polity.

Waldenfels, B. (1990), *Der Stachel des Fremden*, Frankfurt/M.: Suhrkamp.

Waldenfels, B. (2010), *Sinne und Künste im Wechselspiel. Modi ästhetischer Erfahrung*, Berlin: Suhrkamp.

Wallenhorst, N., and C. Wulf, eds (2021), *Dictionnaire d'anthropologie prospective*, Paris: Vrin.

Wallenhorst, N., and C. Wulf, eds (2022), *Handbook of the Anthropocene*, Basingstoke: Springer – Nature.

Weibel, P., and A. Buddensieg, eds (2007), *Contemporary Art and the Museum: A Global Perspective*, Ostfildern: Hatje Cantz.

Wiesing, L. (2005), *Artifizielle Präsenz. Studien zur Philosophie des Bildes*, Frankfurt/M.: Suhrkamp.

Wiesing, L (2008), *Die Sichtbarkeit des Bildes. Geschichte und Perspektiven der formalen Ästhetik*, Frankfurt/M., New York: Campus.

Willems, H., and M. Jurga, eds (1998), *Inszenierungsgesellschaft. Ein einführendes Handbuch*, Opladen, Wiesbaden: Westdeutscher Verlag.

Wittgenstein, L. (1960), 'Philosophische Untersuchungen', in L. Wittgenstein (ed.), *Schriften. Vol. I*, Frankfurt/M.: Suhrkamp.

Wittgenstein, L. (1993), *Letzte Schriften über die Philosophie der Psychologie (1949–1951): Das Innere und das Äußere*, Frankfurt/M.: Suhrkamp.

Wolin, S. J., and L. A. Bennett (1984), 'Family Rituals', *Family Process*, 23: 401–20.

Wulf, C., ed. (1997), *Vom Menschen. Handbuch Historische Anthropologie*, Weinheim, Basel: Beltz (2nd edn, Wulf 2010).

Wulf, C. (2001), *Einführung in die Anthropologie der Erziehung*, Weinheim, Basel: Beltz.

Wulf, C. (2004a), 'Schulfeier und Schulfest. Anerkennung und Vielfalt', in C. Wulf et al., *Bildung im Ritual*, 69–98, Wiesbaden: Verlag für Sozialwissenschaften.

Wulf, C. (2004b), 'Ritual, Macht und Performanz: Die Inauguration des amerikanischen Präsidenten', in C. Wulf, and J. Zirfas (eds), *Die Kultur des Rituals*, 49–61, Munich: Wilhelm Fink.

Wulf, C. (2005a), 'Crucial Points in the Transmission and Learning of Intangible Cultural Heritage', in Laura Wong (ed.), *Globalization and Intangible Cultural Heritage*, 84–95, Paris: UNESCO

Wulf, C. (2005b), *Zur Genese des Sozialen. Mimesis, Performativität, Ritual*, Bielefeld: transcript.

Wulf, C. (2006a), *Anthropologie kultureller Vielfalt. Interkulturelle Bildung in Zeiten der Globalisierung*, Bielefeld: transcript.

Wulf, C. (2006b), 'Praxis', in J. Kreinath, J. A. M. Snoek, and M. Stausberg (eds), *Theorizing Rituals: Issues, Topics, Approaches, Concepts*, 395–411, Leiden: Brill.

Wulf, C. (2008a), 'Rituale im Grundschulalter: Performativität, Mimesis und Interkulturalität', *Zeitschrift für Erziehungswissenschaft*, 11 (1): 67–83.

Wulf, C. (2008b), 'Friedenskultur und Friedenserziehung in Zeiten der Globalisierung', in R. Grasse, B. Gruber, and G. Gugel (eds), *Friedenspädagogik. Grundlagen, Praxisansätze, Perspektiven*, 35–60, Reinbek: Rowohlt.

Wulf, C. (2009), *Anthropologie. Geschichte – Kultur – Philosophie*, Cologne: Anaconda (2nd edn, first edn, Reinbek 2004: Rowohlt).

Wulf, C, ed. (2010a), *Der Mensch und seine Kultur. Hundert Beiträge zur Geschichte, Gegenwart und Zukunft des menschlichen Lebens*, Cologne: Anaconda (first edn 'Vom Menschen. Handbuch Historische Anthropologie' 1997, Beltz; French edn 2002; Italian edn 2002; Japanese edn 2008; Russian edn 2022)

Wulf, C., ed. (2010b), 'Kontaktzonen. Dynamik und Performativität kultureller Kontaktzonen', *Paragrana. Internationale Zeitschrift für Historische Anthropologie*, 19 (2).

Wulf, C. (2013a), *Anthropology. A Continental Perspective*, Chicago: The University of Chicago Press.

Wulf, C. (2013b), *Das Rätsel des Humanen. Eine Einführung in die historische Anthropologie*, Munich: Wilhelm Fink.

Wulf, C., ed. (2016), *Exploring Alterity in a Globalized World*, London: Routledge.

Wulf, C. (2022), *Education as Human Knowledge in the Anthropocene. An Anthropological Perspective*, London: Routledge.

Wulf, C., B. Althans, K. Audehm, C. Bausch, B. Jörissen, M. Göhlich, S. Sting, A. Tervooren, M. Wagner-Willi, and J. Zirfas (2001), *Das Soziale als Ritual. Zur performativen Bedeutung von Gemeinschaft*, Opladen: Leske & Budrich.

Wulf, C., B. Althans, K. Audehm, C. Bausch, B. Jörissen, M. Göhlich, R. Mattig, A. Tervooren, M. Wagner-Willi, and J. Zirfas (2004), *Bildung im Ritual. Schule, Familie, Jugend, Medien*, Wiesbaden: Springer VS.

Wulf, C., B. Althans, K. Audehm, G. Blaschke, N. Ferrin, B. Jörissen, M. Göhlich, R. Mattig, S. Schinkel, A. Tervooren, M. Wagner-Willi, and J. Zirfas (2007), *Lernkulturen im Umbruch. Rituelle Praktiken in Schule, Medien, Familie und Jugend*, Wiesbaden: Springer VS.

Wulf, C., B. Althans, K. Audehm, C. Bausch, M. Göhlich, S. Sting, A. Tervooren, M. Wagner-Willi, and J. Zirfas (2010), *Ritual and Identity. The Staging and Performing of Rituals in the Lives of Young People*, London: Tufnell.

Wulf, C., B. Althans, K. Audehm, G. Blaschke, N. Ferrin, I. Kellermann, R. Mattig, and S. Schinkel (2011), *Die Geste in Erziehung, Bildung und Sozialisation. Ethnographische Feldstudien*, Wiesbaden: Springer VS.

Wulf, C., and E. Fischer-Lichte, eds (2010), *Gesten – Inszenierung, Aufführung, Praxis*, Paderborn: Wilhelm Fink.

Wulf, C., M. Göhlich, and J. Zirfas, eds (2001), *Grundlagen des Performativen. Eine Einführung in die Zusammenhänge von Sprache, Macht und Handeln*, Weinheim, Munich: Juventa.

Wulf, C., and D. Kamper, eds (2002), *Logik und Leidenschaft. Erträge Historischer Anthropologie*, Berlin: Reimer.

Wulf, C., and C. Merkel, eds (2002), *Globalisierung als Herausforderung der Erziehung. Theorien, Grundlagen, Fallstudien*, Münster: Waxmann.

Wulf, C., and B. Newton, eds (2006), *Desarrollo Sostenible. Conceptos y ejemplos de buenas prácticas en Europa y América Latina*, Münster, New York: Waxmann.

Wulf, C., J. Poulain, and F. Triki, eds (2006), *Europäische und islamisch geprägte Länder im Dialog: Religion und Gewalt*, Berlin: Akademie.

Wulf, C., J. Poulain, and F. Triki, eds (2007), *Die Künste im Dialog der Kulturen. Europa und seine muslimischen Nachbarn*, Berlin: Akademie.

Wulf, C., J. Poulain, and F. Triki, eds (2011), 'Emotionen in einer transkulturellen Welt', *Paragrana Internationale Zeitschrift für Historische Anthropologie*, 20 (2).

Wulf, C., S. Suzuki, J. Zirfas, I., Kellermann, Y. Inoue, F. Ono, and N. Takenaka (2011), *Das Glück der Familie: Ethnographische Studien in Deutschland und Japan*, Wiesbaden: Springer VS.

Wulf, C., and G. Wiegand (2011), *Der Mensch in der globalisierten Welt. Anthropologische Reflexionen zum Verständnis unserer Zeit. Christoph Wulf im Gespräch mit Gabriele Weigand*, Münster: Waxmann.

Wulf, C., and J. Zirfas, eds (2003), 'Rituelle Welten', *Paragrana*. Internationale Zeitschrift für Historische Anthropologie, 12 (1).

Wulf, C., and J. Zirfas, eds (2004a), *Die Kultur des Rituals. Inszenierungen. Praktiken. Symbole*, Munich: Wilhelm Fink.

Wulf, C., and J. Zirfas, eds (2004b), *Innovation und Ritual. Jugend, Geschlecht und Schule*, Zeitschrift für Erziehungswissenschaft. 2. Beiheft, Wiesbaden: Springer VS.

Wulf, C., and J. Zirfas (2004c), 'Performative Welten. Eine Einführung in die systematischen, historischen und methodischen Dimensionen des Rituals', in C. Wulf and J. Zirfas (eds), *Die Kultur des Rituals. Inszenierungen. Praktiken. Symbole*, 7–46, Munich: Fink.

Wulf, C., and J. Zirfas, eds (2005), *Ikonologie des Performativen*, Munich: Wilhelm Fink.

Wulf, C., and J. Zirfas, eds (2007), *Pädagogik des Performativen. Theorien, Methoden, Perspektiven*, Weinheim, Basel: Beltz.

Wulf, C., and J. Zirfas, eds (2014), *Handbuch Pädagogische Anthropologie*, Wiesbaden: Springer VS.

Wulff, Helena, ed. (2007), *The Emotion. A Cultural Reader*, New York and Oxford: Berg.

Wunenburger, J.-J. (1995), *L'imagination*, Paris: Presses Universitaires de France.

Wunenburger, J.-J. (2012), *Gaston Bachelard, poétique des images*, Paris: Mimesis.

Wunenburger, J.-J. (2013), *L'imaginaire*, 2nd edn, Paris: Presses Universitaires de France

Zinnecker, J. (1975), *Der heimliche Lehrplan*, Weinheim, Basel: Beltz.

Žižek, S. (1997), *Die Pest der Phantasmen. Die Effizienz des Phantasmatischen in den neuen Medien*, Wien: Passagenverlag.

Zur Lippe, R. (1974), *Naturbeherrschung am Menschen. Vol. I: Körpererfahrung als Entfaltung von Sinnen und Beziehungen in der Ära des italienischen Kaufmannskapitals. Vol. II: Geometrisierung des Menschen und Repräsentation des Privaten im französischen Absolutismus*, Frankfurt/M.: Syndikat.

Index